BOTH ARE TRUE!

Evangelical-Liberal; Science-Religion; and other seeming conflicts, which are actually mysteries, paradoxes and dualisms of a Biblical but mystical Christian Faith.

by
Ray Lewis

Order this book online at www.trafford.com
or email orders@trafford.com

Most Trafford titles are also available at major online book retailers.

Note for Librarians: A cataloguing record for this book is available from Library
and Archives Canada at www.collectionscanada.ca/amicus/index-e.html

Printed in the United States of America.

ISBN: 978-1-4120-8539-7 (sc)

Trafford rev: 11/17/2010

www.trafford.com

North America & international
toll-free: 1 888 232 4444 (USA & Canada)

DEDICATION

To Rose,
my inspiration and support.

INTRODUCTION

...by these, my son, be admonished: of making many books there is no end; and much study is a weariness of the flesh. (Eccl. 12:12)

Duly humbled by the above admonishment, I went ahead with preparation of these essays. I like to write, and I have a small file of other pieces that I've done from time to time. (I won't be collecting them into a book, unless I perceive a demand for it.) The last chapter, "Bears", was one, and only after its completion did the notion of using it in a book occur to me. Accordingly, of the chapters you have here, it was the first one written. I had started it by December, 1995 (and since then very little has been changed or up-dated). Many things contributed to the multiple delays and slow progress. Despite some subsequent drastic changes in the country and the world, little of what I wanted to say has had to be modified (some commentary on current events can be found in Chapters 10 and 12).

I don't know Latin, Greek or Hebrew, and my excursions into comparative linguistics, especially in Chapter 11, are presumptuous, even by my own lights. But some of those concepts have been fermenting in my head for more than forty years, since I first came upon the identity, in these languages, of breath and spirit, expressed in a single word. I depend upon *Young's Analytical Concordance to the Bible* for these and other insights into Scripture. Accordingly, I use the King James Version of English Scripture, because Young's Concordance uses it—and because I love it, and my stubbornly conservative bent makes it difficult and distasteful to change. I know it's supposed to be a less accurate translation than the newer versions, but the differences I've noticed are often trivial; I'll take the risk that somebody might challenge me on this ground.

Chapter 5 on Homosexuality was written perhaps 2-3 years ago. The thoughts on left-handedness were my own. But only this week I discovered an article, "Everyone Entitled to Equality: Homosexuality as Normal as Being Left-handed" (Deb Bridge, in Calgary Herald, July 4, 1996). Though it antedates my own writing, I protest that I did not then know about it and did not plagiarize it.

Finally, as a psychiatrist, I am not entirely blind to my own character traits. Accepting St. Paul's prescription of "… kindness, humbleness, meekness …" (Col. 3:13), still I have to confess to harboring some streaks of anger and grandiosity. I have come to some recognition of when and how and why these tendencies came to be, but I have mastered them only in part. I most certainly do not write with the intention of causing hurt or offense. But I have to say what I need to say in the way I'm able to say it—I don't have some other way. So I apologize in advance for anything herein that you take to be *ad hominem*; that was never my intention (except in the case of a few named individuals).

Ray Lewis, June 1, 2006

CONTENTS

CHAPTER 1

MY PERSONAL TESTIMONY

There is a religious war going on in our country for the soul of America. It is a cultural war, as critical to the kind of nation we will one day be as was the Cold War. (Pat Buchanan, at the Republican Convention, 1992)

Wars, armed or cultural, are not the ideal way to resolve disagreements. Americans, whether liberal or conservative, have far more in common than we have differences. "Debate", maybe, but not war, when neither side is really wrong—both are more true than false—and I'd like us to stop demonizing one another; to quit quarreling and get back to work.

Though this is not a book about myself, I appreciate that Christians may be a little more likely to accord credibility to one who knows Jesus Christ as Lord and Savior, as I do, and who additionally likes what is (in my mind) a "conservative" outlook on public affairs. Christians, like other people, will "consider the source", so a brief testimony seems in order.

Following my mother's death, my legal guardian—my Great-Aunt Sally—sent me to the Episcopalian Sunday School in respect of my mother's Episcopal affiliation. Aunt Sally was in politics; an elected county official, and for some years vice-chairman of the Republican State Committee.

Remember the old Trans-Lux movie theaters? Forerunners of CNN and other continuous-news TV stations, they showed no feature or cartoon films, but only newsreels, *March of Time*, and similar current-events productions. There was this New Yorker cartoon, in which one Swanky, Well-Dressed Socialite Lady is saying to another SWDSL, "Come on, we're all going to the Trans-Lux to hiss Roosevelt". Not funny?—I guess you had to be there. Well, believe me, I and my young friends literally and loudly hissed Franklin Roosevelt whenever his visage appeared on the silver screen. Looking back, I'm not proud of that; but I want it understood that I was brought up Republican, as well as Episcopalian!

During my pre-medical studies in college, and continuing through some of my medical school years, I experienced some emotional problems; not at all serious, as I see now, but very troublesome to me at the time. That may or may not be relevant to this story—the details certainly not—but I did become involved with a Fundamentalist Baptist church during that whole period of time—and that is relevant! I suppose that nowadays I could just as well have ended up at Jonestown or Waco, or drifted into some other cult like the Moonies or Hare Krishna. But instead, I drifted—or rather was led—to the Baptist Church instead of whatever alternative might have been available back then. Such groups, specifically including the Church, can help sustain troubled souls. It did for me, and I'll always be grateful: not only for the help and support it provided me, but for the fact that it did so within a Christian tradition; for I do not equate it with the various heretical cults that prey on the lonely and confused.

From the first, an elderly lady named Helen, doubtful of my salvation, took me under her wing and began the process of my Christian education. I don't claim any verbatim memory of my introductory conversation with her, but it had to go a little bit like this:

Helen: What church denomination are you?

Me: Episcopalian.

Helen (no doubt smelling trouble): Well, where do you go to church?

Me: I haven't been going much since I'm in school and need study time. I've gone to Riverside Church a few times.

Helen: What! You go listen to Harry Emerson Fosdick?

Me: Yeah, I think he's pretty good.

Helen (becoming alarmed): But he's a Modernist!—how can you think he's good? Are you a born-again Christian yourself?

Me (at least as flabbergasted as Nicodemus must have been): What?!!!

Helen (beginning to sense the extremity of my ignorance and worrying that I may be unsaved): You have to be born again. Do you accept the Lord Jesus Christ as your own personal savior?

Me (genuinely puzzled): Doesn't everybody?

Well, you get the idea. She told me about clergy and theologies that deny the Virgin Birth or the Divine Inspiration of the Bible. I balked when she said some of them don't even accept the divinity of Christ; she had to take me to the library and get out a book (I believe it was by Fosdick himself) to prove it, for the author had written just that.

During the interval between college and medical school, at Helen's urging I took a correspondence course from Moody Bible Institute, and for the first time got a sense of what it meant to study the Bible. I had long since come to understand that "whosoever believeth" (John 3:16) meant me. I attended, and eventually joined, the Baptist Church and was (re-)baptized in it. Helen was disappointed that I had no notable "conversion" experience; but really there had never been a time when I was not a believer, and she gracefully accepted that.

She was, as I thought of it, a classic "old maid", and she got somewhat possessive and demanding, wanting me to sit with her in church, and getting a little resentful of the church's young people, including an occasional girl friend, that I'd associate with. She began to seem a nuisance, but I felt such gratitude for her help, and reluctance to cause her any hurt, that I accommodated her as much as I could. In my senior year of medical school I became engaged to marry, and following that, and especially after starting internship a few months later (which really did greatly tie up my time) Helen gradually faded from my life.

But before that, she had become far more than a "nuisance". Her initial revelations to me about Modernism had been so jarring, yet so abundantly true, that she became—as we would say it today—my spiritual "guru". From her I learned the sinfulness of smoking and drinking, gambling and bridge, movies and theater. As to these things, the minister and my young friends at church reinforced the same lessons—which in my mind added to Helen's credibility. So when she began leaning on me to "witness", her word held the same authority. Having no other model or knowledge, I thought it meant to do what she did. She would initiate conversation with strangers or acquaintances (as she had with me), and with little ado would ask, "Are you saved?" or something only slightly less confrontational.

I knew there was something wrong with this—I couldn't understand what—but I simply could not do it. This became a conflict sufficiently grave to contribute to my eventual disillusionment with the Baptist Church and with Fundamentalism in general.

For one thing, it seemed to me that this problem was spiritual, yet nothing about the church or within it offered me any help. At each church service I sought a Bible reading, a prayer, a hymn, a sermon—anything that would provide me with greater understanding. But it dawned on me in time that there would be no help. The church was not set up for, nor had any intention of providing, any such help to its members. Its sole purpose was "witness"—to bring unbelievers into the fold. What could the church leaders have said if I'd been honest with them about my problem? I guess, "If you can't play ball, get off the field" or something to that effect. Of course I should have said the same thing to myself and then taken my own advice. But I felt under such compulsion to witness—such driven obligation to the church's purpose—that I couldn't at the time contemplate a defection.

I attended Baptist Youth and the Young Adult Sunday School when I could, but found that their focus was the same. Anyhow, speaking up in a class or group and saying that I was ashamed to witness (that is, to talk to people like Helen did) was as much as to say I was ashamed of Christ. I myself thought that's what it meant, and it all seemed pretty sinful.

Also, as I actually perceived only later, the personal turmoil that had helped propel me to the church had largely been resolved (that wasn't clear at the time, I suppose because my new problem with the church itself had become as large and as stressful). There were other changes. Part way through internship I married and we found a neighborhood Reformed Church whose interim pastor was a seminary student and an old friend of mine, who was emerging from his own Fundamentalist upbringing. We attended there until I finished training and left town. But for the first time in years I had friends and associates who were not Fundamentalists.

Then came the Korean conflict; I was appointed a medical officer in the Air Force, and was initially sent for training to a graduate school of Public Health. The Christian friends we made in the new location were Southern Presbyterian.

Of consequence too, was a course in Public Mental Health—called "Mental Hygiene" at that school, but it dealt with what later became Community Mental Health. All my previous exposure to psychiatry had left me thoroughly unmoved; but Mental Hygiene interested me. I did end up, after the Air Force and three years further training, becoming a psychiatrist.

New experiences, new reading, new thinking and new ideas, and new people coming into my life, all had their influence. But one single experience became my spiritual Rubicon. I don't remember when it occurred; I think it was actually before I finished medical school, and it certainly colored all the other subsequent experiences. Here's how it happened:

A crucial tenet, indeed the cornerstone, of Fundamentalism—at least as I understood it—was belief in the literal, verbal inspiration of the Scriptures, and consequently their infallibility. Now, I had read just a little of Thomas Paine and Albert Schweitzer, and had uncovered a few problems on my own, like the age and length of rule of King Jehoiachin as given respectively in the II Kings (18 years old) and II Chronicles (8) accounts; or like the story of the sun quite impossibly standing still at Joshua's command, thus giving him extra time to complete his slaughter of the Amorites. I never had believed the universe was created in 6 days.

Not long after I met Helen, we had a conversation in which she herself inadvertently contributed some seeds of doubt, though neither of us realized it at the time. I had expressed interest in the book of Ecclesiastes, and if she had simply accepted that and let the matter drop, nothing more would have come of it. But she was concerned that I might take the Preacher too seriously: "That's only a man-made, human philosophy", she said.

"You mean, not divinely inspired? Why is it in the Bible?", I asked.

"Of course it's inspired. It's a divinely inspired account of a human philosophy."

I've never been quick on the uptake, and that ended the discussion. I am an "I should'a said" kind of guy—like so: "You mean God inspired Solomon to write something He Himself considered false, so that we would have a perfect, infallible account of what we shouldn't believe—but failed to inform us of what it is we're reading, so that we really can't tell it's something He doesn't believe? Did Solomon himself not believe it, and only wrote down what God directed, though knowing it was untrue?— and why would God speak untruths? Or if Solomon really did believe it, and the words in Ecclesiastes are divinely inspired though they represent the author's own beliefs, does that mean that the falsehoods in Solomon's mind were put there by God through divine inspiration?"

But the rationalizations and evasions which must be familiar to many Christians facing these questions were good enough also for me, and I maintained at least a shaky conviction of the inspiration and historicity of Scripture.

Then one day I read II Kings 2:23-24, in which Elisha cursed little children for teasing him; whereupon they were torn up by bears. I may have seen this before, but now it caught my attention. I read it again; I thought about it; in my mind I slowly, deliberately, almost defiantly pronounced to myself the words, "I don't believe it!—*I cannot believe this*".

Surprisingly (to me) I felt no conflict over it. No loss of faith, but rather relief and freedom, as though liberated from some terrible barrier to faith. The tension between what I knew to be true, and what I believed—or thought I should believe—had to end somehow, and it felt good.

Later, when I joined the Presbyterian Church, I encountered a formula that was thoroughly satisfying: the Bible is the "only infallible rule of faith and practice". I believe, without evasion, rationalization or conflict, in the central article of faith and practice that the Bible sets forth: that Jesus Christ is the Son of God and my Lord and Savior; but I do not believe that God ever sent bears to tear up naughty children.

I suppose that here is the place to add that my first-impression response to this passage was naive. After all, the Bible doesn't just tell us about she-bears; it also tells us "whatsoever things were written aforetime were written for our learning" (Rom. 15:4). That statement is a guide to "faith and practice", and if I believe it's infallible, then my thoughts about Elisha, bears and God, have to be re-visited. My first reaction was not analytic but simply judgmental, and we must not sit in judgment (Matt. 7:1) —not on man, and not on the Word of God, either!

More than naive, my reaction was therefore one of sinful pride. A Christian scholar may legitimately study the authorship, the theological, etymological, scriptural, historical, scientific, and even mythological aspects of a Bible passage; but he is not thereby excused from his obligation to learn from it what he can of God's way of faith and practice (II Tim. 3:16). Studying God's Word is one thing; judging it is not seriously different from judging God Himself: this is the arrogance of unbelief.

As it happens, this passage about Elisha lends itself rather well to the present subject, which is why it's set forth in the last Chapter, which is devoted to an exposition of it, and it provides an example of how even a non-scholar may take the Bible seriously, learn from it in simple faith, and not have to fret about peripheral questions or answer challenges of the skeptics.

Since the day I encountered that passage, I hope I've been able to "grow in grace and in the knowledge of our Lord" (II Pet. 3:18); but I have no other major turning-points to report. I think I'm no longer a Fundamentalist. I believe the fundamentals of the faith, in my own way and to my own understanding, but I don't think they want me. I used to belong to the Christian Medical Society, a membership I valued, but back around the early fifties they adopted a new statement of faith to be affirmed by members and candidates. It included the term "substitutionary atonement of Christ" as an article of faith. There's a fine theological line here—one that I was much interested in at the time—as to who or what was changed by the Atonement, i.e., God or man. The substitutionary theory holds that God changed, that His need and intent to punish sinners was altered in view of Christ having substituted his own death for ours. But an alternative view is that God remains completely steadfast—forever unchanged and unchanging—but that *we* are changed: freed from punishment by being no longer sinners, Christ's blood having cleansed and regenerated and redeemed our lives; made of us new creations, born again—not as some kind of legal fiction, "sprung", as it were, by a technicality, but in reality becoming a new creature in Him. (I realize there is Scriptural support for either side; and I think this may be an example of a mystery in which two incompatible propositions are both true. I'll explain that in the next chapter.)

Anyhow, I wrote a letter to CMS and explained that I had this uncertainty about theories of the Atonement and could not whole-heartedly subscribe to one of them—the one which actually had less meaning for me than the other. I said it appeared they were not trying to include Christian medical professionals, but to exclude them, and that they should consider adopting a historic confession such as the Apostle's Creed. I knew this would have opened the door to non-Fundamentalists, so that they probably wouldn't consider it. Indeed they wrote back quoting some Scripture that purportedly backed their theory of the Atonement.

In short, Fundamentalist doctrinal conformity even in controversial matters, is itself a fundamental of their faith, and it's clear that I'd be a contaminant (but then, I never did believe you had to be a Fundamentalist to be saved).

At risk of being tedious, I think I owe at least some of my readers to whom it matters, a brief account of my political evolution.

Since age 21 I voted Republican consistently until 1960. But not that time! Since Richard Nixon's "Checkers" speech in 1956 I had considered him unstable and probably dishonest. I told myself "just this once" I had to vote against a Republican candidate, which I did, in favor of Kennedy.

I had opened a private office practice of psychiatry, but in the early '60's I began to feel a little dissatisfied—and more so as time went by. I got involved in the planning for a Community Mental Health Center for the County, and it recalled to me that Public Mental Health is the thing, and the only thing, that had made psychiatry appear interesting. In 1964 I left the office and went to work in a nearby state hospital—and I loved it! The relevance of all this will appear shortly.

Also in 1964 I looked forward to resuming my Republican affiliation by voting for Governor Scranton of Pennsylvania for president. Unfortunately, he wasn't nominated, and I had to vote against either the Roosevelt-type liberal, Lyndon Johnson, or the overly conservative Barry Goldwater of Arizona. Later I lived in Arizona, and know now that Goldwater got terribly bad press coverage, both alarmist and slanderous.

Still, I don't regret voting against him (as I did). His "Extremism in defense of liberty is no vice" gave me the willies. I feared the extremists of those times, and I fear today's, and I distrust their sympathizers, high and low.

I obviously had to vote against Richard Nixon in 1968 and 1972. In Arizona I was director of statewide community mental health programs within the State Department of Health. I later served pretty much the same role for Detroit-Wayne County, Michigan. I had dealings with Model Cities; my wife with Head Start and WIC (Women's, Infants', Children's programs). I was deeply involved in Comprehensive Health Planning activities; I worked with people in the National Center on Crime and Delinquency and the Law Enforcement Assistance Administration, as well as the National Institute of Mental Health. I did not at that time give much thought to the "Great Society's" huge expansion of Federal programs, Federal largesse, or its public cost. All these various agencies worked in cooperation with, and sometimes with contributions to my own area of responsibility, and I supported them and got what I could out of them.

At the same time, perhaps paradoxically, I had a serious distrust of government programs! I could see that some of them weren't working very well; some of them simply poured money into the multiple levels of bureaucracy that they themselves had fostered. Though a government agent myself during that time (1964—1973), and responsible to establish mental health centers throughout the state, or county later on; I NEVER attempted to set up a government-operated program. We always worked through private nonprofit local boards, providing them with professional expertise, guiding them through the grant-preparation and bureaucratic mazes, and supplying as much funding as we were able. But always the governance of "our" clinics was local, private (nonprofit) and autonomous. That's how I still believe it should be.

I decided to vote for Jimmy Carter in 1976, because I was attracted by his manner and, I'll admit it, by his frank Christian confession; and I also valued Rosalyn Carter's sincere interest in, and serious dedication to, mental health matters.

I've never gotten over wishing I could be a Republican again—but I can't, and in my view they have never offered us a man worthy of the presidency since 1956, except Gerald Ford (I did not vote against him, but for Carter, and it wasn't an easy choice).

In 1980 I voted for John Anderson, "sort of" a Republican. Ronald Reagan did have credentials. He was an orator of the caliber of Roosevelt and Churchill. He faced serious problems, and in our deadly struggle against inflation within our borders and the Soviet Union without, he could have, like Churchill, offered us "blood and toil, sweat and tears" and left us cheering and ready for sacrifice. I can never forgive him for instead pandering to our national greed—quick killings for big business and Savings and Loan moguls, lower taxes for all, and his abusive disparagement of what he regarded as the "Welfare Cadillac" poor; and all the time spending money in amounts that dwarfed Lyndon Johnson's extravagances on Viet Nam and the Great Society. It has been known since the days of Franklin Roosevelt that you can manufacture a short-term "fix" of economic depression and other woes by massive governmental spending. It worked well for Reagan, who left us with a quadrupled national debt! He may well have knocked down the last pillar of the Evil Empire, and stabilized the economy; but our grandchildren will be paying off the indebtedness that he also bequeathed.

I had rather admired George Bush Sr.'s valiant defiance (in the primary campaign) of Reagan's doctrinaire "voodoo economics", and I was greatly shocked and disappointed when he totally abandoned his own beliefs and principles in order to become acceptable as Reagan's running-mate. I note that he is referred to as a "yes man" by Ronald Reagan's press secretary, Larry Speakes, in his book *Speaking Out*.

I was in England during the 1988 Republican National Convention, and a puzzled Blighty turned to me at a lunch counter and asked why George Bush would select a nonentity like J. Danforth Quayle as his running mate. I said, "It's obvious: he's got no character himself, and can't afford to be upstaged." 'Nuff said about my vote against George Bush for president.

I would dearly have loved to vote against Bill Clinton, but they just made it too difficult. I miss being a Republican. I recently came across this (www.gathering-the-family.com): "Every gun that is made, every warship launched, every rocket fired signifies in the final sense, a theft from those who hunger and are not fed, those who are cold and are not clothed. This world in arms is not spending money alone. It is spending the sweat of its laborers, the genius of its scientists, the hopes of its children...This is not a way of life at all in any true sense. Under the cloud of war, it is humanity hanging on a cross of iron." (Dwight D. Eisenhower, April 1953). Now there was a Republican!—(though I know my Aunt Sally hated him). How am I to understand that a man of such sensibility, one who broke a 20-year Democratic stranglehold on Presidential politics, came to be replaced as the Republican model and hero by Ronald Reagan? (Maybe Ike was too *liberal*). Anyhow, I also miss being a Fundamentalist. I don't think I ever stopped trying to be a political and religious conservative—though I may have gone through some ambiguity in the 1960's. As best I could ever tell, conservatives offered no alternatives to the "Great Society"—only opposition—and neither then nor now is it clear how they would propose to deal with society's social problems. Though we can now look back and see that "big government" programs are not the answer, it was not so clear then, especially when the only alternative seemed to be doing nothing.

Remember the context of those times. World Communism appeared to be on the march. It made its gains, not by telling the truth—promising people a tyrannical dictatorship—but by promising food, work, jobs, and medical care; and by pointing the finger at America—the "poster child" of class warfare—of exploitation of the poor by the rich! To me, it was only being responsible when the leadership tried to make us clean up our act, with our being as viciously and almost universally hated as we were back then. We were seen as practically a standing invitation for people to try Communism. Now we see that government cannot erase poverty—not here and not in Russia—but we tried; and only thus do we learn such lessons.

I miss the Fundamentalist church also. Its people really care, in a culture that seems to be interested in little more than pleasure and making money. What they care *about* is a matter for further discussion, and through this book I hope to establish conversation with them.

CHAPTER 2

A FEW THINGS I NEVER LEARNED IN SUNDAY SCHOOL

Here are some "miscellaneous" observations, mostly by way of orientation to some "points of departure" for many of the subjects to be discussed in later chapters.

I AND WE

Know ye that the Lord he is God: it is he that hath made us, and not we ourselves...
...the Lord...created thee, O Jacob, and formed thee, O Israel.

(Psalm 100:3; Isaiah 43:1)

When I was a child I had to memorize the 100th Psalm (and others), and I always puzzled over the phrase, "Not we ourselves". I could see where it's appropriate to be told that God made us, but who ever had to be reminded that we did not make ourselves? American culture is so rigidly and extremely individualistic that, even as a small and fairly un-philosophical child, I automatically interpreted things in terms of myself as an individual. I believe many or most Americans would do the same. Even if, in this passage, the plural "we" is used, still it seemed to be telling us that "we", one by one as individuals, did not create ourselves. I used to try and visualize a bit of nothingness, a non-being or non-something which had no existence whatever, a nothing, a nonentity, somehow making itself into something—a person. The very notion is ridiculous, and I could not understand why in the world it was necessary for Scripture to refute it. The point is not that doing so is untrue; rather it is so self-evidently true as to be an absurd thing to say!

I see now that it doesn't mean what I thought. "We" does not refer to us as individuals. It means *we the people of God*—the Church; or in David's day, the Nation. "We", the Israelites of his time or the Christians of today, did not "make" the Body that defines us. God made the nation of Israel, and He created the Body of Christ, the Church, not "we ourselves", and it does indeed seem appropriate that we be reminded of it.

Thinking in collective terms does not come easily to individualistic Americans—especially Protestants—who are expected as single individuals to obtain their own salvation, and one by one be responsible for their Christian walk through life; and then alone stand before the Judgment.

Now, I don't dispute any of this. I wouldn't know how: I'm American too, brought up, as I already showed, in a culture of individualism in which "every bucket stands on its own bottom", as a governor of Arizona once told me, and such individualism is, to us, self-evident.

But is it Biblical?

Not entirely. Not to David or Isaiah it wasn't. Throughout the Old Testament, individualism as we know it in America today is seldom represented, and I believe it was no part of the usual thinking of the people in those times. It is the nation of Israel that is saved or lost, punished or rewarded. "OK", we moderns would say, "but that's because of the sin or virtue of the individuals who comprised that nation."

Again, I'm in no position to show how that's wrong, if it is. I only tell you, that is not what the Bible says; at least not often and not consistently, and certainly not in Psalm 100. In Chapter 8 I'll discuss this at length, because it is of fundamental importance—to our country, to the theme of this book, and to American Christianity. Here, I only want to introduce the word "communitarian", the term used by George Washington University's Amitai Ezioni and others to identify their proposed alternative to philosophical individualism. For now, my only point is that in our Sunday Schools—Episcopalian or Baptist—we are taught American individualistic values and we grow up seriously deficient in the Biblical idea of community.

Now let's think about some more seldom-spoken (and perhaps rarely understood) matters of faith and practice. I want to take up the question, alluded to before, of how two opposite statements can both be true.

MYSTERY, DUALISM AND PARADOX

He hath abounded toward us in all wisdom and prudence; having made known to us the mystery of his will, according to his good pleasure which he hath proposed in himself: that in the disposition of the fulness of times he might gather together in one all things in Christ, both which are in heaven, and which are on earth. (Eph. 1: 8-10)

St. Paul liked the term "mystery", and used it no less than 20 times in a number of different contexts. He called the

Resurrection (I Cor. 15: 51) and the union of man and wife (Eph. 5:32) mysteries, and he spoke of the mysteries of iniquity and also of godliness (II Thess. 2:7, I Tim. 3:16). The language of the above-cited text is somewhat ponderous, and its meaning is itself perhaps a mystery! Attempts at explaining it are handicapped by the general lack of attention given by the Church to its own mysteries. Perhaps we see no point in discussing what by definition we don't understand—what is a mystery to us—or perhaps, as I tend to see it, modern people, and especially Americans, prefer to think we have all the answers, or at least that we will in due time, after the next scientific breakthrough. We really hate to admit there are things we cannot and never will explain; that even our faith is full of mystery! And though St. Paul affirms that it is, we don't learn about it in Sunday School! St. Peter himself had a little trouble with St. Paul's epistles "in which are some things hard to understand" (II Peter 3:16). I confess that other translations of the Bible support my interpretations of this text less clearly than does the King James version. But I've seen none that contradicts it, nor offers a meaning so different as to invalidate what I'm saying.

So here goes.

St. Paul here seems to be saying that in God's own time, those things that are (or so appear to us) separate or opposed shall be unified—brought together as one in Christ. He says God has made known a mystery, as it were a vision: things that are earthly, that here are divided, paradoxical, inimical, incompatible, at war; "all things" that in a thousand ways are in conflict, shall in Christ and in God's time be resolved and pacified and unified. If so, then our task of fulfilling God's purposes must include that of creating unity—of healing the breaches. For the very Heaven and earth—if we may reconcile St. John's vision in Revelation with St.

Paul's—are no longer to be separate and divided; indeed they both pass away, and are replaced by the new heaven and the new earth, which themselves are not divided but one: the New Jerusalem, the dwelling-place of both God and man (Rev. 21:1-3).

What are some of the paradoxes, or mysteries, that must some day be reconciled in Christ?

Think of the Trinity. We believe in one God. We believe that in God there are three persons. Nobody can explain that. In the old days, Arius, Sabellius, and Marcellus of Ancyra (that I know of) tried to explain it. Their theories were all denounced as heresies—yet there was none to take their place. Nobody knows how one God can be three Persons; but we know that *both are true!*

We are assured that in the world to come, such polarities as day and light *vs* night and darkness will be abolished; as will good and evil, war and peace, sacred and profane, land and sea. Sorrow, crying and pain God shall wipe away; and also their opposite, happiness and pleasure?—for these are all human and temporal entities, emotional and perhaps inappropriate to beings "absorbed in prayer and praise" as the old hymn puts it (Rev. 21-22). (I didn't say *Joy,* our best earthly approximation of what Heaven is like.) It appears to me that even gender will be "gathered together in one", in St. Paul's terms: children of the resurrection are to be "as the angels in heaven", meaning, as I infer, neither male nor female (Matt. 22:30); "And as we have borne the image of the earthy, we shall also bear the image of the heavenly" (I Cor. 15:49).

There is much more. We have a Redeemer who is both God and man. You know that's not possible!—he can be God, or he can be man; but we have faith that *both are true!*

The Gospel tells us that weakness is strength. It intrinsically and expressly values poverty, weakness, death and suffering, and simplicity of mind (or "foolishness", as St. Paul terms it) as the source of life and power. Think about this magnificent paradox, stated so often in so many ways:

"Blessed are the meek: for they shall inherit the earth" (Matt. 5:5).

"Except a corn of wheat fall into the ground and die, it abideth alone; but if it die, it bringeth forth much fruit." (John 12:24), and likewise St. Paul: "...that which thou sowest is not quickened, except it die..." (I Cor. 15:36). And he said, "...when I am weak, then am I strong." (II Cor. 12:10); and, "...the wisdom of this world is foolishness with God." (I Cor. 3:17); and, "...not many wise men after the flesh, not many mighty, not many noble, are called: but God hath chosen the weak things of the world to confound the things that are mighty; and base things of the world, and things which are despised, hath God chosen, yea, and things which are not, to bring to nought things that are..." (I Cor. 1:26-27).

Hear Jesus again: "...whosoever will be great among you, let him be your minister; and whosoever will be chief among you, let him be your servant." (Matt. 20:26); and, "...he that is least among you all, the same shall be great." (Luke 9:48).

And he told us, "...become as little children..." (Matt. 18:3); and "...receive the kingdom of God as a little child..." (Mark 10:15, and Luke 18:17).

Israel was about as no-'count a nation as they come, 5/6ths of it already having been destroyed by Assyria; yet to this land—rather than mighty Babylon, Persia, Macedonia or Rome—came the Savior of the world. And Jesus himself, lacking power, education, or anything of value beyond the clothes on his back—in fact, to employ today's language, an itinerant homeless beggar or hobo, who was disgraced and executed for the heinous crime of treason—was resurrected from death to life, that he might become, beyond all earthly reckoning, that very Savior and Lord: the ultimate mystery and paradox!

And look at the Sacraments. Some see baptism as little or nothing more than a testimony—something performed, or rather accepted, by the individual himself to testify that he's saved. Others see in baptism, not something the individual does at all, for whatever purpose, but something done *to* him by God and the Church: the outward, visible sign of an act of God, not man, of an inward and spiritual grace. I find no Scriptural basis for disproving either theory; I suspect that *both are true!* And since the practical matter of infant *vs.* adult baptism hinges on which way we look at it, I conclude that a person or a church may decide what it believes and act accordingly, without negative reflection on those who decide and act differently, and even more so, without stirring doctrinal and denominational warfare!

And then there's that other great sacrament of the Church, Holy Communion. Without appreciation of mystery, we can make no more of the Eucharist than a mere symbol of Christ's body and blood. In fact, generations and multitudes of Protestants have found this sufficiently satisfying; and who will assert that when we partake of the Sacrament—the means of grace—that the Giver of grace may withhold or begrudge it because our understanding is and always will be imperfect?

Yet I'm reminded of Flannery O'Connor who, upon being advised by a fellow dinner-party guest that the Eucharist is a "healthy symbol" retorted, "Well, if it's a symbol, to hell with it." I'm sure she was reflecting the Roman Catholic version of the Real Presence, the actual body and blood of Christ in their real, concrete and material constitution, having been "transubstantiated" from bread and wine. I have no interest in picking any doctrinal quarrels with Roman Catholics, especially because—even though I can't accept the idea of transubstantiation—I do believe in the Real Presence. To me, the Sacrament is a means of grace and not merely a symbol thereof.

But I said "merely" because Holy Communion, whatever else may be said about it, is expressly a symbol of Christ's body given and blood shed. As such, "to hell with it" is inappropriate, because *both are true!* We celebrate Communion "in remembrance" (Luke 22:19), just as we celebrate Memorial Day in remembrance of those other sacrificial deaths of our national heroes, and our Buddy Poppies and our bread and wine are symbols to make remembrance meaningful. But that's not all: there is at the same time Christ's Real Presence, brought about not by physico-chemical transformation of the elements, but just as miraculously, by their consisting of his *mystical* body and blood. Though the notion of mysticism sounds fuzzy and insubstantial, it really isn't. The many mysteries of our faith are so because we can't fully comprehend them, and not because they aren't real. (Is the Trinity real, though a mystery?) And we don't solve the riddle by just declaring it all symbolic.

And how about this?—the Reformation itself derived from Martin Luther's mantra from Heb. 10:38, "The just shall live by faith"; and by various companion texts such as Eph. 2:8, "by grace are ye saved through faith". He called the Book of James "an epistle of straw", because it says, "Can faith save?...faith without works is dead" (James 2:14-26) Note the contradiction—and the mystery; for both are Scriptural—and widely supported elsewhere in the Bible; and *both are true!*

Unbelievers sometimes cite such paradoxes as barriers to faith—as their excuse or pretext, that is, for unbelief. The fact is that Christianity is thoroughly realistic in this respect; it shares in the character of our world, which is inescapably riddled with contradiction. There is in some Oriental philosophy a concept we call "dualism", by which every aspect of the universe is considered to be matched by its equal and opposite entity: *yin* and *yang* as some call it, typified in such elements as male and female, day or light and night or dark; by good and evil, heat and cold, creation and destruction, war and peace, life and death. A similar notion is reflected in Zoroastrianism, in which the Good and Evil deities are equal and opposite; and in a limited way in some Western philosophy such as that of Rene Descartes, whose dualism was mainly concerned with that between body and soul.

Our capacity to perceive the world is pretty much limited to the dualistic. We know, without in the least understanding how, that body and mind are a unity, and we express that knowledge in words like "psychosomatic". But I think, as this same word actually reveals, we persistently conceive and speak of them as a duality. Even in the scientific realm, we understand that the creative, progressive or evolutionary history of Nature, which has generated a universe and organized its specialized forms, has throughout been opposed to its destructive and dissipative tendencies, collectively known as *entropy*. In fact science has by now pretty well agreed on the existence of "anti-matter", all the particles of which are oppositely charged, relative to the ordinary matter that we know; and which, on making contact with the latter, would result in total annihilation of both.

We know that non-Euclidian and traditional geometry are irreconcilable and contradictory, and yet *both are true*. We know that light is radiated in the form of a kind of particle, called a *photon* or *quantum*, but that the selfsame light is also being radiated in wave form similar to radio waves. You can prove the actuality of both types of emission by measuring the light in different ways; for *both are true!*

The Bible itself seems to me a paradoxical mystery. It was written by fallible men; yet we say it is the perfect and infallible Word of God. An oxymoron indeed—a statement that is internally self-contradictory. We propose to resolve the contradiction with the theory of divine inspiration, and there is undoubted Scriptural justification for this. But as you shall see, I think we go overboard with it. Meanwhile, if you ask me how I can order my life and stake my salvation on St. Paul's assurance that we are "saved by grace through faith" (i.e. not by works), yet poke fun at his ideas on women and sex (Chap. 4 *&* 5), what can I say? It's a mystery to me! Skeptics have sold us on the idea that nothing can be the Word of God if it contains unscientific errors, yet they believe that parallel lines may cross (Lobachevsky) though knowing they cannot (Euclid). Why can't I know that the story of Joshua commanding the sun to stand still is scientifically absurd, yet respect it as the Word of God, for whatever He may want to say to me through it?—or the story of Elisha and the bears, or of Creation?

Here are some more paradoxes: we saw, in the last previous section of this chapter, how the claims of individualism and community co-exist—both valid, yet easily conflicted. We know that, in the words of William Safire, "God does not micromanage the universe"; yet we are equally sure that "prayer changes things." And how about determinism—or predestination, in John Calvin's terms—vs. free will? There are Scriptural proof texts for both; answers have been proposed, but none satisfy. Theologians tend to come down on one side or the other, trying not to think about Scriptural and scientific considerations to the contrary, and forgetting that in the context of a mystical faith, we don't have to quarrel over things that we cannot know.

St. Paul leads me to believe that the multitudinous mysteries and contradictions of this world will be resolved in the next. But for our purposes now, the important thing is for us to recognize that the contradictions and mysteries do exist. The search for dogmatic certainty will usually fail as this or that proposition encounters its equally forceful opposite. As you read on, you will see some more instances which illustrate the ambiguities of life and doctrine (though not of faith); and the uselessness, not to say foolishness, of creating conflicts over them.

LOVING GOD IN THE 21ST CENTURY

Herein is love, not that we loved God but that he loved us... (I John 4:10)

In the above verse is illustrated one of the most stark contrasts between the Old and New Testaments. Under Law, the necessity to *love God* is the first and greatest commandment, according to Jesus (Matt. 22:37 etc.) Note, though, that even if he here quotes Moses with approval, he makes no such commandment himself. Instead, he answers a question not asked, telling us what the second commandment is: to love thy neighbor as thyself.

I do not say—nor did Jesus, nor Sts. John, Peter, Paul and James who also spoke on the matter (Eph. 1:8-10; James 2:14-26)—that there's anything wrong with loving God. But let's be right careful when we think about what it means. Jesus told Peter what it means: Peter protested three times, with increasing desperation, that he loved Jesus (John 21:15-17). Jesus never did accept his claim; in what almost sounds like a rebuke, he only responded, "Feed my sheep", which is to say, "Take care of my people", which is to say, "Talk's cheap—put up or shut up!"

Today we'd call this an "operational definition"—explaining an abstract concept in terms of the actions or operations that produce it. For example, I could say that Patriotism is my first duty as an American citizen. But what does it mean? To some, it means emotional flag-waving and hatred of foreigners. To me, patriotism is only realized when we vote, obey the law, work and support our families, give military or other service as the country requires, pay our taxes, and raise our children to do the same. We would not say that any or all of these things are "more important" than Patriotism; only that they constitute its operational definition. Likewise, though Jesus confirmed that nothing is greater than loving God, his concern was that we understand what that means.

Loving God does not mean persecuting the Church, as the ancient Jews and Romans thought. It does not mean persecuting Jews, as the Church once thought; nor torturing and killing Protestants, as Torquemada thought; nor Roman Catholics, either, as Calvin, Cromwell, and other Reformation leaders thought. It does not mean persecuting Methodists, Mormons, Muslims, Moonies; or women who obtain abortions or clinic workers who provide them; or Galileo; or science teachers who believe in Evolution; yet all religious persecutors certainly believe that they love God and are working according to His purposes. And sometimes centuries have to pass before it becomes generally accepted how wrong they are!

Jesus said, "A new commandment I give unto you, That ye love one another" (John 13:34), and in the same discourse he repeated himself three times (John 15:12,17) .

Now, if I tell you I got a new shirt, or a new piece of furniture, or a new kind of flower to plant in my garden, you'd assume I had added the new item: I've *supplemented* what I already had. But if I say I got a new house, or a new wife, or that the nation of Ginsoak has a new government, you would understand that a very major change has occurred—in some cases you'd call it a revolution!—the old has been entirely discarded and replaced; the new does not add to the old, but *supplants* it.

New Testament writers do not command us to love God, and the reason, I submit to you, is simply that a revolution has taken place. We are not subject to any such new commandment or ancient law. We are under Grace (how easily we forget that!) and the "new commandment", the only one, supplanting all others, is to LOVE ONE ANOTHER. St. Paul understood this; he wrote, "... all the law is fulfilled in one word... Thou shalt love thy neighbor as thyself" (Gal. 5:14). If we love our neighbor, we have fulfilled Christ's commandment, and St. John assures us that in doing so we show our love for God: "Whom to love is to obey." (John Milton). And loving one's neighbor is not abstract or sentimental, but active, consisting of the performance of loving deeds. Actual, concrete deeds: feeding the hungry, healing the sick, visiting the prisoner.

This is not an arbitrary law of God, imposed on us to make religion difficult. It's what love means, and is equally true of God's own love, which consists of deeds, not sentiment: "He maketh his sun to shine on the evil and on the good, and sendeth rain on the just and on the unjust", and He "so loved the world that he gave his only-begotten son" (Matt. 5:45; John 3:16). After all, no matter how generous, kind and thoughtful we are, we can only use these qualities to do loving deeds to our fellow-men, not to God. He has no needs of us, or desires, except that we supplement His own loving deeds to mankind. "Go and do thou likewise" (Luke 10:37); "...let us not love in word, neither in tongue; but in deed and in truth." (I John 3:18).

In past centuries we could love God by killing the Turk, the Jew or the heretic—or so we thought. In the 19th and early 20th centuries, many Christians thought that loving God meant to promote the Social Gospel—to bring the Kingdom of God to earth through establishment of a liberal or socialistic political order or alternatively, they thought that loving God meant opposing Modernism and witnessing to the unsaved. More recently now, it seems that loving God has become much more sentimental; our "warm and fuzzy" response to a good time of Christian fellowship or a beautiful performance of Gospel music; or by the emotionality of our abhorrence of street crime and drugs, or immorality and abortion, of evolution and secular humanism and Bill Clinton: the more keenly we *feel* the more we love God. In the 21st Century we need to know better than this: that we are not commanded to love God at all!—but that we may yet do so, singularly and solely by loving His creatures, by doing to them as Jesus exemplified; and that *we are liars* if we claim on any other basis to love Him (I John 4:20—5:3).

After some internal debate, I thought I should add this, for I may sound hypocritical and "holier-than-thou". Yes, I'm a physician—a healer—and a mental health bureaucrat—a professional do-gooder; but none of that counts. I, and the auto mechanic, the secretary, the housewife, the lawyer are obligated to do our best at the work to which God led us; but no brownie points accrue to any particular line of work, or at least not to mine. I've made a good living at my job, and I don't believe that "doing well by doing good"—helping people at no cost to myself, or even at a profit, is what our Lord had in mind.

When I speak of loving God through loving deeds to man, I mean deeds done at a cost. I think the cost is supposed to be sacrificial, and painfully so ("give till it hurts"). It may be at the cost of money, time, pleasurable activities, or any kind of mammon; but I do believe we are supposed to sacrifice something. And not just at Lent; but rather it's what St. Paul called the "way"—around the calendar and around the clock, our way of life, because love is more than what we do, it's what we are.

I'm of an age to look back and judge my own record; and by the above standard I haven't much to show. If I ever sound like I'm preaching at you, please believe me—it's because of what I know, not what I've done; because I have learned too late that I've done too little to show the kind of neighbor-love that Jesus asked of us. If you think that sounds like "do as I say, not as I do"—I'm sorry to say, you may be right. Look to Jesus for your example, not to me.

WWJD

... what I would, that do I not; but what I hate, that I do ... the good that I would, I do not; but the evil which I would not, that I do ...when I would do good, evil is present with me ...O wretched man that I am! (Rom. 7:15-24)

"What Would Jesus Do?" is a great motto, and the youth movement by that name holds real promise. The choice between good and evil is pretty clear during our maturational years. Some choices are tough to make, but they are seldom ambiguous. Everybody knows right from wrong when it comes to the "temptations of youth": drugs, tobacco and alcohol; cheating, shoplifting and sex; snobbishness toward the uncool; seeking pleasure over studies and conformity over dignity. There are so many, it seems to me that without reliance on Jesus and the commitment to seek his guidance—to ask "what would Jesus do?"—that any final attainment of real morality is greatly against the odds.

I guess it has to be that way; maturing surely means not just strengthening the body but toughening the character; and the more rigorous the exercise, the better the outcome. It should be self-evident that drugs and alcohol, which anesthetize both conscience and judgment, make it impossible to grow in responsibility and capacity for moral choice. It is less obvious, but equally true, that frequent or habitual choice of the "wide gate and broad pathway", in any area at all or in multiple areas, likewise retards maturation.

So much—so very much—could turn on our seriously entertaining that question, "What would Jesus do?" So why didn't St. Paul ask it? Why his sense of evil-doing (or if you prefer, his guilty conscience), as he expressed it in Romans, chapter 7? There's a simple answer and a complex answer.

The simple answer is, he wasn't a teen-ager! If you've read with care up to now, you've seen that we were talking about WWJD as a means of helping Christians through their developmental years to become responsible and to develop personal powers of choice by which to fulfill ethical responsibilities. As I pointed out, most choices during those years are not complex or ambiguous—the ideal "practice field" for honing skills!

But later on in life it does get complicated. And that's the second reason for St. Paul's problem. Here's one way to look at it:

We've started to talk lately, in connection with various public matters, about the "law of unintended consequences". It just means that for many (or for most or all?) of the things we do that appeared to be good and desirable, we come to find out they also had a negative or destructive side, that we simply didn't foresee. I think that is how somebody like St. Paul can see the presence of evil in all his efforts to do good.

The all-time poster child of this law is Karl Marx, who in theory intended nothing but benevolence for the working man—a casting off of his chains—a Utopian society organized by all, supported by all, for the benefit of all. Yet he generated in practice, all unintended, the most destructive regime since Tamerlane.

Unintended consequences are easy to see when speaking of government: an anti-poverty program that didn't benefit the poor; a military enterprise that saw us victoriously through the Cold War but left us with the very military-industrial complex which, in prospect, so frightened President Eisenhower that he had so vigorously to warn us against it; a tax cut that marginally boosts the economy but nearly bankrupts the government.

Even Adam and Eve only meant well in taking a fruit that was "good for food, and that was pleasant to the eyes, and...to be desired to make one wise" (Gen. 3:6). With hindsight, we are able to see the downside!—but they did not.

From their day, to the time of St. Paul, right down to the present, our attempts to do something good and constructive and beneficial and loving often merely make matters worse than they were before.

"...so little knows
Any, but God alone, to value right
The good before him, but perverts best things
To worst abuse, or to their meanest use." (John Milton)

There's a trap here, one that we weren't warned about in Sunday School. We know we're supposed to be honest with ourselves and God, and own up to our sins and confess them. But they don't tell us about all the ways we have to deny and rationalize our guilt. Take an example:

Imagine a woman contemplating divorce. She will almost always have some conflict about it—will feel at least a little guilty; will have some sense that it's wrong. But as we know, if she really wants a divorce, she will get it. And once having done so, she'll say, "It was a tough decision, but I think I did the right thing." Now suppose that the ex-spouse had been unfaithful, non-supportive, abusive and violent to her and the children; and finally abandoned the family completely. Who is going to argue with her and say, "No, actually what you did was wrong"?

I'm using an extreme example to make my point, because in fact almost nobody (not even I) would say that. And yet, as a general proposition, nobody believes that getting a divorce is virtuous. We all know that divorce is indeed a great evil, a societal wrong as well as a cause of individual harm to its victims. So by what logic do we contemplate something so wrong and still say, "I did the right thing"? How does an evil that I might see you do become right if I do it myself? That's the trap; there's no avoiding it, but there's an answer.

Martin Luther said, "Love God and sin boldly". I can't say with authority what he meant by that, but here's what it means to me: If you love God (which is to say, if you love your neighbor—as we discussed earlier) you will make choices which at least are not wholly selfish. They will almost inevitably have a downside—will involve some evil or other, if not in the action itself, then in its unforeseen consequences; and you have to become aware of that, if you're to be honest with yourself and God. We only add to our guilt when we try to deny or rationalize the evil we do. But you can't do *nothing!*—you have to decide; and having decided what to do, confess your sin and do boldly what you have to do, and trust to God that He has not led you "into temptation"—to the selfish or comfortable or easy or profitable choice; but to the lesser of the available evils.

It seems to me that (after adolescence) there is rarely a moral dilemma in which we must choose between good and evil. If those were recognizably the alternatives, there'd be a lot less evil done!—because many or most people would not knowingly and deliberately choose to do evil instead of good.

Understand, I'm talking about a true and consequential *dilemma*, in which we are deeply and genuinely conflicted, puzzled, willing to do what's right but utterly confused about what that might be. Obviously, we all make choices, repeatedly and all day long, and often if not habitually we choose to do wrong—and often are not even conscious of it. These are not the *dilemmas* I speak of, because these choices tend to be made easily and thoughtlessly, usually from laziness or selfishness or mere force of habit, with little or no consideration of moral issues, nor with any hesitating indecision therefrom.

Rather, a true dilemma is between two evils, such as between a divorce and an intolerably destructive marriage relationship. Usually we decide on what we *want* to do; always we rationalize and deny its evil nature and pronounce it right rather than wrong. Luther, as I understand him, urged us to acknowledge with St. Paul that evil is always present with us; boldly choose an action based on love and not selfish wants; hope it is the lesser evil and stop telling ourselves it's right!—(rather then wrong).

Incidentally, ethicists quarrel about whether morals are relative or absolute. That is, have we a moral code governing all situations and all people, under which wrong is wrong, regardless of time, place, person or circumstance? Or must each choice be evaluated as its own case: can what's wrong for one person in his circumstance, be OK for another in his own setting? Was it wrong for Dietrich Bonhoeffer, the German Lutheran pastor, to participate in a plot to assassinate Hitler, or for WW I hero Sgt. Alvin York to go to war in spite of his own belief that it is wrong to kill? Or, even though it would be wrong for me to kill, were their decisions justified for them, in their time and place and under their circumstances?

It's clear that *both are true* (see previous section). There is a universal moral law, as St. Paul spells out in the first chapter of Romans. There is no time, place, or human culture in which cowardice, dishonesty, disloyalty, child abuse, or numerous other evils have been considered right. We mentioned the unambiguous moral choices that face adolescents; and I maintain that there is no way that a kid can honestly rationalize that it's OK for him to shoplift or smoke, while knowing it would be wrong for anybody else.

But when we get older and our lives get complicated, it's not so simple. That's why we have dilemmas!—and one person's decision in any moral crisis may not be right for another. However, I doubt if Bonhoeffer would have claimed that it was right and virtuous to murder Hitler; or that Sgt. York would claim the dozens of bereaved German widows and orphans that he created, as stars in his crown. Their choices were clearly for evil, though, as I would maintain till my dying day, absolutely the lesser evil of the alternatives available to them in their time.

Our Sunday School lessons always told us that we should do the right thing, and follow the Golden Rule, and avoid the wrong. They taught us specific "thou shalt nots" that were sinful, and so allowed us to believe that other things we do are OK. But I have learned that most everything I do has a downside that often is harmful to myself or others; and above all in a serious moral conflict or dilemma there is seldom a "right" choice. When I struggle and agonize over which is the "right" thing to do, I am setting myself up to be able, after I've done it, to say I did the "right" thing. And yet, if I knew that it were *really* right, I'd simply do it (usually), and not have any dilemma at all. There can be exceptions, as when the conflict involves actions that may be dangerous or expensive, and our struggle is not with conscience but feasibility or fear. For most of us today these situations are rare.

For most of us, most of the time, most of what we do is, just as St. Paul complained, partly or wholly evil. We still have to do it, as Luther pointed out, because that is what the world is like; but we don't have to deceive ourselves. Abraham Lincoln understood this (quoted in *The Prairie Years,* by Carl Sandburg): "The true rule in determining to embrace or reject anything, is not whether it have any evil in it, but whether it have more of evil than of good. There are few things wholly evil or wholly good. Almost everything is an inseparable compound of the two; so that our best judgment of the preponderance between them is continuously demanded."

Here's how Albert Schweitzer put it: "The good conscience is an invention of the devil."

Now I want to take up some matters of religious and public policy as they relate to Christian principles.

CHAPTER 3

THE ENVIRONMENT

The earth is the LORD'S and the fullness thereof...(Psalm 24:1) *The earth does not belong to us: we belong to the earth.* (Chief Seattle) *What's the use of a house, if you haven't got a tolerable planet to put it on?* (Henry David Thoreau)

Oh God, help us not to despise or oppose what we do not understand. (William Penn)

I don't know how often Christians get involved in environmental advocacy, or conversely—given their affinity for Republican causes—how negligent of it or even oppositional they may be. I have a feeling it isn't "high priority" with many or most; but I think it should be, and I'd like to talk a little about why. We'll start with a discussion of man's relationship to the animal kingdom.

MAN AND ANIMAL

(humans) themselves are beasts. For that which befalleth the sons of men befalleth beasts; even one thing befalleth them: as the one dieth, so dieth the other; yea, they all have one breath; so that a man hath no preeminence above a beast: for all is vanity.

All go to one place; all are of the dust, and all turn to dust again.
(Eccl. 3:18-20)

I have no doubt that my mentor Helen (see Chap. 1) was right, that Ecclesiastes sets forth a human philosophy, and a dark and pessimistic one (as to the question of its divine inspiration, that shall remain a mystery!) You get the feeling that King Solomon finally became so surfeited with "gold and silver, ivory, and apes, and peacocks ...seven hundred wives, princesses, and three hundred concubines" that he finally began to ask what it all means—and couldn't think of an answer. Yet he was wise in spite of all, and his conclusion, as set forth in Ecclesiastes, is that none of it means anything!—and it's hard not to agree. (We know that in Christ, life has both joy and meaning; but in wealth and mammon and the pursuit of earthly values of pleasure and gain, there is neither: Solomon was right!).

It may be merely his pessimism that causes him to equate man with beast; but pessimists may yet be wise. We'll talk later about any differences there may be, but first I want to establish that we are full-fledged members of the animal kingdom. I'm not talking about Evolution, which purports to tell us *why* it's so. I'm more like discussing "why not".

Though the wisest man of antiquity said that "a man hath no preeminence above a beast", yet there seems to be a driven human need to believe ourselves superior. Such a belief is clearly refuted by Scripture—at least in King Solomon's contribution to it—but more pointedly by Harvard University's brilliant paleontologist and prolific author, the late Stephen Jay Gould. He was, of course, a dedicated evolutionist, though with a difference—as we shall see—and he claimed that a big reason why

Evolution is so distasteful to many people is that they can't stand to be dethroned. Accustomed to seeing humanity as some kind of grand climax or ultimate achievement of Nature, or perhaps as separately and specially created apart from and superior to Nature, we may perceive Evolution as a leveling doctrine, one which establishes what Solomon asserted: man is a beast! I think Gould was at least partly right about at least some people. In our self-importance, even arrogance, we think ourselves superior to Nature; of a different order entirely. We cannot accept being really and truly animals, a part of the world and even of the animal kingdom.

We do have a better nervous system (including brains) than the peacock, but are not more beautiful; and it is only our subjective prejudice—one man's opinion, so to speak, though it's Everyman's—that makes us value brains over beauty (and our true animal nature may be demonstrated by the fact that—at least in our courtship behavior—we often *do* value beauty over brains). People still are revolted at any allegation of biological kinship with monkeys, thus demonstrating their belief in their own self-importance relative to "lower" animals. It seems to me that a careful study of the Bible could disabuse us of this.

In the first place, no arrogance or self-importance *ever of any kind* is countenanced by Jesus. It is the very core of what he most fervently denounced—hypocrisy and self-righteousness.

Secondly, consider two passages selectively quoted from Scripture to make my point (look it up—the language I've omitted does not contradict what I included):

...The LORD *God formed man of the dust of the ground ... And out of the ground the* LORD *God formed every beast of the field, and every fowl of the air... dust thou art, and unto dust shalt thou return.* (Gen. 2:7,19; 3:19)

Solomon in all his pessimism was only quoting Scripture! Man was made in God's image (Gen. 1:26; see below) but Christians and others easily confuse two different matters here. "God is a spirit", Jesus told us (John 4:24) and the statement that we are made in God's image cannot mean that He is made in ours!—that He possesses hands or feet, ears or genitals (such as to make Him of one sex or the other). God has given us a brain, rather than the beauty of the peacock or the strength of the elephant or the speed of the cheetah or flight like the albatross or even, for most of us, the wonderful loyalty and devotion of the dog! He has given us our gift of a brain, no more wonderful than the peacock's tail, but unique among all gifts: it is compatible with a soul or spirit—and *that* is the image of God in us. Our bodies are not constructed in the image of God—Who is a spirit—but more like that of a chimpanzee or gorilla. Jesus knew this: "the spirit is willing but the flesh is weak," he said (Matt. 26:41) and "a spirit hath not flesh and bones" (Luke 24:39). Hear St. Peter: "all flesh is as grass...the grass withereth" (i.e. is mortal) (I Pet. 1:24). St. Paul said, "the flesh lusteth against the Spirit, and the Spirit against the flesh: and these are contrary the one to the other" (Gal. 5:17), and in many other places he avers the earthy, or animal, nature of our bodies (Rom. 8:4-9; I Cor. 5:5; 15:44-49; Gal. 4:23; etc.)

The Bible tells us that in our essence we have, or *are,* spirits, and are like God in that respect. But it *does not teach* that in our mortal nature, we are anything but one among many creatures. I am one life, placed among countless other lives of countless diverse forms, each in its own way superior to me—though none with the ability in arrogance to *think* itself superior!

And I have a theory too, that if we weren't so secretive and uptight about sex—if we ever really opened up and thought about it—we'd recognize the act as a very animalic bit of behavior. I have little doubt that this reminder of our animal nature is one reason for the historic frequency with which it has encountered disfavor within Christianity. Now let me tell you something else about our place in Nature.

WEEDS

Sir, didst not thou sow good seed?...from whence then hath it tares?...An enemy hath done this... Gather the tares...and burn them (Matt. 13:24-30)

Did you know that among some ecological biologists the term "weed" is not limited to certain forms of plant life such as the bindweed and ragweed? As reported in Harper's Magazine, October, 1998, by David Quammen, the term as they use it encompasses all sorts of species, both plant and animal, which possess "weedy" characteristics: "...they reproduce quickly, disperse widely when given a chance, tolerate a fairly broad range of habitat conditions, take hold in strange places, succeed especially in disturbed ecosystems, and resist eradication once they're established. They are scrappers, generalists, opportunists. They tend to thrive in human-dominated terrain because in crucial ways they resemble *Homo sapiens:* aggressive, versatile, prolific, and ready to travel".

Quammen's essay goes on in quite pessimistic tone to discuss man's progressive destruction of natural wildlife habitat, with resultant mass extinction of species—not only leaving nothing but weeds of both plant and animal persuasion, but also leaving only the "disturbed ecosystem" in which they thrive. It is indeed gloomy to think of the day in which bird life will be limited to the crow and the house sparrow, the starling and the pigeon; when wild animals will be gone, all but rats and mice, skunks and coyotes; when the only wildflowers will be the mustardweed and thistle, and the woodlands taken over by kudzu vine and Ailanthus (the perversely named "tree of heaven". Anybody who has observed this unlovely, evil-smelling weed-tree invading a woodland, or who has attempted to eradicate it from his property or fencerow, will agree that it should instead have been named for what George Bernard Shaw called "the alternative establishment"!) Naturally, this futurama will include hordes of houseflies, Japanese beetles, grasshoppers, cockroaches, fire ants and Africanized honeybees; not to mention unforeseeable kinds and numbers of bacteria.

Talk about "ready to travel"—note that of the 18 species named above, 10 are not New World natives, but imports, mostly from Asia.

According to Quammen this scenario is controversial, not necessarily inevitable. Unfortunately for the optimists, their prediction that all will be well is not based on an alternative scientific interpretation of facts (because the facts of mass extinction are well-known and undeniable) but on the expectation that man's own inventiveness and technological mastery will suffice to save the world. I don't find that a very comforting thought.

For those are the very things that have brought about the whole predicament. You may already have noticed from Quammen's listing of weedy characteristics that the ultimate, most vicious weed of all is mankind himself. He is the sole reason for threatened mass extinction of most remaining species. The only limit to his power of destruction is other weeds!—the very things whose extermination he deliberately seeks but can't accomplish!

If you're incurably optimistic, I recommend David Quammen's article (in which he provides some further reading that sounds pretty sobering), because we need to take seriously our future and the earth's.

Whatever that may hold, the conclusion for us here and now seems unavoidable: I am not only one life among many, I am also the first among many weeds, and I take over earth space far more rapidly, completely and destructively than dandelions and crabgrass can take over a lawn. Belief in our separate and superior status over all other life allows us to deny or ignore that fact, though we risk destruction along with the other tares of Nature. The parable of the wheat and tares surely means what Jesus said it means, so you are free to dispute the following exegesis; though I think it only supplements but does not violate his intent. If we humans are indeed the tares of God's field, must we not come under judgment for choking out most of the life that God has planted around us? In our driven proclivity to weedy behavior, do we act as children of the Kingdom, or of the Wicked One?

Anyhow, the burden of proof is clearly upon anybody who claims that mankind is separate and apart from—not to say superior to—the rest of the animal kingdom. His superiority is only in the greater threat he poses. His relationship to Nature is about like that of the gypsy moth to the apple orchard: he will consume it utterly if not stopped; and that according to Nature's laws and from inside Nature's system—not from outside as if by some kind of invasion by a superior force.

Yet the Bible tells us of man's "dominion" over Nature. We have to think about what that means.

DOMINION

God said, Let us make man in our image, after our likeness: and let them have dominion over the fish of the sea, and over the fowl of the air, and over the cattle, and over all the earth...and God said unto them, replenish the earth and subdue it: and have dominion...over every living thing. Thou madest (man) to have dominion over the works of thy hands: thou hast put all things under his feet. (Gen. 1:26-28; Ps. 8:6-8)

Though we've just proved Scripturally that man is not superior to animals, still the word "dominion" does not imply equality! Indeed, the above Psalm was quoted by a congressional representative in a committee hearing, in opposition to an environmentalist who testified in support of a bill; and in denial of our obligation to the wild things of the world. No more stark rendition could be made, of an interpretation of Scripture that would excuse man from, or even set him in opposition to, the conservation and protection of Nature, because of his supposed "dominion" over her.

As far as I know, Jesus never directly addressed our relationship to the natural world, though he told of how God cares for birds and plants (Luke 12:24-28)—suggesting that we should, too. Most explicit references are in Genesis. The passages cited above seem to sum up what many Christians believe, that "dominion" means to rule somebody or something, to exercise power and lordship over them; and we have acted like very bad rulers, inflicting upon Nature death, slave labor, and even extermination, purely and merely at our whim.

How would the dominion of a good ruler be different? The prophet Daniel used that word most prolifically (Chapters 4,6,7). He refers to Nebuchadnezzar (Chap. 4) and to the envisioned future kingdoms (Chap 6,7) as having "dominion", and there can be no doubt that the word means earthly power.

But Daniel also knew how power is to be used: "...break off thy sins by righteousness, and thine iniquities by showing mercy to the poor..." he advised Nebuchadnezzar (Dan. 4: 27). So dominion exercised in the manner of the world's principalities and powers is "iniquity", according to Daniel. Instead of that, the king is to use his power to protect his poorest and least consequential subjects. Protect from whom? From those who would hurt and exploit them—the rich and powerful.

Look: God alone has ultimate dominion. Ask yourself how He exercises His powers; what kind of rule He imposes over His territories. Isn't it a rule of kindness? Refer to the verses from Luke 12, cited above; God's dominion over Nature is revealed in His caring and protection of it! Can we really think that our "dominion"—in flat opposition to God's own—entitles us to destroy wild environments and slaughter their inhabitants? Scripture tells us that man's dominion is a gift of God, and we know that His gifts are not to be wasted or abused.

Nebuchadnezzar's punishment of insanity and banishment was not for his power, but for his pride, arrogance, self-importance; for claiming for himself that which had been given him by God (Dan. 4:25-37). As Daniel put it, his mandate sounds a little like that imparted to mankind in Genesis: "...the God of heaven hath given thee a kingdom, power, and strength, and glory. And wheresoever the children of men dwell, the beasts of the field and the fowls of the heaven hath he given into thine hand, and hath made thee ruler over them all." (Dan. 2:37-38)

It is true that throughout history man has used his powers to hurt and exploit and destroy; and there's no doubt we use our dominion over Nature in the same way. But can any Christian argue that this is the purpose of God's gifts? Can we deny that such behavior is a remnant of the "old man" in us (Rom 6:6)?—or do we think it's a "fruit of the spirit" (Gal. 5:22-23)? The greater our power, the higher our capacity to do good—to save life instead of destroying it, to feed the hungry, clothe the naked, even as God does the ravens and lilies—not to despise them and exploit them for gain. In exercise of our own dominion, we should heed the admonition given to Nebuchadnezzar. Instead of his arrogance, pride and self-importance, he should have been finding ways to "show mercy" on the multitudes of poor and enslaved in his kingdom. Today we take comparable pride in the great civilization we've established by both conquest and in peaceful growth; no doubt the lesson of Nebuchadnezzar should be telling us something about our own arrogance, pride, self-satisfaction and attitude of superiority (see previous section, and also Chap. 6).

But we're still exploring the meaning of "dominion" over wild creatures. Is there some reason to think that we are excused from the obligation Nebuchadnezzar bore, to protect—show mercy to—the weakest and most vulnerable? And what species other than weeds is *not* weak and vulnerable when confronted with ever-expanding cities and industries?

Exactly how and in what sense is man's "dominion", conferred upon him in Genesis, supposed to be drastically different from Nebuchadnezzar's? Were we given authority and power to brutalize and exterminate in the manner of kings and dictators, rather than to cherish, nourish and protect? The world of Nature that God made would surely be no worse off if it didn't have Man to cut its forests, pollute its streams, and butcher its passenger pigeons and dodos. Man had no need to receive any special "dominion" from God, in the sense of power to rule and destroy. We already had all that in our size, strength and intelligence, and in those other qualities obtained in the Garden, though not originally endowed by God. The only reason Nature needs any kind of ruler to exercise dominion is that explained by Daniel: to receive his protection and stewardship. God did not grant dominion over His world only to subdue it, but to protect it from harm, even as Nebuchadnezzar's power and dominion incurred for him the obligation to protect the poor. What irony, that 99% of the harm done to God's world comes at the hands of Man—that the main thing it needs protection from is its designated protector! It seems pretty clear that our pride, self-importance and above all, our Nebuchadnezzar-like *lust for power* underlie our interpretation of Genesis. There may be no other portions of Scripture which are so universally interpreted to give mankind license rather than responsibility; and I don't think we should so interpret these, and put them in contradiction to the rest of the Bible. Our "dominion" is not of earthly power, but stewardship, and here the New Testament does have something to say. Read the parable of the faithful and unfaithful servants (Matt 25:14-29), and reflect on Jesus' view of those who do not care for the things entrusted to them.

NOAH

The Endangered Species Act is the Noah's Ark of our day. (Calvin De Witt, University of Wisconsin professor of environmental studies and co-founder of Evangelical Environmental Network.)

Another portion of Genesis that sets forth man's relationship to the natural world is in the story of Noah (Gen. 6-7). It is always taught that the Ark is a type of Christ, the means by which man is saved from destruction and the wrath of God. In the New Testament, Christ's references to Noah do not clearly say as much (though I Peter 3:20 and II Peter 2:5 may seem to), but he makes Noah's escape from the flood of no greater or different significance than Lot's escape from Sodom (Matt. 24, Luke 17). I certainly accept the Ark's typology as St. Peter understood it. Yet it is only the symbolic meaning of the story, and the symbolism of a text should not obscure its literal content.

To save the human race from destruction, a simple houseboat would have sufficed. The Ark was expressly made to save animal life from the destruction brought about by man's wickedness. How appropriate to our thesis!—as Dr. DeWitt points out, our wickedness once again threatens the natural world with destruction. We attribute no significance to Noah's saving the animals, only the humans; yet is this not the clearest example of how man's dominion is to be exercised?—to save creatures rather than to destroy them?

After the flood, God made a covenant not to "smite any more every living thing" (Gen. 8:28). Note that His promise was not just to mankind. The covenant, which Fundamentalists interpret only as God's dispensation of grace (i.e. to humans) was actually to "all flesh", the entire animal kingdom, no more so to man than beast (Gen. 9:9-11, repeated in vss 12, 15,16,17).

That is, it's God's will that "all flesh" be preserved from destruction. As in other areas of life, it usually happens that we manage to defeat His purposes; but we haven't changed them. He has delivered the entire animal kingdom into our hand (Gen. 9:2). The "dominion" thus conveyed expressly provides for its use as a food source, but that doesn't cancel the protective covenant elaborated in the succeeding verses.

Here's what Jesus said about dominion: "...princes exercise dominion...*but not you*...whosoever will be great ...let him be servant" (Matt. 20:25-28, emphasis added). Noah was actually servant to the animals, butler, cook, waiter and housekeeper. Man's greatness, his dominion, is shown neither when he domesticates nor when he exterminates creatures, but when he accords them "Reverence for Life", in Albert Schweitzer's terms, and uses his powers to save and protect them. Schweitzer became a physician to save human life; but he grieved that in the process he became a "mass murderer of bacteria" (*The Philosophy of Civilization*, 1923).

I do believe that sensitivity to Life, such as this, is Scripturally mandated, and that the foregoing discussion (except where noted) is conservative and sound Biblical exegesis. I believe that Christians should be foremost in the ranks of those attempting to conserve the natural world, and its dwindling plant and animal species and forests and wild lands.

For our purposes I only want us to understand that humans have a responsibility, imposed by God, to be part of the world and its protector. But I'd better clarify and limit what we're talking about.

RIGHTS AND RESPONSIBILITIES

Who knoweth the spirit of man that goeth upward, and the spirit of the beast that goeth downward to the earth? (Eccl. 3:2)

Ecology is a vast subject, and I don't want to get distracted with detailed discussions of different aspects of it—water, air, wildlife, global warming, and on and on. There are many worthwhile environmental organizations, some more radical, theoretical and political, others more practical and outcome-focused. There are even organizations based on our religious responsibilities to Nature: Christian Environmental Council, Evangelical Environmental Network, Christians for Environmental Stewardship, Christians Caring for Creation,

Target Earth. There's also Evangelicals for Social Action, though their interest is somewhat more on poverty and family issues. I know nothing of these beyond the mere names, but I wanted to convey that if you feel any stirring of concern for Life, you are not alone, and may want to consider joining with others through such organizations.

There are other groups that are at best peripheral, and in my view opposed, to a Scripture-based philosophy of Man-in-Nature. Of some number of these, the most prominent is PETA—People for the Ethical Treatment of Animals. Here's the problem: ethical treatment—which who would dare oppose?—is, in their view, based on "Animal Rights" (and what I have to say applies generally to that kind of view, and not to this or any other specific organization as such).

Now, I've claimed that humans are animals, but animals are not all human. Every kind of animal is different, and in the case of humans, differences are not just structural, in the sense that you can tell from my body structure that I am not a goat or guppy. The further difference is that a structural feature, the brain, enables possession of a non-structural entity that is even more singularly unique: the human soul or spirit. There's a linguistic device called "anthropomorphism" (Greek for, approximately, human form), by which a non-human thing or entity is regarded as human. Examples are our tendency to refer to a nation or a ship as "she", as if it were a human being—a woman; or to portray literary or comic-strip characters: Reynard the Fox, Peter Rabbit, "Snoopy", "Garfield", "Pogo", "Krazy Kat", as having human characteristics. As a linguistic or literary device, it is colorful and entirely proper. As a basis for policy, attributing human qualities to non-humans is disastrous and totally irrational.

Our concept of "rights" goes back to our Declaration of Independence and Constitution; elsewhere in the world it is likewise based on humanistic or religious philosophy. To my knowledge, these are always called "Human Rights" and have never encompassed animal rights. Nor do any higher religions generally claim for animals a soul and an afterlife. Not even Animal Rights advocates have linked rights with responsibilities, though that should be fundamental to any concept of ethics. The only way to avoid the anthropomorphic fallacy is to acknowledge the fact that animals are not human; not political, as to have rights; nor spiritual, as to possess souls; nor ethical, as to bear responsibilities.

They are *animals*: loved by St. Francis of Assisi, revered by Albert Schweitzer, admired and respected by whale-watchers, bird-watchers and Indians, by Jacques Cousteau and John James Audubon and William Beebe and Rachel Carson, and by all conscientious ranchers, cowboys and farmers (but not counting workers in the execrable "factory farms"); hunters, fishermen, and other people of awareness and good will. Insistence that we treat animals with respect comes not because they are human, but because *we* are: to do otherwise is "inhumane" and brutalizing. "We have a moral obligation to other species. The only reason for saving them is that it's right" (Russell Mittermeier, PhD, Harvard paleontologist and president, Conservation International). No other animal takes responsibility for saving another species. Humans are different, as even King Solomon began to recognize!

I can't see much reason for other movements, either, like the vegetarian. The Old Testament certainly doesn't contemplate it; the New Testament Good Shepherd either was an idiot, or else he knew perfectly well that the sheep to which he gave his loving care and tenderness were being raised for slaughter. It didn't keep him from loving them. (Albert Schweitzer saw no moral difference between killing a plant or an animal for food.)

Apart from all that, though, we ought to think about our priorities of food production and distribution. With the widespread famine conditions in Africa and elsewhere, both acute and chronic, is it morally justifiable for us to devote a huge proportion of our grain and soybean production to fattening hogs and steers, as we currently do?—while human beings are starving? Whatever else you may think of vegetarianism, it's well-established that we *can* live on far less meat than we do—whether or not we'd be healthier if we did. (The same could be said of devoting immense tonnages of corn to production of ethanol to feed our cars, instead of using it to feed the hungry.) A moral question, to which I've not heard, nor can offer, any ready answers; but a question worth asking.

Some of the most practical conservationists are hunters and fishermen. Some delicate-minded city folks who associate animal life with cute little puppydogs and fuzzy little pussycats believe sportsmen to be bloodthirsty and cruel. Maybe that could have been true of the old-time meat-hunters who exterminated the passenger pigeon and nearly did so the bison and many waterfowl; but that's history (we hope). Nowadays it appears a similar threat exists against ocean food fish, whose numbers are so depleted through over-fishing—especially the large species such as tuna and swordfish—that not only their continued availability as human food sources but even, in some cases, their continued existence as species, may be running out. I don't so much finger the fishermen in these cases. They are only trying to make a living, and the scarcer the fish, the harder they have to work to catch enough of what remains to be able to keep beans on their tables.

I fault governmental policy-makers and their food-industry financiers for allowing this situation to develop and for looking the other way as it progressively gets worse. Anyhow, I think the sportsman has an extra special responsibility for protecting and preserving wildlife; but I see no biblical, rational or ethical reason why he should not be a sportsman.

Love for and protection of life is a Christian duty, Biblically mandated and magnificently exemplified by some of our greatest humanitarians, from St. Francis to Albert Schweitzer. But Life does not exist in a vacuum. It exists in an environment or surroundings, be it ocean and stream, forest, range, wetland or tundra. I cannot claim to love a person if I am intent on destroying his home or starving him. Nor may I destroy the environment in which wild things reside, nor passively allow others to do so, yet still claim to care about Life.

CHAPTER 4

FEMINISM

Let the women learn in silence with all subjection... I suffer not a woman to teach, nor to usurp authority over the man, but to be in silence. Let your women keep silence in the churches: for it is not permitted unto them to speak...And if they will learn anything, let them ask their husbands at home: for it is a shame for women to speak in the church. ...the head of the woman is the man...neither was the man created for the woman, but the woman for the man. ...to avoid fornication, let every man have his own wife...it is good for [the unmarried and widows] if they abide...but if they cannot contain, let them marry: for it is better to marry than to burn.

(II Tim 2:8-12; I Cor. 14:34-35; I Cor. 11:3-8; I Cor. 7:2-9)

Not in my current study of the Bible, nor ever in my long years of interest in and reading of the Gospels, have I found any single word by Jesus that would put down, minimize, disparage, or in any way whatsoever diminish the respect, dignity, worth, importance, nor indeed the equal status of women compared to men. Clearly set forth are his loving dealings with Mary, Martha and Mary Magdalene, which fail not in the slightest of the love he likewise showed to his male disciples. But the most telling indications of his attitude toward women are revealed in his words upon female sexuality and sexual sin—the single most touchy and alarming topic for men, and subject of the greatest taboos that are held by them toward women.

To the shacked-up Samaritan woman (John 4:1-26), he merely said, "Thou sayest well, I have no husband...he whom thou hast is not thy husband". Maybe this was a rebuke—an awfully mild one if so—but it really seems to me he was kind of kidding her for her embarrassed claim that she had no husband. And there the issue was left.

To the woman who committed adultery (for which she—but not necessarily the man—was sentenced to death under Jewish law) he merely told her, "Neither do I condemn thee; go and sin no more". (John 8: 3-11)

For that matter, when a divorced woman has sex, even though Jesus says it constitutes adultery, he does not blame her but rather the husband who abandoned her! (Matt. 5:32)

Now, I am most emphatically not one of those who draw distinctions between Jesus and St. Paul, and end up concluding that the New Testament contains two different and often contradictory Gospels. These were very different men, with different missions to very diverse audiences; one the Jewish Messiah, the other God's apostle to the Gentiles; who each taught in his own style the things that served his evangelistic goal. A different Gospel?—no, not at all, but one Gospel: preached by the incarnate God who spoke all truth, and preached also by a fallible man who in important ways was a product of his own Pharisaical background—as he proudly pointed out at times (Acts 23:6; 26:5; Philippians 3:5)—who (so unlike Jesus in this way) significantly failed to rise above some of the beliefs and prejudices inherent in his cultural background and emotional make-up.

As the above selected verses indicate, St. Paul could reveal dislike and disrespect for women. In some of his writings he holds them to be little more than sexual objects, to be avoided if possible, or "used" (Rom. 1:27) by men who can't "contain". He did not allow widows to join the church before the age of 60, for fear of their effect upon male members (I Tim. 5:9-14). It is this aspect of St. Paul's attitude and teaching that I want to discuss; but we needn't deny that numerous passages from his letters convey the love, gratitude, and respect that he held for many of his female converts (Rom. 16:1-7, 12, 15; and others).

I mentioned in Chapter 2 that we shall see some examples of ways in which the doctrine of Divine Inspiration of Scripture can be misapplied. If St. Paul was divinely inspired to point out that some of his views about women and sex are not necessarily "of the Lord" (I Cor. 7:6, 12, 25) then why has the Church up to, and to some extent including the present day, taken his dogmas and prejudices as the Word of God and the Law of God—while ignoring the words and example of Jesus?

It's true that step by step we have gradually distanced ourselves from St. Paul's narrow, rigid views. Even back when I was a kid, women were permitted to "teach" (in Sunday School, where their only authority was over children, not men!) Many years later it began to be permissible for them to appear in church without a hat (despite St. Paul's warning—I Cor. 11: 5-13; though here also he disavows any divine order in the matter—v. 16). Now women are, in some denominations, serving with clear authority as deacons, elders, ordained ministers or bishops.

In others they are still barred from any post entailing authority over men, and this policy is always justified scripturally as the law or commandment of God—based upon the opinions of St. Paul, the man who denounced religious law more impassionedly and logically than any other personage of history!

Feminists are right to protest such nonsense. In the Church, as in business, industry, education, medicine and almost all aspects of life, feminism's quest for women's equality is both fair and Scriptural.

I say "almost". There are several reasons for hedging:

There is continuing uncertainty, and not just on my part, about women in the military. Women universally are likely to be victims of violence and fighting, not its perpetrators, and are seen by both sexes in most cultures as the mediators, compromisers and peacemakers. They may well have a genetic predisposition for this; whether or not it is that, or only cultural in origin, such a disposition places them in not only a necessary but a morally superior position, compared to men who, as a whole, are lacking it. I don't think any characteristics which make women superior should be sacrificed to make them equal! Still, I wouldn't want to relegate military or other women to their traditional roles of nursing, cooking, cleaning and typing. So there is uncertainty; and in resolving it, I'd like to hope that Christians and others would think first of what is best for society—not what is most convenient or economical or flattering, or even what's most politically correct or gratifying in the short term for women.

Militant feminism's quest for what they call "equality" does take a few strange twists. Chastity used to be another territory guarded by women; they were trusted to do so by men who, however driven their insistent assaults against that territory, nevertheless punished any failure to defend it, by labeling and categorizing the woman; regarding her with disrespect, disgrace and opprobrium. (Read *The Scarlet Letter*.)

This was not fair to women, who were expected to repudiate their own sexuality, or to men, who had no need of learning to be responsible, hence mature, in sexual matters.

But the sexual revolution ignited by feminists' challenge to this inequality has left us nearly without any sexual ethic at all. Modern teenage girls are as mortified to admit their virginity, in the occasional case where it exists, as a proper girl in the 1800's would have been to confess the opposite. The idea is not original with me that liberty—sexual or other—ought to mean the freedom to maintain one's own moral beliefs and to make choices accordingly, without social pressure to some alternative standard. I don't hear many feminists complaining about the extravagances and distortions to which their rebellion against sexual double standards has led us. Again, I believe with the late Ashley Montague in *The Natural Superiority of Women*, and I would like to see them use their strengths to try and civilize us men, and not lower themselves to equality with all our most disreputable tendencies.

Feminism has its strange quirks in the religious area, too, A Presbyterian minister was trying to teach her congregation the ancient Russian Easter greeting. Instead of "Happy Easter", Russians say, "Christ is risen", to which is made this response: "He is risen indeed". This is a grand and beautiful tradition, and I wish with all my heart that it could become an American one as well. But the minister in question had to doctor it a little, and she asked the congregation—which we can imagine didn't know any better—to respond, "Christ is risen indeed"—eliminating "He" by way of purging any suggestion of his masculinity.

Now, I realize that God is not a male—nor a female either. We think of God as a Person, yet there is no personal pronoun in English for the unspecified or common gender. In English grammar, a noun of masculine, feminine or neuter gender may be antecedent respectively to the pronoun he, she, or it. When a noun is of common or unspecified gender, it properly is antecedent to a masculine pronoun: "Somebody dropped his watch"; "Did every student turn in his homework?"; "God is a spirit: and they that worship him must worship..." (John 4:24).

I don't defend this; I think it unfortunate, but it's a fact of life, and I haven't seen any sensible solutions to the problem. I have seen or heard God referred to as "She"; I am startled but not offended when I do: it is unusual and not proper grammar, but that's all. Not being a woman myself, I do not understand why one might be offended if God is referred to as "He". Perhaps I would, if I had been raised to understand "he" as a word meaning somebody who wanted to dominate and control and put down or hurt and disregard me and other "she's" of the world. That understanding, of course, ought to change.

Brian Wren, a British Reformed pastor, wrote a book on this problem, *What Language Shall I Borrow?*, in which he discussed the "Patriarchal" trend in Judeo-Christian tradition: the references to God as male, whether "He", or as "Father" or even "Husband" (of Israel). He wrote, "Patriarchal Christianity is in danger of worshipping an idol, and we are not protected from idolatry by the fact that much of our God-language is Biblical." That is, if God has no gender in the human sense, then it's a false god that's called "He", "Father", etc. He is right to the extent that the imperfections of English grammar cannot be justified merely because they are Biblical; it could not be otherwise, since our Bible is written in English! He is wrong, of course, to imply Jesus' idolatry on account of his customary reference to his Father in heaven. One feminist attempt to deal with this, *The Inclusive New Testament* (1994, Priests For Equality, Brentwood, MD), does a magnificent job of de-masculinizing the text. It's a great effort, and I do endorse it. But it substitutes "Abba" for every reference to "Father" in the Gospels. Not good enough: "*Abba*" (Hebrew or Aramaic) is the diminutive of "*Ab*", Father. It is never translated into either Greek or English; the only reasonable approximation of its meaning would be "Daddy"—which is more tender and personal, but not less masculine, than "Father".

Some women may have emotional antipathy to "He" because it has meant so much pain to them; and some to "Father" when that word denotes somebody absent, or brutal, or sexually molesting of them. We can sympathize, but we can't doctor our language, or history, or theology—or Scripture—to accommodate them, or construe a simple quest for their equality to mean that Jesus Christ, a historically documented male, may not be called "he".

Nevertheless, I think Christians are wrong to see feminism as a threat or an enemy. It does not, or should not, deny fundamental gender differences. We belong to the animal kingdom: men, like bulls and roosters, will always be bigger, stronger and meaner than women, who in turn will always be more nurturing, loving, cooperative, sympathetic and peaceable than men. Feminism, at least in its less shrill manifestations, does not deny these things, but only opposes men taking advantage of them. As I see it, men have historically feared women's superiority, and over-compensated by using their greater physical strength to impose on and dominate women; feminism seeks to right the wrongs that mens' domination has fostered.

As for the more fanatic and far-out aspects of radical feminism, let's take a lesson from history. In the days of feminist pioneer Elizabeth Cady Stanton, women were in a much worse state, legally and socially, than in the 20th Century, which saw a modern re-birth of the movement. It seems to me that, had the feminists single-mindedly pursued suffrage, women at large, and many sympathetic men, might have rallied behind them and perhaps accomplished something. As it happened, they did not; the activists accomplished no significant reforms whatsoever, because you know what they did do? They had to get themselves embroiled in the slavery controversy, and they came out for Abolition.

Now, there's nothing wrong with Abolition, and everything wrong with slavery. The feminists' stand was moral and compassionate; it was also their kiss of death. No southerners, nor very many northerners, would support what appeared to be a bunch of Abolitionists, an unpopular and even feared minority, right up to the Civil War. Lincoln despised slavery as much as anybody, but he rightly saw political suicide if he identified himself with Abolitionism. The feminists were no more compassionate than he; we can all be thankful that he was not as self-defeating as they.

Today's feminists have likewise decided that it's not good enough to pursue their fundamental goal of women's liberation and equality: they must also come out for abortion and homosexuals' rights! Well, homosexuals are no more popular now than Abolitionists were back then. Feminists who hitch their wagon to that star, not to mention that of abortion-rights groups, will, like their 19th Century forebears, go precisely nowhere.

Just as in the issue of slavery, I do not say they are wrong on such matters—only self-defeating—and I'll devote chapters to some comments on these subjects. Some of the more crackpot feminist notions need to be opposed—or more likely just laughed at—but for the purpose of summarizing this chapter, I just wish that Christians—in their personal, religious, and political thinking—did not fear and oppose women's liberation. I wish, as the Promise Keepers seem to be suggesting, that we men meet the challenge of women's superiority, not by putting them down, but by becoming better people ourselves.

CHAPTER 5

HOMOSEXUALITY

Thou shalt not lie with mankind as with womankind: it is abomination..If a man also lie with mankind, as he lieth with a woman, both of them have committed an abomination: they shall surely be put to death.. God gave them up unto vile affections; for even their women did change the natural use into that which is against nature: and likewise also the men, leaving the natural use of the woman, burned in lust one toward another, men with men working that which was unseemly

(Lev. 18:33, 20:13; Rom. 1:26-27)

Discussion of almost no other subject is more likely than this one to invite accusations of irrationality: of injecting emotional feelings into what should be matter for objective treatment. So I have to start with a personal confession.

I don't like homosexuality. Thinking about sexual activity between men induces discomfort, perhaps about on the order of thinking about vomit—so as a rule I think about something else. It's not intolerable; not horrifying, frightening or outrageous, but just not a thing to dwell on. I must be slightly attractive to these people, because they've come on to me many times. I've never been upset at their advances, not even when in the Army I was surprised by a Christian buddy who pawed me and copped a feel. It really didn't bother me—the act itself, though I brought it to an abrupt halt—but I knew we couldn't be friends, and that felt bad. (Of course we really *could* have continued as friends, but I thought his attraction to me would be a problem. And there were plenty of other people with whom I could maintain uncomplicated friendships. And also, to tell the whole truth, I despised him for being "queer".)

I resent the use by homosexuals of the term "homophobic" for people like me; simple prejudice is not a mental disorder like claustrophobia or acrophobia, as if my beliefs and attitudes might change if I'd take maybe Valium or Prozac. I resent their perversion of the word "gay". Why don't they want to be called "homosexual"? But I guess there's an excuse for using "gay". They won't be called "homosexual" anyhow, but a whole variety of demeaning and insulting slang epithets. Maybe they have a right to choose their own label.

Actually, nobody should be calling anybody anything; it's nobody's business. My own sole desire in the matter—both before and after the "gay pride" and "coming out" movement—is that I not have to deal with it. "Don't ask, don't tell" suits me fine (if only we could ditch the punitive consequences of "telling"). I don't want homosexuality discriminated against and persecuted, but I also don't want it flaunted. I do understand that there has been and still is a lot of prejudice and no little persecution (and as will be discussed, some of it unfortunately based on biblical language, or interpretations thereof). To the extent "gay pride" means an attempt to end this, we ought not to oppose it. But I am quite satisfied to find that a person is a good friend, or a good worker or soldier or teacher or team-mate or whatever, and I don't need and I do not want to know, and please God not *discuss* his or her sexual orientation!

But if I'm going to write about it, I have to deal with it! So leaving my cocoon for a few moments, I'll try to see what it all means for Christians.

ORIGINS OF HOMOSEXUALITY

This is not the place for a long, detailed examination of the origins or causes of sexual orientation, certainly not by a non-expert like me. Nevertheless, we do need to identify a few false ideas if we are to talk about reality and not myth.

Homosexuals are not in all cultures considered seriously abnormal. Some Native American tribes, for example, merely assigned them women's work instead of hunting and warring, but didn't otherwise concern themselves much about it. I understand homosexuality was pretty much open and accepted in ancient Greece.

Our own views are partly shaped by those of Sigmund Freud, but both he and we start from millennia of Judeo-Christian tradition—one of suspicion and disapproval, as indicated by the earliest Judaic writings on this subject, and Christian writings as well, cited at the head of this chapter. Freud labeled it a form of neurosis; what today we'd call a "disorder" but at the time a clear implication of mental abnormality. Our general stigma against mental illness must contribute a lot to our prejudice against homosexuality. (Freud himself was not as psychologically oriented as most of his followers. He was a neurologist by training, and always believed in a structural—"organic"—basis for mental disorder.) This may have been the first time that homosexuality had been defined as an abnormality rather than either a normal deviation, or else a sinful perversion. For Freud, neurosis was in principle curable, though in the case of homosexuality he confessed that he didn't know how, since psychoanalysis didn't work with these people. At one point he opined that changing a homosexual's attraction toward the same sex would be just as difficult as changing a heterosexual's toward the opposite sex!—and in this it seems he was probably right. In 1972 the American Psychiatric Association removed homosexuality from its diagnostic list of mental illnesses and declared it a normal variation, like left-handedness; and no more of an "illness" than that.

Whether right (as it was) or wrong (as some still think) this solved nothing, because the whole issue of origins is complicated.

It now appears that sexual orientation is partly a genetic trait, present from birth. The problem with that is: if it's in a person's genes and DNA—then why isn't it inherited?—and nobody to my knowledge ever claimed that it is. Yet experience shows that attraction to the same sex usually is present from one's earliest years; not learned, and certainly not elected. It's almost pathetic to hear of otherwise intelligent Christians—or others—speaking of homosexuality as chosen by the individual, as if anybody in modern society would elect a lifestyle involving disgrace and pain, even persecution and loss of rights. Remember that within the lifetime of today's adult homosexuals, they were believed to be criminals as well as mentally ill (the "abominable crime against nature" was not deleted from one state's criminal statutes until 2002, and then with much opposition in its legislature). Does anybody "choose" that? Most homosexuals testify that from the earliest stirring of attraction to other people—even the grade-school "puppy-love" period—their interest was in the same sex. Very often they hated and feared it, and fought against it, sometimes eventually seeking help in therapy—but to no avail.

Well, usually to no avail. There have been reports of reversal, both by treatment and by religious conversion. These are very rare, but they happen. Not only that, but—as is more well-known—there are adults, often married, maybe parents, who discover that, hitherto unbeknownst even to themselves, they are homosexuals. They have been capable of relating to the opposite sex, both in personal and physical relationship; but no longer want to. They will say, "I had no idea what sex was like till I did it with Joe"—and their affections follow their desires.

Then there are the equal-opportunity bisexuals; they can have it AC or DC, as they say, with no driven compulsion either way.

A bisexual apparently is free to choose a male or female partner on some or most occasions; but with that sole exception, *none of what I'm describing implies free choice.* Sexual orientation appears to be one of the things which, although partly or mostly genetic, is not a total-opposite character such as male or female. It is probably more like height, which is also determined by genes, but along a continuum or scale, with infinite gradations between the extremes of short and tall. Most of us are probably nowhere near the extreme, if there be any such thing in the matter of sexual orientation, but instead contain at least a smidgen of bisexuality. This is classically illustrated in prisons, where thoroughly macho inmates, in an extreme case of sexual deprivation, are able to turn to each other; even though, prior to incarceration, they couldn't have even imagined any such thing, and likely would have been violently angry at any suggestion that they were capable of it.

So this much is abundantly clear: children are not "recruited" into homosexuality by adult homosexuals, whether teacher, scoutmaster, or real or adoptive parents. It's the old story: either you've got it or you don't. Even if it's a matter of degree, as discussed above, you're born with what you've got—not sold it. The notion that homosexuals should not be teachers, youth workers, parents, or anything else by reason of sexuality, is pure prejudice.

There is a crucial and clear-cut distinction, however, between homosexuality and pederasty. Since a child might be molested by adults of its own sex, we may think of them indiscriminately as "homosexuals", but it simply isn't so. The child-molester is a totally different case and should be dealt with through whatever criminal, social and civil policy measures are needed to keep him or her away from children. (Even here, it is worth pointing out that their victims are traumatized—hurt, damaged—perhaps severely, but they are not "recruited". They do not themselves become homosexuals or perverts because of these early-age experiences.) Like some or a lot of our behavior, that of child-molester may be genetically determined, in whole or in part. That has nothing to do with the questions at hand.

The so-called "XYY" genetic abnormality has for many years been known to abound among violent criminals, and at least a suspicion is justified, that these people have, along with physical "XYY" characteristics (tall build, mild mental retardation, coarse features, etc.) a genetic predisposition to violent behavior. I have never heard, and hope I never do, any suggestion that their criminality be therefore excused. People with handicaps are expected to compensate for them, even if the handicap is genetic and behavioral. Normal sexuality is also genetic, yet people lacking suitable sexual outlet are expected to control themselves. Child-molesting tendencies, regardless of genetics, must no less be contained, and external control imposed if they are not, including whatever duration of penal or other institutionalization may be necessary to protect the public.

None of this has any bearing at all on homosexuality.

The fact is that most of our negative, rejecting and condemning attitude toward homosexuals is solely prejudicial. But there is one way in which they have contributed to their own unsavory reputation, and that is the utter promiscuity of some of them, in their sexual activities. If homosexuals are going to clamor for marriage rights, for ordination to the clergy, and for equal treatment in other respects, then they should conform to at least the loose standards of sexual morality that apply to other people, and more fundamentally, adopt at least the conventional views of sex as the expression of love and commitment—even if not of marriage (since we've ruled that out in their case). Nobody need contend that such ideals are universally accepted, nor widely practiced; yet they have not disappeared.

It may be that relatively few homosexuals habitually "cruise" for partners or otherwise engage in such promiscuous patterns, I don't know, but a reputation is hard to live down. It may not be fair, but it is rational, to point out that if they seek respectability they may have to be "respectable", maybe even more so than the rest of us. It isn't my job to prove they aren't a menace to community morals, it's theirs, and allowing themselves—or tolerating in their compeers—utter self-indulgence and promiscuity merely because they're free of worries about pregnancy is not the highest recommendation. It is probably hypocritical of us, if we demand a higher degree of chastity of them than we expect of ourselves, but that's the kind of society it is. It's the only one we have; it's the one in which they claim to want integration and acceptance, so it has to be on our terms, not theirs. They are in no position to flout the rules of society even more egregiously than the rest of us do, if they're going to make demands on us.

But meanwhile, what about the policy issues?

LEGAL ASPECTS

I think it's clear that I have found no basis for discrimination of any kind in all of the several arenas, and specifically in work, including work with children and ordination to the clergy. (I hope to have made it clear that child-molesters, even if they are "celibate" priests, are completely excluded from this discussion.) Regarding ordination, I'd only say that the usual expectations of chastity should apply, no less than to any other ministers or priests. I can't think of any reason to make homosexual activity an exception to our ideas about fornication and adultery (cf p. 79.)

Unlike any other "minority" matters, homosexuality presents us the issue of legalizing their marriage. We can't afford to ponder this question at our leisure, because it's looming over us right now, and it may be one that we're not ready to answer.

Our Constitution and Bill of Rights most certainly were not written in contemplation of this matter. So if the founding fathers gave no answer to a question not asked, we can only try to understand the general principles they did adopt, and see if we can apply them. But first of all I want to make a distinction.

The legal and religious issues are different. A clergyman is said to "marry" a couple, but this is only true legally, because a justice of the peace can do the same thing. Jesus told us that "God hath joined together" a man and wife (Mark 10:9), and though this can occur in a church, it is not of the Church, because when he said it, the Church did not yet exist. When they say "I do"—when they make their certain and final and eternal commitment (or maybe it's when they are physically joined, as St. Paul suggested in I Cor. 6:15-17, assuming that "one flesh", properly attained, is supposed to constitute marriage), God does His work of uniting them. When the clergyman then "pronounces" them man and wife, just as a magistrate would, he is making it legal, but not he and not the Church caused it happen in its inner, spiritual reality. (I know the Roman Catholic and some sacramentally oriented Protestant or Orthodox churches would disagree; but that's my opinion.) So if it's God Who joins people together in marriage, not the Church, then when the Church refuses marriage, it is actually outside its jurisdiction—just as if it tried to refuse somebody a driver's license. The truth is, we cannot know whether God would likewise "marry" a homosexual couple, but I suggest that the burden of proof is on those who claim He would discriminate!

Legally, the issue is equity. If the Founding Fathers had been asked, "Is there any group, ever, of whatever description, who *as a class* are to be denied equal rights and protections of law?" we have to think they'd have said "NO". (Though that's not counting slaves—about whom they of course did decide to look the other way.) Whatever the benefits and burdens of marriage, I doubt if the Constitution allows us to deny them to anybody.

I realize that we don't think of marriage as a device for securing certain rights, yet that is one primary reason for homosexuals to claim, or us to consider, any legalization of their unions. Still, I doubt if we're ready to redefine marriage, and make it mean something different from what it traditionally has always meant—not only under the Constitution, but since the earliest of Judeo-Christian times and probably since the beginning of the race of man.

I think it might be possible to create a new category of legal relationship—perhaps a status of being "bonded" rather then "married" (in a relationship thus known as "bondage"?—I don't know) that when legally sealed would confer the rights and responsibilities of marriage—I suppose including the necessity of divorce in case of its dissolution—but without doing injustice to the vast majority of us who treasure not only our own marriage, but the name and idea and institution of marriage, and don't want it opened up to any kind of redefinition (see Appendix).

I'm somewhat less sure of the legalities than I am that the churches should open themselves to the fellowship of believing homosexuals and, in case of their couples, to recognition and blessing of their union. But I don't think we're ready, even in church, to call it "marriage"; and before we ever do, we'd better know what we're about.

HOMOSEXUALITY IN SCRIPTURE

So let's think about the Scriptural approach to this question. Even if I have some emotion about all this, I truly don't believe that any of the foregoing discussion sounds seriously unbalanced, either in condemnation of homosexuality or in over-compensative charitableness toward it.

I can't say as much for St. Paul. There's no evidence that he based his remarks to the Romans (quoted in this chapter heading) on Old Testament Scripture (when he does very frequently cite Scripture, he generally makes it clear that he's doing so). Given his cranky attitudes about proper sex, as we saw in the last chapter, we'd hardly expect to find him expressing much tolerance for homosexuality. As to the former he frankly admitted he was giving his own opinions, and in the latter case I think we may make the same assumption.

This is going to annoy some readers who think I have less respect for the Bible than they do. I don't believe that's so; anyhow, if any of them believe the earth rotates around the sun, they have already disavowed one Bible verse (Joshua 10:12), and in principle they have endorsed the right and duty to be rational—to use your head—when interpreting Scripture. This is discussed further in Chapter 10.

St. Paul is very explicit in some other epistles. In I Cor. 6:9 he includes "abusers of themselves with mankind" in a detailed list of "the unrighteous" who will "not inherit the kingdom of God"—with idolaters, thieves and extortioners. In a similar list found in I Tim. 1:9-10 he includes "them that defile themselves with mankind".

Some observations: St. Paul makes use of such lists in several epistles. There are at least two others in which no reference to homosexuality is made: I Cor. 5:10-11 and Gal. 5:19-21. Though the two I cited previously are unequivocal, still homosexuality is not included as consistently as fornication and adultery. He seems to be less obsessed with it than with heterosexual sins.

Also, I'd like someone a lot smarter than me to explain something. Fornication, adultery, and homosexuality apparently are listed by St. Paul as separate sins. Query: Can a homosexual ever be guilty of fornication or adultery? Or is he immune to them, if we accept the strict construction of them as heterosexual sins? If homosexuals' reputation for promiscuity is at all realistic, why shouldn't those who engage in it be considered fornicators, as would a heterosexual person behaving similarly, only with the opposite sex? And if that term can be properly applied in these cases, how about adultery, in the case of a committed relationship in which one partner betrays the other? And if that term can be so applied, does it not implicitly confirm the existence of a marriage-like state between two such persons? I have to say that, as with his other pronouncements on sexuality, St. Paul reveals more prejudice than rationality.

There's a hint here once more that he is contradicting the words of our Lord. What did Jesus mean by this: "There are some eunuchs which were so from their mother's womb: and there are some eunuchs, which were made eunuchs of men: and there be eunuchs, which have made themselves eunuchs for the kingdom of heaven's sake" (Matt. 9:12)? Unless you believe, like the old Russian Skoptzi, that "eunuch" means that Christian males must castrate themselves "for the kingdom of heaven's sake", you have to assume that Jesus here speaks more broadly of the inability of a man to relate sexually to a woman: by castration indeed if "made eunuchs of men", and by self-sacrificial commitment to chastity (without castration), as in St. Paul's own case, by those who "made themselves eunuchs for the Kingdom's sake".

But "from their mother's womb"? I think he may have been talking about homosexuality. A boy-child literally born without testicles would be pretty rare, and he would still not necessarily be impotent, whereas a homosexual would. In any case, this might seem to have been the place for Jesus to denounce homosexuality, if he had so intended.

The meaning here is a little obscure, certainly, but if it is possible that our Lord was talking about homosexuality, it is not possible to infer any condemnation of it!

As to Old Testament words on the subject: I've stated before that we as Christians love, respect, study and learn from all the Scriptures. But especially concerning the Judaic rules and regulations, whether those regarding circumcision, Sabbath-keeping, abstaining from pork, or exacting the death penalty for homosexuality, we do not consider them literally as "the Law of God", binding on us. There is one law, and one law only, that governs Christians: Love one another.

Consider Leviticus 20:13, requiring execution, as cited above. Let's postulate that under the law of love we would not put people to death because of their sexual activity. Would this mean that homosexuality is no longer an "abomination" to God? Did He, in modern jargon, "get over it"? Or is there an abiding principle which, under Christianity, holds believers to even higher standards than under Old Testament rules—just as Jesus taught us higher standards that transcend legalism, regarding divorce and adultery, taking oaths, taking lives, and taking vengeance (in Matthew, Chap. 5, e.g.)? If so, then he and St. Paul are both saying that O.T. laws are now superseded: by what, we talked about in Chapter 2.

The problem with identifying "abominations" is that the word is used in considerable profusion in the O.T. In Leviticus, Chapter 11, the word is used eight times, all with regard to the dietary laws, by which eating of certain kinds of animals is called an abomination. Above all else, worship of idols and other gods is repeatedly and emphatically denounced as abomination. But also, offering a flawed animal in sacrifice to God, offering money obtained from the sale of a dog, remarrying one's previously divorced wife after her second husband's death, or maintaining dishonest weights by which to cheat another; all are identified as "abominations". Some of these we can agree are wrong. Some of them, like worshiping idols, we don't do, mainly because we'd think it stupid. Others are merely puzzling, and we eat pork, lobster, and even rattlesnake; and for the most part marry whom we please, without much legalistic concern over God's view of the matter.

So is homosexuality an "abomination" of the same class of seriousness as idol worship?—or is it more like eating shrimp or oysters ("Whatsoever hath no fins or scales"—Lev. 11:12)?

The thing is, even Jesus' elaborations of moral principle are not to be read legalistically. We do kill when we think it justified, even if we don't think it virtuous but only a lesser evil. Similarly, we do divorce and remarry; and we swear oaths. If we have any qualms of conscience at all in such matters, we quite easily assume that we are not under law but under grace, and we "sin boldly" with greater or lesser consciousness of our need of grace and forgiveness.

I can't find a biblical basis for our negativism about homosexuality, nor any reason to believe that tolerance of it will endanger either the nation or the faith. Many will continue to dislike it, as I do, but we will have to be responsible for our own attitudes, and not claim they're inspired by God.

MARRIAGE

That being so, let me return to the religious aspect of homosexual marriage. I've talked about the legal question, suggesting that a relationship could be recognized under the law, even if we stop short of naming it "marriage". If there's any reason why all these same considerations could not also apply in the Church, given all of the same conditions, it's a reason that has escaped me. If the work of uniting a couple is indeed God's work and not our own, then only He knows whether He's willing to do it as readily for Jim and Harry as for Dick and Jane. My view of marriage theoretically would make it possible for a couple to get married as privately as they got engaged, and to do it in the living room or in a bar or in bed; but we don't accept that. We expect them to have the simultaneous benefit and obligation of making it legal in a public commitment, and few of us are so "modern" as to think that doing it or not is a matter of indifference.

If we think chastity and faithfulness are values, should we not expect the same of homosexuals? And if we do, should we not do what we can to foster it, as we do by solemnizing marriage for a heterosexual couple, with vows of permanence and faithfulness? And if we do not precisely know the mind of God in the matter, should we err (or sin) on the side of inclusion and assistance—or on the side of rejecting and excluding and stigmatizing?

I can't help comparing the situation with that of marriage in the Roman Catholic Church. There, getting married is a sacrament of the church, like baptism—not something you do, but something the church does to you. Logically and inescapably you can't undo it, any more than you could unbaptize yourself. You can get a civil divorce but in the eyes of the church you're still married, and any subsequent sexual activity is adultery. You can still do it, because the church provides for confession, penance and forgiveness, such as to allow continued membership in good standing. But remarry?—*no way*, because that would constitute more than casual or even repetitive sin, but actually a declaration of intent to commit adultery repeatedly and regularly and life-long. The parallel is almost exact: we condemn homosexual and adulterous acts both as sinful, yet the perpetrators of them are permitted continuing fellowship (at least in the more accepting churches, in the case of homosexuality). But permitting their marriage would appear to be the opposite of forgiving their purported sin, but rather blessing it.

A Roman Catholic would probably say, "Yeah?—what's the matter with that?" Not much, really; their view of marriage has good Biblical justification (except for the sacramental overlay) though I object to its legalistic application. But from the typical Protestant point of view, forbidding a loving couple's marriage means requiring that their sexual union be extra-marital, which defeats the goal of chastity and morality. We are accustomed to amusing ourselves with this Roman Catholic paradox, but we ought to recognize the same thinking in ourselves, as to homosexuality.

In cases like this, where the Bible offers no laws but only forgiveness, mustn't we also "sin boldly" in this as in other matters; and in humility choose the lesser evil, as between blessing unconventional relationships or discriminating against them?

It is not clear whether such relationships are truly "marriage" or not, either in the attitude of parishioners or in platonic reality, if there is any such thing. I do believe we're free to call it what is most acceptable to all. I believe a clergyman is free to "pronounce" a couple's union whether that has any legal force or not. I believe the churches should lead society in matters like this, not follow. They should be first to renounce discrimination and exclusion; and to condemn, not the homosexuals, but those who wave the Bible at them and who claim to know the law of God and what's an abomination and what's not; and the cruelty of those who picket Matthew Shepherd's funeral with "Matt in Hell" and "God hates Fags" placards, with his bereaved parents looking on. These people, if I identify them correctly, were a church group led to Wyoming by their pastor. If that's accurate, then this is the same pastor who says that homosexuals should be put to death, because that's what the Bible says; but please, *do not* react to that just yet. Before you either laugh or cry, reflect that he is only taking the Bible literally and seriously; one of the few who do so scrupulously any more (that I know of). He really believes what he says he believes: that the Bible, all of it, cover-to-cover, is literally inspired, infallible, and unexceptionably applicable to us today. Of course, he and we also ought to reflect on St. Paul's verdict (Gal. 1:8,9) upon anybody who wants to impose Old Testament law on Christians: "Let him be accursed". That's the Word of God, too.

Let's be a little more honest. Yes, homosexuals' souls are in peril; not because God hates them but because we do: so we deny them fellowship and exposure to Christian love and the gospel of love. Come on: if God can love the aforementioned pastor (and I have to suppose He does though *I* can't) then I believe He also loves people even if they are emotionally and sexually southpaw. And if He does, then we should too.

May homosexuals come to Christ "Just as I am", or was that hymn written only for a certain class of sinner? (and which class?—are we so sure it's us, with so much hatred in our hearts?—or is it them, the despised and rejected?) Are we not called, like Jonah, to minister to those we despise? And must we not, like him, repent of our rebelliousness in refusing to do it? What is the likelihood that homosexuals might come to Christ, when we assure them in his Name that God hates them? Besides the lost blood of Matthew Shepherd and others, do we also have lost souls on our hands? How and when did their redemption come to be less important to us than their condemnation?

But common-sense still tells us there's something wrong.

Suppose we imagine a homosexual couple, born-again Christians like my buddy back in Army days, leading exemplary Christian lives in all other respects, living together in love and faithfulness. Wouldn't almost everyone agree there's still something wrong with this picture?—and it's the crux of the whole matter: they are not married! No less than with a heterosexual couple, you aren't supposed to live in sin!

Of course it is utterly hypocritical to deny homosexuals the right to marry, then find fault because they aren't married! If you believe our Lord disapproved of homosexuality (though he never said so), go back to your Bible and learn what he says and thinks about hypocrisy!

But suppose we found, or at least believed in, good social and religious justification for refusing homosexuals marriage (or anything tantamount to it)? Do we refuse them fellowship until they renounce and disrupt their loving relationship? What a grotesque turnaround, when the Church has to disapprove of love!

So what can I say? For the uncharitable attitude I hold toward homosexuals, as I confessed at the beginning of this chapter, it is I who need their forgiveness and God's. How can I condemn people "for whom Christ died", when I myself nailed him to the cross, as surely as if I had personally swung the hammer?

But if you can, go ahead: you don't have to answer to me.

CHAPTER 6

MATERIALISM

We wrestle not against flesh and blood, but against principalities, against powers, against the rulers of the darkness of this world, against spiritual wickedness in high places. (Eph. 6:12)

In this and succeeding verses (13-17) and in other places, St. Paul makes use of the athletic or military metaphor: physical combat as a model of our struggles against sin and temptation, the lust of the flesh, the lust of the eyes, and the pride of life (I John 2:16). Thus it is no great surprise to find him warning us in this passage that we'd better know who our opponents are!

It is not rare but common, that Christians identify this or that person or group or organization or institution, or set of ideas or behaviors, as an enemy of the nation or of the faith, or even as *the* enemy: the Antichrist. (I can remember when Benito Mussolini, the self-proclaimed founder of the revived Roman Empire, was generally regarded by Fundamentalists as the Antichrist.) Yet on analysis, or merely on hindsight, these "enemies" often boil down to what St. Paul calls "flesh and blood". Though I may be wrong, and though there may be individual exceptions, I believe that it is not usually possible to identify concrete, personal *rulers of darkness,* as distinguished from the spiritual and mystical forces that beset us. But what we can do is consider why some of our frequently-designated targets are not importantly, or at all, our real enemies.

The distinction is a crucial one, and not just because St. Paul said so. Take Communism, for example. I will not be discussing it at any length, because the need for that is about over. Yet it helps to illustrate the distinction I'm making.

Think of it this way: Communism is a cultural *system* in which food, housing, jobs, education and medical care are proposed not as mere necessities or means, but as *ends:* as ultimate values. The problem is not that Communist governments are militantly atheistic—though the Soviet Union certainly was; or ruthlessly dictatorial—though they always are; but that it is the opposite—almost a mirror image—of Christianity. It proposes, as Christianity does, the creation of a "New Man"; but its ideal is of human dedication to the State, to supplying the material needs of society. It promises a future "Workers' Paradise" (of this world, of course) in which even the government "withers away"—no longer needed because of universal dedication of all its citizens to securing the common good of all: "from each according to his ability, to each according to his need", and without any necessity for any socially-imposed rules or coercion.

The Christian New Man or Woman is likewise concerned with the material necessities of fellow human beings, but their concern is based on love; not on loyalty to a society or social order, but to a divine Lord who had these same concerns and taught us to have them too. One can see why Karl Marx, and after him the Soviet Union, embraced atheism, and perceived Christianity as an ideological rival and hence an enemy. They flatly declared their philosophical base instead to be *dialectical materialism.*

So there's no doubt that Communism shows us a perfect example of "spiritual wickedness" against which, and against its powers, we were called upon to "wrestle". There's no doubt that Christians in general (except for some Modernist cranks) were strongly anti-Communist. It is not quite so certain that our witness was as clear and powerful as it ought to have been. In fact, the struggle, for the most part, was carried out on a secular level, as a (cold) war against the Soviet Union. It has been a long, hard and expensive war, and I certainly share in America's pride at our victories achieved. But wars, whether cold or hot, are against *flesh and blood*. The war was not really against wickedness, but against another country. To be sure, we liked to tell ourselves that our battle was against Communism. And indeed, Communist ideology was a weapon in this war; it was often exploited by nationalistic leaders to organize and unite their people against us. But that's *a political* war. After all, we counted anti-Soviet Yugoslavia as a cold war ally, regardless of her Communist government. Likewise, when it became clear that China had completely broken with the Soviet Union, we made haste to befriend her. In 1918-1921 we participated in an undeclared "hot" war against the Soviet Union, along with Britain, France and Poland; yet we allied ourselves with her in 1941-1945.

That is not a history of principled opposition to the Communist system, but of very ordinary big-power international politics! The spiritual war is different. We "wrestle not" against nations; the rulers of darkness are not the rulers of China or Cuba, and not Islamist fanatics and terrorists either (if they wantonly kill us and other people, then in doing so they no doubt serve a "ruler of darkness", but they themselves are flesh and blood; God's erring children—about like ourselves. After all, in the verses quoted above from St. Paul's letter to the Ephesians, he lets "flesh-and-blood" Romans off the hook, even though they were busily throwing Christians to the lions.)

We're not concerned here with philosophical materialism, the doctrine that physical matter is the only reality and that all processes and phenomena derive from it. Also, the materialist dialectic—a wacky invention of the German philosopher Frederick Engels—is irrelevant to our purposes, and I should think even Communists wouldn't believe it any more. My sole object in all this discussion is to set forth an example of a "flesh and blood" enemy that we confused with a spiritual one. We'll be talking about others, against which we waste our material, spiritual and political resources. I believe it is our materialistic frame of mind itself, that tempts us to do so; sometimes we don't even think from a spiritual standpoint about what kind of struggle we're in. It's so much easier to identify things that people *do*—the homosexuals or the unmarried pregnant or the addicts—and having pronounced such doings sinful, we condemn the *behaviors;* isn't that what the Pharisees did in earning Jesus' disapproval? I mean, that is not different from condemning the *people* who so behave. That is a "flesh and blood" war against a materialistically-defined enemy, and it stems from our own bondage to the world, the flesh and the devil.

Let's get down to cases. There are two aspects of materialism. It is a "preoccupation with or stress upon material rather then intellectual or spiritual things" (Webster). Example: preoccupation with Christmas as an occasion of getting and giving things rather than as a spiritual celebration. For our purposes materialism is mostly subsumed in the notion of wanting stuff and getting stuff, whether concrete stuff like a new fishing rod or dining-room set, or what we might call functional stuff, like a job promotion, or abortion, or listing in the social register. At this level, we're talking about a kind of *behavior*, though it's understood that behavior includes a mental component: not just putting your money down and buying stuff, but also the ideas or mind-set that motivates you to do so, whether from need—such as hunger—or envy of somebody else's stuff, or pure covetousness or lust.

Secondly, there's a deeper aspect, more important because more basic than materialism in the behavioral or dictionary sense. There may be a conscious, deliberate philosophy, an ethical-social doctrine that the only, or anyhow the *highest* values or objectives in life are those of material well-being and the furtherance of material progress. This materialistic philosophy may sound familiar because it's pretty much the same thing we were just saying about Communism. It is neatly set forth by George Bernard Shaw in the introduction to his play, "Androcles and the Lion", in which he unapologetically refers to his ideas variably as either Christian or Communist; in fact he believed that true Christianity *is* Communism. But materialism doesn't have to be Communist, because it has been adopted, or more or less nearly approached, by revisionist interpretations of Christianity that equate redistribution of wealth and material progress with establishment of the Kingdom of God. Nor does it have to be associated with the kind of behavioral materialism that was described in the last paragraph; there have been cells of Communist true believers in dialectical materialism, whose personal lives were ascetic.

And finally, it doesn't have to be conscious, a deliberate philosophy; it can be the unacknowledged basis for our beliefs, and hence behaviors, in most areas of life: our business and professional, financial, social, recreational and household activities. It is not necessary, and in America it's probably rare, for people to define themselves and their values as materialistic. I think of Imelda Marcos, who accumulated 5,000 pairs of shoes. Can you believe she did so on principle—because of believing that the highest values in life consisted in such egregious self-indulgence? I suppose she said, "I have the money; why shouldn't I spend it on things I want?—you can't take it with you!" Don't most of us say the same thing, as soon as we have enough surplus money to face decisions about what to do with it? Even if we tithe, we are likely to have that same attitude about the rest of our resources.

So we can talk about wanting and buying stuff, or talk about the attitudinal outlook that getting stuff is very important, or even *the* most important, value in life, and it may sound as if they were both the same thing. And in our own lives we tend to adopt the behavior and ignore or deny the attitudinal basis for it. Yet Jesus told us it's what's in the heart that counts, because that's where the behavior comes from. We're not good at talking about this. Taking it seriously might require renouncing some things. And "things"—our *stuff*—is the crux of the matter. Though we may have fewer shoes than Imelda, we are really just like her if our hearts are the same.

Societal (as distinguished from individual) materialism is not limited to Communist society. There are very serious materialistic strains in our own civilization. They are mostly cultural (rather than governmental, as with Communism) and thus are a part of our normal and customary, inner-driven roles, behaviors and outlook within that culture. If the culture of materialism were imposed by a wicked governmental system it would be easier to identify and resist than when it has actually become a value, a sought-after aspect of our society. A Christian witness persisted in Russia through all the years of Communist persecution; but except for a few Brethren—Amish and Mennonite "plain" people—where is the anti-materialistic sub-culture in America? It is the very question raised by the foremost spiritual voice of Russia during that whole period—that of Alexander Solzhenitsyn—who was as critical of American materialism as of Communism and its *gulags* in his own land.

For 21st Century American Christians, I do believe that materialism is an adverse "principality", the kind of "spiritual wickedness" warned of by St. Paul. Materialism is not less worldly or evil in America than in Russia. Every bit as urgently as in a Communist country, materialism requires a counter-struggle, and no hot or cold war can win it for us.

Let's think some more about what this means.

The Amish and Mennonite groups by their very existence are a rebuke to us, and for this we need them; but they do not provide a model for society at large. The pursuit of simplicity can become a fetish, as it was with the Shakers, or it can be off-target. That is, the Mennonites and Amish have a healthy and admirable contempt for a lot of the features of American life that most of us consider important but that are in fact worldly and objectionable. The Amish, in particular, are admired by almost everybody for their fiercely determined adherence to a way of life uncluttered by modern consumerism or even conveniences. But the core of spirituality that motivates these groups can easily be overlooked (how often have you seen a TV documentary about the religious faith and beliefs of the Amish, rather than about the externals of their way of life?) The Mennonites are likewise remarkable, to general public perception, neither for faith nor works, but for plainness of dress, especially the ubiquitous bonnet.

I use the term "off-target" because our faith, witness, and works should proclaim Christ, not just draw attention to themselves. Conspicuous consumption is not the "target", but is only the external manifestation of corrupted, materialistic values; and its converse, conspicuous plainness, is also external, even though it be a manifestation—as in the Mennonites I have known—of a pure faith and non-worldly values. Nevertheless, it does not in the main point the observer to Christ, but to itself.

I digress. The topic is not some sect or other, and the digression is only made to show that the problem of materialism, and of establishing and maintaining a witness that points away from it and toward Christ, is so complex and difficult as to elude simple or external solutions. The "Beatnik" and "Hippie" movements of the '50's and '60's likewise abjured materialism; but lacking spiritual foundation (except for a few "Jesus freaks") they eventually either gave up the struggle, or evolved into Weathermen or Black Panthers or other forms of futile radicalism.

Again, there is little evidence of any sustained, unified and meaningful non-conformist anti-materialistic movement in America. The Evangelical-Fundamentalist groups are resoundingly known throughout the Nation, their voice loud, clear, and to some alarming: but what is it saying? It speaks mostly of politics, telling us to give our vote to the party of Big Business—as materialistic as any Communist cell—to diminish or abolish public programs for health, welfare and environmental protection; to cut taxes (so as to "boost the economy"—but really to leave us more money to spend on ourselves and our individual materialistic pursuits). It identifies problems in the areas of abortion and homosexuality, problems which it calls "moral" but to which it proposes political solutions. That voice shows not the least concern, to any outsider's perception that I've heard of, about rampant materialism, not to say about personal faith or social justice. I believe most of the constituents of that voice are themselves so caught up in the culture of consumerism and materialistic pursuit as not to notice that anything is missing from their message.

But the old warning still stands: "Ye cannot serve God and mammon" (Luke 16:13). If we serve God He is our king and ruler; and mammon no less so if we serve it instead. I interpret St. Paul's term "principality" to reflect this. A principality is the domain of a prince—a ruler—and he or that which rules us is he or that against which we must wrestle whenever he or that is not God. "Tis a gift to be simple, 'tis a gift to be free", sang the Shakers, and no less so in our day and in our churches and denominations we must seek to be free from the domain of mammon, free of the materialism that would clog and clutter our lives with shopping and spending and getting and coveting and shopping and discarding-and-replacing and accumulating and shopping and collecting and competing and conforming and keeping up with the styles and the fashions and worrying, worrying, worrying about whether we're doing it all successfully and whether we can keep it up and still survive in old age, and whether we can equip our children to become equally trapped in the selfsame rat race; but never worrying about Mother Teresa's sick and impoverished babies; or Albert Schweitzer's and St. Francis' animal friends or the poor, scarred, devastated earth we've left them to live in; or the sick or the addicted or the imprisoned—both in jails and in city ghettoes—or the widowed and orphaned and demented and prostituted and handicapped, or—*of course,* since we're blind to it—about the state of our consumer society and our covetous souls: choking to death on our untold riches but spiritually starving. Larry Gaffin said,

"Having enough is more important than having it all." And, "...give me neither poverty nor riches..." (Proverbs 30:8), and

"...where your treasure is, there will your heart be also." (Luke 12:34) We do not lack fair warning.

I once had a nurse on my staff, a divorced mother with a son to raise, who liked to display—and even brag a little—about her household furnishings. She'd wear what she called "grungies" to look poor and facilitate price-haggling, and she'd go to the used furniture outlets to get what she wanted. Her home had been mostly furnished in this manner. Her pieces were obviously functional, and (though I'm a man and hardly equipped to judge) they did not seem at all unattractive after she did a little finishing work on them. Though I personally admired all this, I do believe it was considered a little strange by those who knew that she actually made a decent salary. I've known cheapskates and skinflints, and I know those terms simply don't apply; she just thought expensive new furniture a waste of money, and she had her priorities.

How about the guy who said, "I went up to clean the attic, but my heart wasn't in it, so I went fishing." We know what that means, about where your heart is. We know, don't we, that in both individual and civil life little gets done if our heart isn't in it. According to Jesus, you can tell where somebody's heart is by where he puts his money (Luke 12: 34). We know it too. What else could it mean, such sayings as, "Put up or shut up!" or, "Put your money where your mouth is!" Conservatives who claim to be "compassionate" but who use their power to shred programs intended to alleviate human and environmental stress, and who tax the poor and the working man for money to give away to the rich—and who bray about their Christian convictions—will have to explain some day to their Maker—not to me—where their heart was all this time.

A local newspaperman, around the Christmas season a few years ago, wrote about an essay submitted by a small Muslim boy. Telling what he thought about Christmas, the kid said he felt rather left out; but it didn't matter, because all he really cared about was his own celebration of Eid al-Fitr—the end of Ramadan, the month of fasting that may come more or less around the same season. He liked it better, he said, "because it's a religious holiday". Isn't that remarkable?—first, that he would think a religious holiday is better than a secular one; and then, that he'd consider Christmas secular! Is there something wrong when our greatest Christian celebration somehow escapes being perceived as a religious occasion? The reason, of course, is that it's not one! "Christ Mass", immemorially represented in the Church calendar, is intended to mark the Savior's birth. It once meant what John Betjeman wrote:

No love that in a family dwells,
No caroling in frosty air,
Nor all the steeple-shaking bells
Can with this simple truth compare
That God was man in Palestine
And lives today in Bread and Wine.

No celebration can add to, but it may easily detract from, the truth about what began that night in Bethlehem.

But Christmas, in its derivative spelling, or Xmas, (with the "birthday boy's name crossed out", as Ray Romano put it) or Chrismukkah (as it's sometimes called by those who think Hanukkah is a comparable occasion and contemplate a joint celebration of it) or Yule (anything to avoid reminding us of Christ) or Holidays (as in "Happy", intended to be inclusive also of New Year's, as well as Hanukkah, Eid al-Fitr and Kwanzaa) is a feature of the secular calendar. As a secular occasion, it is observed—unlike religious holidays—by the government. Its family celebrations are identical, as between those of Christian and irreligious families, except for many of the formers' more or less ceremonial visits to Midnight Mass or candlelight services. On Christmas itself, many or most churches are closed; and who would go, if they were not?—we are far too busy with decorations and presents and dinner and other stuff.

Children, inevitably, like being given toys and other presents. How could Christmas not be identified by them as the day of gift-giving? That is what all the excitement's about, and in what family are the kids not advised that the supernatural personage responsible for it all is Santa Claus? Maybe in the mind of a child of five or six or so, the red outfit may become supplanted by a white robe, and the guy with the long white beard who sees and knows all, and who judges and punishes or rewards naughty or nice, is re-identified as God; but both are henceforth banished from our thoughts and our celebrations of the season.

Persons and families who are already Christian no doubt find in Advent services a religious glow that helps to build up the holiday excitement; and they may select Christmas cards that quote a Scripture verse or express a pious sentiment; and they may attend their children's Sunday School Christmas pageant or other such celebration; but most of this is within the circle. To the unchurched who don't look for it, the evidence of a religious basis for their holiday is mighty scarce.

Easter is no different, though less consequential in American life (if not in the Christian calendar). The word "Easter" in Acts 12:4 represents the Greek *pascha* (cf. "Paschal Lamb", the atoning Christ). The word is always translated "Passover" elsewhere in Scripture, being the Greek equivalent of the Hebrew term for that feast, *pesach*. In early-day England, the Christian Paschal came to be known as Easter, the name derived from Old English *eostre* or *eastre*. It substituted for a pagan spring festival in honor of Ostara, an Anglo-Saxon fertility goddess. Hence the significance of eggs: the reproductive zygote. Beyond that, the chicks and bunnies, the hyacinths and daffodils and lilies—all are pagan symbols of spring and by implication, of fertility. Small wonder that in a materialistic society the occasion easily lends itself to commercialization.

Would that individual and cultural materialism were limited to our fertility and mid-winter festivals! Our national holidays have been similarly hijacked by commerce and recreation, though the naive observer could, with a little diligence, detect a modicum of patriotic pride and dedication on Independence and Memorial Days and others. Day-to-day, though, look where our hearts are, as indicated by where our money goes:

According to the 2001 World Almanac, we spent $44 billion a year on jewelry and watches in 1998, and that much again on shoes; $54 billion on tobacco products, a like amount on "toilet articles and preparations"—and you can bet that is mostly male and female cosmetics, not soap and toothpaste—and a similar amount also on toys and sport supplies; and as much again on "commercial participant amusements" including, I guess, bowling alleys, golf course fees, skating rinks and the like. We spent $38 billion to watch things: movies and spectator events such as concerts and sports. We spent $244 billion on clothes. I grant that at least some expenditures in each of these categories can be justified—except tobacco, though as a former smoker, I have a lot of sympathy for people who can't quit. But together they absorb over 10% of personal expenditures. Compare it with 1.7% for education, and 2.8% for religious and welfare activities. Many of the categories I didn't include consume a much greater share, and some of these are certainly subject to scrutiny for possible extravagances that betray a covetous and materialistic bent: housing, food, and car expenses among others. Where would you say the heart is, of a family or individual whose budget reflects the same proportionate expenditures?

A physician, Peter Whybrow, M.D., has written on this matter, *American Mania* (New York, W.W. Norton, 2005), with the subtitle, *When More is not Enough*. He even highlights our dietary extravagance, as reflected in the national epidemic of obesity: recommended reading for the concerned.

I say all of this, not to condemn anybody or to sit in judgment on any thing or things that anybody owns or desires. As I said, hardly anybody is consciously and deliberately materialistic as a matter of principle. People born and raised in a culture where Mammon is king might be considered just a trifle deviant if they completely failed to integrate the social norms into their own patterns of thought and behavior. Especially people brought up poor, such as during the Great Depression, may grow up somewhat fixated on acquiring things, as though forever hedging against hunger and want. But I would like to get across the notion that we have a problem; that we do not wrestle with materialism as we ought, but rather accept it while looking elsewhere for spiritual enemies to fight; and finding ones that do not cause us any discomfort or require any sacrifice, that are not fundamentally spiritual, and that do not even threaten the faith—or our own souls! (including—but not limited to—the various "enemies" identified in the chapters of this book). But I have to emphasize that if the problem involves social norms, it's bound to need a social solution, in which I think the Church ought to be involved and even take leadership (not least by setting an example).

Meanwhile, we've got a problem!

The Shaker hymn's proclamation, "'Tis a gift to be simple", seems unavoidable. To become uncluttered you have to stop cluttering, and victory over materialistic clutter comes, not when we stop doing it, but when we stop wanting it—when your heart is in the things that endure, and the things around you that need Christian nurture and service.

In many of these chapters I want to tackle at greater or lesser length some of the often troubling aspects of our national life that I believe do not deserve the attention, not to say opposition, they tend to get from conservative Christians, and whose defeat would be of only marginal if any benefit to either our spiritual or national well-being. I want to do this because it seems to me they "clutter" our Christian witness, every bit as much as financial extravagances clutter our budgets.

Here are some examples of "clutter": Pat Robertson asserted that the recent earthquake in Haiti was simply the latest in a nearly unbroken series of catastrophes visited upon that nation as a result of a pact with the Devil they made in 1802 whereby they obtained freedom from the French; and then some Fundamentalists claimed that the desolations of 9/11/01 were brought upon us by ourselves because of such things as homosexuality and abortion. I understand these spokespersons later recanted; but beyond being asinine, such words are a horrifying embarrassment to the cause of Christ, because these people speak in his Name. No matter how much you may hate those things (and that's none of my business, so I'm not trying to change your feelings about them) they are not worthy targets in our spiritual war. If defeated (which is almost certainly impossible anyhow) no soul would be brought to Christ thereby (would it?) nor the physical or moral strength of the nation enhanced. They are "flesh and blood" targets, against which we should "wrestle not". We bring only disrepute upon ourselves and the Name of Christ by vain oppositionalism against targets which are not truly spiritual (unless to a specific individual personally involved in these matters) and are irrelevant to our struggle against principalities and powers. We clutter up our witness with it.

I want this understood: my object in discussing these topics will not be to convert or persuade, as to any issue. I'd be surprised if any people changed their opinions because of reading these chapters, and that's OK. All I want is to show that there is a different but legitimate Christian view of the issues; that they are not the "enemy" against which St. Paul urged us to wrestle; and that we preach a false gospel when we identify Christ with our foolish and futile crusades.

Orthodoxy is the repository of true faith, and rightfully maintains its guard against heresy—as it wrestled so faithfully against all the Modernist/revisionist fads of the nineteenth and early twentieth centuries (the remnants of which still persist). But it must be equally vigilant against erecting its own beliefs and standards and declaring them to be orthodox; against mistaking them for the true faith it is dedicated to preserving; against stagnating in them when challenged by new, sometimes liberal, maybe radical, truths. That's what the Pharisees did. That's half the story of St. Paul's ministry, in which he struggled as much with conservative Christians—the Judaizers—as with the heathen. That's the story of the Reformation, of Galileo, of the English Puritans. It was the orthodox faithful, under the spiritual leadership of the great Cotton Mather who in 1692 killed 20 alleged witches. It was the liberals of the day and later, who led in abolition of criminal sentences against witchcraft, and eventually to the understanding (contrary to certain express Biblical texts) that the whole doctrine of witchcraft was phony. Indeed it is a materialistic fallacy ever to think you can combat spiritual enemies by punishing or killing, or even controlling, flesh and blood.

It's my belief that the very definition of Pharisaism is the use of religion to condemn and control or punish the purported sins of other people as a way of avoiding confrontation with—denying— our own iniquities. I believe it is especially attractive in a materialistic society. If we truly accepted what St. Paul called "the mystery of iniquity", we could understand why Jesus concerned himself, not with the concrete sin of the woman taken in adultery, but with the spiritual sin of those who condemned her (John 8:3-11).

I'm afraid we are at least as materialistic as that; or else we might take an interest in people's needs instead of their sex life. (In saying all this, I acknowledge that I commit the very thing that I'm criticizing. I do regret that; but I can't not say it.)

In Chapter 12 I'll talk more about some of the problems we face in contending with the "principalities and powers"—both imaginary and real. I hope we can devote our efforts to them, and not clutter our message and drain off our energies and our credibility in battles we cannot win, and generally should not win, and that would serve Christ and the nation little or not at all, even if we did win.

I know from experience that a struggle against Mammon is a difficult and lonely undertaking—one that attracts little understanding or respect from others. For that matter, it's hard to see how a single individual's victory in it, however good for his own soul, could have very much public impact, by way of enhancing America's moral and spiritual life. So I wanted here to identify the enemy and establish that it's worth contending against; in Chapter 8 we'll think about the place of community in fortifying the struggle of individuals.

As St. Paul warned us, we have to know who our enemies are. That, incidentally, means knowing who they are not!

But civilization has made so much materialistic progress; that is, it has so improved the material circumstances of our lives, that "Progress" has become seriously over-valued and thoroughly identified with Materialism itself. We have to deal with that before moving on.

CHAPTER 7

EVOLUTION—*NOT!*

...evolution argues that...humanity will continue to go forward (Economist Julian Simon)
...the trend of civilization is forever upward. (Dr. Endicott Peabody, Groton School headmaster)

We'll talk about Darwinian—i.e. biological—evolution in Chapter 9. The above citations negatively signal the subject of this chapter, which is, "Why Evolution has Nothing Whatever to Say about the Development of Humanity and Civilization". I think the discussion is warranted, precisely because sentiments like those expressed by Peabody and Simon are widespread, and because of their falsity they need to be refuted, and because, being false, they give biological evolution a bad name. It has enough problems without being saddled with psychological-social-anthropological nonsense.

One of the most popular and, especially in America, by far the most influential peddler of the Theory of Evolution was the philosopher Herbert Spencer. So inspired was he by Darwin's book, *The Origin of Species* that he constructed from it an entire philosophical system, propounded in a multi-volume set called "Synthetic Philosophy", as well as in many other writings. It's obvious that in one chapter I can't do justice to so voluminous a work (which I haven't read); but in summary, he applied the evolutionary idea of constant development from lower to higher forms, to society, which in that view had to be progressively advancing (and you see this notion expressed in the citations above). Darwin never said that, and his less wild-eyed enthusiasts don't say so either. But "evolution", defined uncritically, is generally accepted as true; and the various illegitimate offspring of Darwin's biological formulations—such as Spencer's—tend to be accepted also. I believe that Christians who want to think seriously about evolution and about policies related to it, need to understand what it is not, before we can think about what it is and what to do about it.

CIVILIZATION

The dictionary tells us that civilization is "a relatively high level of cultural and technological development". That may include, but does not specify, the idea of continued advancement or Progress, or attaining continually higher levels culturally or technologically. Albert Schweitzer, in his book, *The Philosophy of Civilization* (New York, 1950) elaborates: "Civilization ...consists in our giving ourselves...to the effort to attain the perfecting of the human race and...of progress...in the circumstances of humanity and of the objective world". He says that Progress—the continued improvement of both human and environmental qualities—is the essential meaning of civilization, and that it occurs, if it does, as a result of human dedication and effort (i.e. not inevitably as a result of natural law, as Spencer and others claim). It's pretty clear that to assess the matter, we need a historical perspective. You have to look at where we were long ago to see if where we are today represents Progress. In fact, I'm going all the way back to Creation.

We believe that God does not make mistakes—there's no "Oops!" in Creation—so His works are perfect. There is a problem with that, having to do with Man himself, who is surely God's creation, yet far from perfect. So is God infallible, and His works impeccable—or not?

Let's think once more about dualism and paradox, as discussed in Chapter 2. If you had creative power, and took a notion to create rabbits, you could not possibly improve on what already exists. If you made something "better" than a rabbit, OK, let's say you could do that, but it would not be a rabbit! Perhaps we can make a better mousetrap, and it would still be a mousetrap; because that is a human invention which can always be improved. But God's creatures are already perfect. (From a different standpoint, this would not be a true statement; but that discussion belongs in Chap. 9.) There is no improved "rabbitness" beyond what already exists; and if you created something "better", it might be a puppydog or a pussycat if you thought that was something "better", but it wouldn't be a rabbit!

Now suppose you wanted to make Man. If you were a *good* creator, you'd no doubt want to make your Man good like yourself, and not some kind of evil being. To accomplish that, you'd have to do just what you did in creating rabbits: you made them to be physically what they are, and to do instinctively what rabbits do—it's not like you gave them a choice.

So you can't give your proposed Man a choice, either, if one of his qualities or characteristics is that he must be good. You have to "build in" goodness just as much as you "built in" long ears and love of carrots in the other species.

For rabbits, that's OK; but for Man?—see what you've done? You've made a man with no choice; an automaton, an animal like other animals, a machine made of meat. (Of course, some people do say that's exactly what we are—but we won't let those people bother us.) In other words, your Man is not perfect, for all his goodness, but is deficient in the only thing that makes goodness matter: his free choice to be so *even at a cost* of whatever easier, pleasanter or more profitable course of action may have been available. A person without a conscience (popularly called a "psychopath" or "sociopath"), a defective person, without a will to choose what's right, does come to our attention sometimes, in the person of the very worst of humans ever to make the news. Yet if you create a perfectly good man, rather than a totally evil one, you can't give him the ability to choose, either. He must *be equally defective* as the psychopath, if he's to remain perfect. But a defective man is *not* perfect! If you create a perfect Man, he must be a whole Man, complete with free will and moral sensibility. But if you create a whole Man, *he will be,* or become, imperfect. The reason is simple. There's a difference between personhood and godhood. Your whole and perfect Man, as you created him, would start out as a perfectly good creature. But nothing or nobody can be a mere human and yet possess perfect, infallible knowledge and foresight. Those things belong to God alone, and your hypothetical Man is no less perfect for lacking them than your rabbit was imperfect if he lacks a prehensile tail. That belongs to monkeys, and your creation is a perfect rabbit without one, just as your man (in our argument) is perfect without characteristics that belong to God. Your Man, therefore, however richly you've endowed him with conscience and will-to-virtue, and with whatever intensity of his effort to do good that he may engage, he will fail. He cannot always have knowledge of what is good; his choices may not always be clear—between good and evil, rather than between the greater or lesser evils—and he will not always foresee all the consequences of his acts; these can be negative or destructive, even of a seemingly good or neutral act. For one or all of these reasons, sooner or later, your whole Man is going to mess it up, simply, in the first instance, *because he can;* and if he cannot, he is no Man but a yo-yo or a Robo-Tron in the hand of some celestial toy-maker.

Anyhow, it appears that humans, in the nature of their constitution, are going to sin, for we not only lack a perfect knowledge of the nature and consequences of our acts, we also lack the perfect will-to-virtue with which you just now endowed your own hypothetical creation. I have a lot of sympathy for Adam and Eve. Adam, of course, was only trying to please his wife, and you may judge—because I will not—how wrong that may have been (see I Tim. 1:14, "Adam was not deceived, but the woman being deceived was in the transgression"). Eve's motives were more complex: she "saw that the tree was good for food, and that it was pleasant to the eyes, and a tree to be desired to make one wise" (Gen. 3:6). She lacked "knowledge of good and evil" (Gen. 2:17); she did not understand the consequences of her act, having been deceived about that by the Serpent. She did not foresee her own mortality, much less Attila the Hun or Genghis Khan, Torquemada or Tamerlane, Gettysburg or Stalingrad, Auschwitz or the Rape of Nanking or Hiroshima, Calvary or Armageddon.

She did what any of us might do, if we care about human progress and the advancement of civilization: she took action that promised better material circumstances, esthetic or cultural advancements, and intellectual progress. I can imagine her excitement at the Serpent's assurance that their eyes would be opened to possession of god-like knowledge. In modern times she might have founded a university to accomplish much the same things; she anticipated Ezra Cornell, Leland Stanford, Andrew Carnegie, Cornelius Vanderbilt and James and Benjamin Duke. She modeled the Golden Age of Greece, the Renaissance, the Enlightenment, and the American Revolution. Adam and Eve took the very first step in the development of civilization, in furthering the Progress of Man.

And they were punished for it!! Wow. What are we to think about God's view of civilization and Progress? We are advised by preachers that the first sin consisted in (1) rebelliousness—simple non-compliance with God's command, and (2) pride—the self-important frame of mind that feeds rebelliousness. In the third Century A.D. Origen decided that infant baptism was cute; and needing a theological justification for it, he invented the doctrine of Original Sin. It followed from this notion that "little children who have begun to live in their mother's womb and have there died, or who, having just been born, have passed away from the world without the sacrament of holy baptism, must be punished by the eternal torture of undying fire" (St. Fulgentius, 6th Century A.D.) Protestants don't really believe this. We profess it, but nullify it. We say that God loves children and would not condemn one who died at an age of innocence or unaccountability. Now, Original Sin is the doctrine that you can go to Hell because of somebody else's sin, other than your own (namely, Adam's). To say that it applies only if you reach the age of accountability is to say that if you then go to Hell, it is for your *own* sins—those for which you are accountable.

Original Sin is not a Biblical belief (nor are Protestant rationalizations of it). What God really said to Adam was, "... dust thou art, and unto dust shalt thou return" (Gen. 3:19). The curse of God was mortality—death, and He expelled our parents from the Garden, "lest he put forth his hand and take of the tree of life, and eat, and live forever" (Gen. 3:22). That is, *Lest he escape death,* with which I have cursed him. St. Paul explained our relationship to Adam: "by one man [i.e. Adam] sin entered into the world, and death by sin; and so death passed upon all men, for that all have sinned." (Rom. 5:12). I don't know how it could be more clear. We inherit the curse of Adam—death—not because he sinned, but because we do.

Besides being unbiblical, the doctrine ignores the fact that pride and rebelliousness are *not* washed away by either adult or infant baptism; and it tells us nothing about God's intentions for us regarding civilization or Progress. Because that is what it was all about.

Of course, you could say that He was just being arbitrary, like a father at the end of his patience who tells an unruly kid, "Because I said so!" if asked why he must obey. But I have trouble with the idea of a God Who demands obedience for its own sake, with no other reason but that He wants it that way. Even the exhausted father does in fact have reasons—based on what's best for the child—for wanting obedience, even though he despairs of making an explanation that will satisfy the bratty kid, who in any case likely could not understand what's best for him and why.

And in that, I think, we come closer to understanding. Remember the problem in creating Man: if you make him good, he's a mechanical doll; if you make him free, he won't be good. It seems to me that by creating Man innocent—without knowledge of good and evil—God established a hedge or protection against using his freedom in evil ways. Yet a creature who in principle possesses complete freedom, cannot be free in fact if he has no options. Eden may be nice, but it's a gilded cage for one who is supposed to be free but has no choice but to be there and whose life and circumstances he can never change. It doesn't matter that one may lack a compelling reason to change anything: Eden *was* nice! But to be free in fact, not just in principle, one must have access to the forbidden fruit. So Man was free; and at the Serpent's urging, he conceived the idea of Progress!

God's command, then, seemingly so arbitrary, was actually meant to protect humanity—to keep mankind from having powers he didn't know how to use, from destroying himself by the unforeseen consequences of his own cleverness; in a word, from what we euphemistically call "Progress". I think the point is not that God disapproves of Progress (even though it was Serpent-inspired rather than a part of His original endowment) but just that He knew (as we never seem to) what we're likely to do with it. He knew that the genius of Newton and Einstein would lead to Hiroshima, that Plymouth Rock was a step toward Antietam, Ludlow and Wounded Knee, and that Martin Luther would father the Thirty Years' War.

I can't find in this any suggestion that knowledge itself, or increase in knowledge, or attempts at increasing knowledge, or trying to convey knowledge to the young, are evil. The sin was, after all, that of disobeying God, just as we've always been told. That belonged to our first parents alone (though we do emulate them!) What was passed down to us, besides mortality, was the actual change in man's nature from his original innocence, when his "eyes were opened". He can never again be contented with his circumstances. He is torn between a longing for the Eden of his primeval past, and that of the future, whether Heaven, or the "Worker's Paradise" or "Brave New World" or Tower of Babel, that he seeks with driven compulsion to attain. The Serpent's invitation to Progress still rings in his ears. There's no advantage to the Deceiver in tempting us only to sinful deeds, when he can "work us woe" on a much grander scale by seducing us to ever greater Progress whose evil consequences — species' extinctions, atomic warfare, environmental pollution — we still haven't learned to prevent.

You may believe the story of Adam and Eve is literally historical or only mythological, but in either case it presents a striking allegory of every person's story. An infant, upon delivery from the safe, warm, effortless, essentially parasitic existence of the womb, is cold and wet, and is probably spanked into life by an obstetrician impatient to hear that first cry. (You know how it is in mid-winter when you leave a warm house and take a deep breath of frigid air? It *hurts!*—and I've often thought the newborn's first breath must feel like that, too.) Who can doubt that his cry and his struggling, wriggling inchoate movements convey what he cannot speak: "What a bummer this is! I'd rather be back where I came from!" And it goes on; for many years he will come rushing back to his mother's arms to be enveloped in them when the world gets too painful. Unless numbed by the traumas of life, he can never learn to avoid homesickness and separation anxiety and bereavement: the pain of loss. When too old for mother's arms, he will seek other comforts: easy street, the wide gate and the broad path, drugs, alcohol, love and sex, and even religion in search of the elusive Eden. Yet he knows why he lost it in the first place: because he wanted to be a Big Boy or Big Girl; he had to grow and mature and become what his potential enabled him to become; he is forever restless, probing, turning here and there; he seeks learning and experiences and relationships that will further his personal maturation and his social and vocational accomplishments. From this conflict of desires arises the social division between conservative and progressive: between the desire to hold fast to what we have and preserve the traditions and the old values, as against the impulse to Progress and change and improvement, at the cost of leaving behind what seems old and confining.

I do not say there's anything wrong with longing for the imagined Eden of our "good old days", or for any fantasied future Paradise. I only say that Adam and Eve had no such longings at the start, and that these are what we have inherited from their changed nature, and are what accounts for our behavior for better or for worse, and not the stain of some abstract Original Sin that we did not commit. Only devotion to Progress can foster civilization, said Schweitzer, and now we can see why it's so. But we also see that Progress itself is a pretty dubious notion, both negatively and positively charged. Let's look at it some more.

PROGRESS

Back when power equipment was new, a story was told about two sidewalk superintendents watching a steam shovel excavate. One said, "That machine has taken away the jobs of 100 men with shovels." The other said, "Yeah, right, or 1000 men with spoons." I wonder if the shovel or spade, ever did put anybody out of work. But even if it did, it has been an unquestioned blessing to mankind—certainly to me: I've spent a lot of hours wielding one in tasks that I couldn't have accomplished with spoons. Yet we must also feel fortunate that the word "ditchdigger" became obsolete, even if some men encountered hardship as it did.

The British Luddites gave their name to protestors against advancement in industrial methods. During a period of years in the early 19th Century they engaged in sporadic riots, sometimes quite destructive, against textile mills with their labor-saving machinery, and in protest against the alleged inferior products of the machines. Gradual improvement in economic conditions, presumably including new employment opportunities for textile workers laid off when machines were installed, led to eventual subsidence of the rebellion and the triumph of Progress.

While we may not sympathize with their specific quarrel, we have to learn this from it: that Progress comes at a cost, no less now than in Eden. Liberal and Progressive schemes of human uplift, not to mention industrial and business manipulations, may take shockingly little account of unintended consequences; take little thought about whom they are going to hurt. That is how Herbert Spencer's philosophy got carried away from the foolish to the dangerous.

But he was only one of a host who were hit like a thunderbolt by Charles Darwin's *Origin of Species,* published in 1859. Remember that in his time there was no science of biology; both professional and lay interest in living things was subsumed as Natural History, a purely descriptive pursuit with little scientific underpinning beyond Linnaeus' classification scheme, with its implicit but not understood hint at relationship between species. Physics had been a modern science since Isaac Newton (1642—1726) and his laws of motion and gravity, among other things. Chemistry also had attained its modern framework with the atomic theory of matter, originated by John Dalton in 1808. But fifty years after that, there was no theory, no structure, no concept by which a study of living things could be organized. It is quite justifiable, and shouldn't be surprising, that when one suddenly appeared in Darwin's theory, it should have been accepted wholeheartedly and enthusiastically (maybe a little bit too much so!—but that's for Chapter 9.)

What he himself did not expect, and ambivalently objected to throughout the rest of his life, is what has come to be known as *Social Darwinism,* a school of thought which held that society has evolved on Darwin's evolutionary or biological model. At the beginning of this chapter I mentioned Herbert Spencer's work. His ideas were popularized at a most remarkable period of time: when business and industry were growing almost explosively under the influence of the Industrial Revolution (with the aforementioned "Luddite" sort of consequences to the detriment of the common man); during the golden Victorian age of Great Britain's economic and international grandeur; and during America's post-Civil War mania of geographic as well as economic expansion. What could have been more welcome than the voice of the profoundest philosopher of his day (according to his reputation at the time), when he argued that all such great advancements in industrial capacity, economic arrangements, national expanse and political power—all resulted from the operation of natural law upon society; all these things had to be, because the necessity and inevitability of Progress are ordained in the nature of the universe.

I needn't remind very many of my readers that a lot of leaders of the religious community also hopped on the bandwagon. It suddenly became necessary to consider religion, too, as an evolving phenomenon; "the faith which was once delivered to the saints" (Jude 1:3), having come to us by revelation "once", obviously did not square with an evolutionary process of gradual development. The entire history of man's relation to the Numinous was now interpreted as evolutionary in nature; as a natural— rooted in Nature—progression from a postulated cave-man state of fear leading to animistic beliefs, through idolatry, polytheism, monotheism, to the current enlightened situation. In this view Evolution, the necessity of continued progress ever onward and upward, must lead to re-formulation of the Kingdom of God from a spiritual state "within" the believer (Luke 17:21) to a socialized political-economic system. As the late A. Powell Davies, Pastor of All Souls Church, Washington, D.C., explained,

(Churches) "must sometime recognize that God can work through natural events in a gradual social evolution. Indeed, this is the way he does work...

"Christianity, Judaism, Buddhism, Islam, Taoism—all the higher religions...have grown in natural ways and evolved with history...

"Surely the same God, the same indwelling Spirit, is at work in all." *(Dead Sea Scrolls,* North American Library, New York, 1956)

If Communism is a "mirror image" of Christianity (Chap. 6) then Social Darwinism must be its diametrical opposite. It glorifies the rich and powerful, while regarding the sick, the poor, the handicapped, the stranger, as unfit and unworthy of survival. Yet these are the very people toward whom Jesus taught us our care and our labors must be directed.

As reported by Columbia University's Richard Hofstadter in *Social Darwinism in American Thought* (New York, 1994), from which the historical elements of this discussion are derived, lay enthusiasts were more likely taken by Spencer's idea that the motor of social evolution is identical to that postulated by Darwin for the evolution of life forms: Natural Selection. Only, that was Darwin's own term; Spencer and all his followers used instead the words *Survival of the Fittest.* Darwin accepted his term—but not his sociology. What a rush it must have been for ruthless and usually thieving leaders of business and industry to have the assurance that they are not evil, or even smart and lucky, but that they are naturally and amorally the fittest. Some even imagined that they were building the Kingdom of God; this seems to have been a particular delusion of John D. Rockefeller and his son— talk about doing well by doing good! And how convenient not to have to trouble oneself over those whom they had trampled down, or what became of them—they were unfit anyhow, and like any trilobite they brought about their own extermination by their unfitness to survive.

(I'm not suggesting that the Carnegies, Rockefellers and Vanderbilts of the time were given to studying philosophy. Condensed and oversimplified versions of Spencer's ideas were widely reported, for example in Popular Science, Atlantic Monthly and other popular publications. As bad as Spencer's ideas were, they probably were made worse by journalistic oversimplifications and distortions, probably in the direction of sensationalizing them; and to this must be added the effect of human nature, our propensity to hear what we want to hear and what serves our purposes.)

The flip side of the coin that glorifies those "fit" to survive, is of course contempt for the "unfit". Spencer himself said, "The whole effort of nature is to get rid of such, to clear the world of them, and make room for better." Another Maryland Simon, Newcomb J., a Johns Hopkins economist (of unknown relationship, if any, to the late Julian Simon I quoted at the beginning of this chapter) wrote, "From an economic point of view the gentleman [giving charity] pays the beggar for being poor, miserable, idle, dirty, and worthless" (from Dr. Marvin Olasky, *The Tragedy of American Compassion*, Univ. of Texas). That is, in terms of economic supply and demand, the good intentions of the "gentleman", such as his desire that there be no poverty, are irrelevant. Putting money into poverty creates a demand for it, same as with cars, cell phones or rock music; so don't do it!

In the natural world, Spencer claimed, being bigger, faster, stronger, more aggressive, even smarter—in short, more *powerful*—conferred survival capabilities; and so in human society does power ensure survival and thus lead to improvement and Progress. At least this is how Spencer was interpreted in America, and it may be something of a caricature. He himself was disappointed with Americans, their excess of hurry and hard labor, their over-emphasis on the gospel of work; in effect, I think he considered them a little immature for the proper utilization of his ideas. But the original perversion remained Spencer's, for Darwin himself made no suggestion that his biological theories held any meaning for sociology. Regardless, cut-throat competition (or competitive throat-cutting), not to mention rugged individualism, now had scientific and moral justification, because even allowing the poor to starve is only elimination of the unfit, and is necessary to continued Progress!

Our quite remarkable technological and socio-political achievements fit in so well with the idea of Progress that it may be hard for some to reject it. I think this means we have inordinate pride in what we've accomplished, at least in making ourselves so well off materially. I mean, civilization has achieved undoubted progress in making people better off than we used to be—especially if we don't count the cost; but Progress as a feature or element of Nature like gravity or hydrogen, is pure fantasy. It anthropomorphizes the universe, attributing to it the restlessness and striving "onward and upward" of our own kind. We got that when our eyes were opened back in Eden, but the universe was moving in its own way and according to its own laws long before that (billions of years before, they're telling us nowadays). The idea of Progress as a principle of Nature is what psychologists call "projection", the attributing of our own feelings or impulses to somebody or something outside ourselves. Psychologists say it has to be motivated—to have a cause—and I think the reason we do it is our vainglory and our cruelty. We strive onward, serving our own purposes, no matter whom it may hurt; enjoying all the benefits of the great Progress we've achieved and untroubled with considerations about what and whom we may have stomped along the way. That is what we "project" out of our own characters and into Nature.

But there it is, a belief so deep-seated that it goes on beyond the awareness, or at least outside the deliberate thought-process, of most people who hold it: that there is in the world of Nature and of human affairs some sort of driving or organizing force by which the course of organic evolution and of human history is impelled onward toward increasing approximation of some imagined ultimate perfect state. The Julian Simon quote at the beginning of this chapter is a perfect example. He was arguing, in the words of his column's title, that "Life Keeps Getting Better", and that it must continue to do so, because that is what the process of evolution requires.

We are greatly indebted to the late Stephen Jay Gould of Harvard for debunking this idea. As to organic evolution, he has in *Full House* (1996) and in countless other writings decisively shown that the idea of Progress is a myth. He points out that Darwin himself expressly rejected the notion that his great theory contained any suggestion of Progress as a natural principle. For that matter, he never used the word "evolution", according to Gould, until Herbert Spencer first popularized the term. In human affairs, Gould takes pretty much the same stand. He has written of the wall paintings of cave men in Europe, and shown that some of it, allowing for crudity of primitive materials, is not inferior in quality to what we ourselves call great art. In the thousands of intervening years, Gould saw little evidence of improvement and progress.

He was a thorough-going evolutionist and his work is not in any way supportive of evangelical or other religious positions (least of all Creationism!), and lest I be regarded as a "shill" (his term) by using his work in causes he didn't endorse, I want to point out that back when he was in knee pants I was reading *The Origin of Religion* (1945) by Princeton's Samuel M. Zwemer. The thesis of this book is that primitive Man was monotheistic and possessed of morals that, like his artistic abilities, were comparable to our own. His descent into animism, idolatry, polytheism, superstition, infant and other human sacrifice and studied, horrifying immorality, all came later. Conventional anthropologists, of course, depict religion as a human invention stemming from primitive Man's fear and ignorance. The trouble is, they weren't there. They don't know what primitive Man was like. They only know that Evolution requires a primitive, elementary beginning and subsequent Progress. The "facts" they believe in and teach their students are not facts at all, but extrapolations based on what the facts should have been if social evolution were true. Something like this: if in the course of growth in human reasoning power you become able to figure out that there is a cause of thunder and lightning, of attacks by wild animals and death of your relatives; and if you don't know that cause, then you have to assume that some unseen agency is involved, and you wonder if it can be influenced and made less threatening, so you invent prayer and sacrifice...and in due time this must evolve into modern monotheism.

But I can remember, back in the same period of time, using the example of Hitler and all his works to ridicule the progressivist assumption that, in our language at the time, "everything's getting better and better". And it wasn't biological evolution we were wringing our hands over, but Modernist religion with it's post-millenarian belief in progress. The idea of intrinsic and inevitable Progress (which, it follows, should ultimately prevail no matter what we do, because of being a natural force like gravity, that we cannot interfere with) is obviously and expressly destructive of both faith and enlightened public policy.

WHY IS THERE PROGRESS?

In spite of all that, we do ride cars instead of horses, we harvest grain with combines instead of sickles, we live in brick houses instead of grass huts or skin-covered teepees, and on and on with our many advancements. I'd be a dope to say there's been no progress made throughout history, yet I've taxed your patience at length to deny it. Actually, what I've been denying is Progress with a capital "P". Here's what I mean:

Belief in Progress as a principle inherent in Nature is not only unscientific, as shown by Gould and others, and an anthropomorphic fallacy, as I mentioned before; but is also irreligious – a naturalistic substitute for true Divinity, an attribution to Nature of creative propensities or even powers which God alone possesses. We recognize that in creating Mankind in His own image, God gave him a measure of creativity. But there is no reason to assume the same for all His unreasoning or even inanimate creations. It would attribute to Nature and natural objects a Force analogous to the human soul that operates to ordain their constant Progress; a Force that the real Creator does not need, and an "other god" that the Judeo-Christian God would not tolerate,

As Gould pointed out, there is in human affairs a factor uncharacteristic of Nature at large: education. Though some species train their young in survival skills, only humans teach things like history and mathematics. The former enables us to profit from the advances and mistakes of the past; the latter offers a framework for designing new improvements.

These disciplines, combined with library science (oral, print and electronic) by which technology and history are accumulated and made available to succeeding generations, almost ensure progress of one sort or another—material, if not moral. But what is only an artifact of civilization cannot be its cause, nor may it be attributed to all of Nature!

There is a philosophical theory called "teleology", which proposes that events of the universe are determined by the requirements of some future goal or purpose; and not by the circumstances that led up to them (which is the opposite theory of causation, called "mechanism"). Mechanism says that a row of dominoes standing on end may all fall down because of each one in turn being struck and overbalanced by the fall of the one preceding it. Teleology says it happens because of some known or unknown purpose that brought it about; presumably whatever purpose existed in the mind of a being who created the original design; i.e. the row of dominoes. Teleology is inherently metaphysical, but is actually necessary to the idea of Progress. It is elaborated in such ideas as *elan vital* (Henri Bergson), *Entelechy* (Hans Driesche) or the "Life Force" (advocated if not invented by George Bernard Shaw). Science has no interest in teleology; it is interested in tangible causes, and it investigates them from a mechanistic standpoint. So whence comes belief in a parallel teleological Progress (even in many scientists, though generally unacknowledged by them and probably not wholly conscious)?

I think, in part at least, from our need of reassurance of our own self-identity as the acme of creation (otherwise, what could be the purpose or goal of Progress?) and of the strangely Marxist-sounding view of history as evolution in miniature, with steps moving onward and upward toward perfection. It seems to me also that it leads to the complacent assumption (perhaps not by many scientists) that public policy decisions (which are only history-in-the-making) must turn out right and inevitably lead to Progress and improvement no matter how much we politicize them and corrupt the process! It allows us to believe that whatever we do now is better than what we used to do; that the crazed jumble of shapes and colors in an "abstract" painting represent progress from the laboriously-worked representations of Michelangelo or Rembrandt; that rock'n'roll is a big improvement over the ballads and folk-music of our past; that we have better playwrights than Sophocles, better philosophers than Aristotle, better sculpture than Michaelangelo, better poets than King David or Shakespeare or Milton; and better theologians than St. Paul or Augustine or Calvin; in fact that any change at all is for the better, whether stimulated by scientific breakthrough or by vulgar demand. It also inspires a belief (even among scientists) in extraterrestrial or "alien" life. To me this is fantasy. Here's why:

The age of the earth is thought to be some five billion years, having begun as a hot—even molten—body which was necessarily devoid of life during at least half of that span of time, until it cooled sufficiently. It seems a sure thing that life could not come into initial existence now, nor during most of the second half of the earth's existence, speaking from a mechanistic point of view. What are the odds that life could have arisen at all, much less that whatever event or circumstance brought it about could have happened at the precise point in time when conditions favorable to life prevailed? And of all the generations of living creatures that have appeared since then, each individual member of which having its own greater or slighter variation from its forebears, what are the odds that a succession of such changes could have eventuated in the life forms of today, or that any of these should have been humankind? Every generation faces unimaginably stupendous odds against any change taking place that moves its bearer in the direction of Progress. The chance that all this could ever have happened at all are incalculably remote.

But the recognition that there are millions of billions of galaxies in the universe, each with millions or billions of stars, at least some of which are likely to be the center of planetary systems like our own Solar System, and at least some of these probably containing planets with moderate temperatures, water, carbon, oxygen, and other necessities of life, as our Earth does; this is said to beat the odds!—to provide such sheer numbers of opportunities for life to develop that the odds against it are overcome. Supposedly every such life-friendly planet would provide an opportunity, in Gould's words, to "rewind the tape"—to develop life, or for life to develop. The belief that this could happen, and that it could result in intelligent life (not to say human or human-like life, which both novelists and scientists seem to expect) is a belief based on the classical formula: since evolution and its assumed teleological motor—the Life Force or Elan Vital or Entelechy—are facts of life and of all Nature, then they must apply to all phenomena in all circumstances in every location anywhere in the universe. Where we have no facts concerning the past, whether the past of the human race, or of the geologic history of the Earth, or the cosmological history of the universe, facts (or at least suppositions) can be derived by backward application of the ideas of evolution and Progress. For myself, I deny that mechanistic principles allow the development of life, not to mention intelligent life, more than once in the history of the universe. For it to have occurred even once is a statistical absurdity.

Such unique events are not unrecognized in science. Quantum mechanics deals with random motion of subatomic particles, and its doctrines necessarily require statements about probabilities, never absolutisms. The statistical probability that you could walk untouched through a brick wall is infinitesimally small; yet solid matter is known to consist mostly of empty space. A fortuitous arrangement, simultaneously of all the atoms in your body with all those in the wall, could in principle allow all of them to pass unhindered beside and through each other. The rise of Life out of the inanimate strikes me as an event of comparable or less probability. Yet it seems we're unwilling to rule out the possibility of extraterrestrial life. It is very seriously expected to have occurred countless times throughout the universe; because it involves what the space-happy scientists in fact provide: a teleological Life Force or something to overcome the odds.

RANDOMNESS AND STRUCTURE

Then what does indeed account for increasing size, complexity, etc. of the life forms we know about, from single-celled bacteria all the way to mankind? If that is not Progress, what is it? And mankind's movement from cave-dwelling primitive to computer-wielding engineer—is that Progress or what?

Buckle your seat belt, and remember that I speak as a Christian!

There is nothing there!—nothing *at all* that might help account for Progress! It's time to tackle a concept that is understandably repugnant to Creationists. It is this: that changes occurring totally at random can result in organization leading to complexity. We're anticipating Chapter 9 on Evolution—what it is—but I think we can't credibly talk first about what it *isn't* by sketching only half the picture. I can't really demolish the idea of Progress in the universe and in human affairs unless I can prove, or at least advocate, some other way that things have unfolded as they have.

And that reason is in the random nature of the universe. That will be explained in Chapter 9, but first I need to advocate it as a valid concept, even for Christians.

Our problem, of course, is that chance (or luck, or randomicity) and the hand of God seem mutually exclusive. Understanding evolution can, and often does, appear to negate any role at all for Creation; and hence its threat to many Christians.

But you have to think about some of the other things that we really do believe. We all know where babies come from, and a frothing, fuming atheist can explain it in accurate, complete and scientific detail, and never mention God; for it is as natural a process for us as for our pets and our livestock and the mosquitoes in our back yard. Yet no Christian mother, nor likely any other, ever failed to thank God when handed her newborn baby! To heck with chromosomes and embryos: we know a baby is made by God and is a gift of God. For that matter, we even thank Him for our food, the production of which is far less mysterious than of our children.

So here's another mystery of our faith: God is both *Transcendent* and *Immanent*. There is simply no accounting for this or rationalizing it. They are utterly contradictory; each standing alone would flirt with heresy, either of Deism or Animism. Yet *both are true*: the High King of Heaven is also He who feeds the sparrows (Matt. 6:26).

In a recent TV debate on Creationism a speaker said that if God organized things ultimately to produce mankind, He was an incompetent bungler. (Notice that he was refuting a *teleological* model of the universe; sound familiar?) Life developed in countless ways that led neither to the evolution of mankind nor of the creatures familiar to us or useful to us. Pterodactyls, trilobites, and all the rest of the evolutionary dead-ends came to nothing, nor bequeathed anything to the eventual appearance of nature as we see it today; they were simply wasted. Unavoidably we're led to consider a purely chance process.

Look: even the atheist who knows all about how babies are formed and born, has to start at conception; the mysteries leading up to that are beyond anyone's grasp. Conception refers to the junction of one sperm cell with a human ovum, or egg. Though only one sperm succeeds in penetrating the egg to fertilize it, it is one of millions that have been deposited there by the father. *No two of them are identical.* It is a matter of random chance which one becomes successful, the same as with donkeys or dolphins that reproduce by the same process.

If a child is made by God, it must be made as He intended it. If its appearance, temperament, even its sex, are determined by a random selection of one among many millions of sperm, then *He is in charge, even of randomicity!*

God chooses His own methods. We have to be careful in prescribing for God what He can and cannot do. "My thoughts are not your thoughts, neither are your ways my ways" (Isaiah 55:8). If you accept divine healing even though expecting it to come about through the ministrations of a doctor; if you think God made your child, even though you know perfectly well whence came the biological spark that kindled its life into existence; then what is so unchristian about it if I believe God also made the world and the universe and all of life through His own choice of a natural process by which to do it—*even if He chose randomicity?*

Here's one way to think of it. If in idleness or boredom you flip a coin, you will not concern yourself overmuch with whether it will land heads or tails, and then perhaps not even bother to look and see which way it fell—because it doesn't matter. But suppose you'd bet the farm on it!—you are very likely to pray for a favorable result, and if you get it, you are certainly going to thank God!

See, you really do believe God can be in charge even of randomicity. If you did not, you would thereby acknowledge something in, or something about, the universe that He cannot control; that is independent of Him and (what I think it would mean) *greater then He!*

Flipping a coin, if done fairly, is an act that renders a purely random result. You know that, and you also know that God could use it to save the farm for you or not, in His sole providence. The criticism of evolution, that it excludes God because of being based upon random changes, merely shows that the critics themselves exclude God by limiting His powers. It's another example of human arrogance: if *we* cannot exercise control over random events, then we think God can't either!

Or else, that they are not truly random. I'm well aware that somebody like Stephen Jay Gould would say that I haven't either denied Progress nor supported randomicity, but only introduced the Supernatural—a teleological God-presence to account for both. And so it appears; what can I say? Only that I find his arguments utterly convincing, else I wouldn't cite them. Especially on the subject of Progress; when I saw his piece on cave art, I felt as though I were reading something by Samuel Zwemer. He makes the point that if we could "rewind the tape" and let evolution happen all over again, there is not the slightest natural reason to expect it would follow the same course, least of all to produce a humanity like our own.

I think that's true. And I think there's no reason for it to have happened in the first place! The odds against life having ever begun, and then having developed the way it did, are monumentally, mountainously, overwhelmingly enormous; so how come it ever happened? Another wise man, Albert Einstein, said "God does not play dice with the universe", but maybe he was over his head on this one. He was objecting to Heisenberg's "uncertainty principle", a complicated theory of quantum mechanics, because he thought it incompatible with his theory of relativity. It stems from the random motion of subatomic particles, as a result of which the position and velocity of a particle cannot both be known. Of randomicity and order, it seems *both are true*!

I had entertained the idea of randomness of the universe for a long time. Preparation of this chapter, reading, studying, thinking have persuaded me of it; but they haven't converted me to atheism. So I believe that the universe, from its creation, to the motion of atoms in the water flowing from my faucet, to my own conception, are random events—the result of pure chance. I also believe that every aspect of it is ordained by God, the Creator and Sustainer of the universe. *Both are true!*—for I also believe God has given us fair warning that there are mysteries we cannot explain (cf God's discourse to Job, as summarized below). So there is no conflict between science and religion, if both are true. Scientists should believe in God for their soul's welfare; but they need not do so as scientists, nor postulate any sort of divine (or natural) entelechy in their study of Nature; nor may they ever settle for "mystery" in their search for explanations. They should do what they're trained to do: think and theorize, observe, explore, test and experiment. (I know, even if they don't, that the closer they come to truth, the nearer they approach God.) And we should continue what we do: worship and serve God. We are clearly called upon to apply His Word to our beliefs, our Church and our lives; but I see no justification for trying to apply it as a measure of scientific validity.

I can think of one weak illustration of purposeful chance. Suppose I attach a spray nozzle to my garden hose and turn on the water. The water will rush out and the drops be distributed totally at random. I have no control over the location at which any drop of water will fall. I am in charge of the *process* of watering my garden, but not of any individual drop of water. What I'm in charge of is a collection of many purely random events: the emission of countless drops in a completely unpredictable, irregular pattern. Yet I am able to use this random process purposefully, and the fact of my purposefulness—incidental and irrelevant to the mechanical process of water distribution—does not make it any less a random process.

Of course if I lived in the East none of this would apply. Instead, I'd be indoors looking out my window at rainfall accomplishing the same thing in the same manner. As you'll see shortly, I wanted to use the metaphor of the gardener. Yet what could be more random than the weather? It is basically unpredictable. Our forecasts—of decreasing accuracy up to seven days, and mostly guesswork after that—are not forecasts at all, but observations of what actual weather events are currently happening, as determined by instruments dispersed globally; and then adding educated guesses about the extent and imminence of their appearance locally. One reason for the unpredictability is that these events can be set in motion by random occurrences, whether of major or minor initial consequence: the so-called Butterfly Effect, "the notion that a butterfly stirring the air today in Peking can transform storm systems next month in New York" (James Gleick, in *Chaos*, Viking, New York, 1987). To the mathematician, the idea of Chaos parallels that of Randomness. To a simple mind like mine, they are not very easily distinguishable; but Chaos is not random: it is orderly, though unpredictably so, to our present knowledge. It's been called "order masquerading as randomness". The fairly new mathematical discipline that studies it deals with exactly such things as how the movement and distribution of liquids are determined. For our discussion I'll stick with the term "random" because it's familiar both to me and to Creationists—even though Chaos, being orderly and thus created, might be easier for people to accept. Besides, I don't know enough about Chaos or its mathematics; and to underscore my ignorance, I confess to thinking that out of all the millions of butterflies fluttering their wings countless times through countless days in countless locations, it seems a random chance which one will generate perturbations that escalate into weather patterns, whether or not we were able to fathom the mechanisms by which such escalation occurs in the first place. Yet all that is still a matter of ignorance (not knowing how something works doesn't prove it's untrue). If it be so that Chaos is the order of the universe rather than randomness, then that's the way it is. I can't see that it demolishes my argument.

The hose analogy is of course a poor one, inasmuch as I hold it and direct its spray!—and I can't be in charge of the process unless I do. But it still may illustrate what I mean about purposive "use" of randomicity. Maybe it would be helpful to think of God as the great "gardener"—as holding a figurative celestial "hose" out of which spewed elements and particles in all their multitudinous extravagance, whose random or chaotic dance engendered a universe and a life-nurturing planet and a spiritual race of beings, just as efficaciously as my spray of water drops irrigated my own little garden plot. Notice that if I could really exercise control through some kind of mechanical determinism, and make each drop of water to fall in order—say a checkerboard or herringbone pattern—it wouldn't accomplish anything more or better, as to the objective of watering my garden.

A potentially promising insight into all this has been proposed by Baylor University's William A. Dembski, in "Randomness and Design" (2002; see www.discovery.org). As an official of the Discovery Institute, his work is no doubt an attempt to lay a mathematical and philosophical foundation for a theory of Intelligent Design. In itself, that notion has not stirred up much interest on my part. Despite denials, it strikes me as an attempt to insert the supernatural into science (even if true in some sense, it is about as scientifically meaningless as "God created the world"—also true, but no more susceptible to scientific study than any other metaphysical proposition; which is to say, it can never be more than an article of faith). Dembski, however, only studies randomness itself (in the cited article). At least to my knowledge, he suggests no intervention in ongoing natural developmental processes by any Intelligence. In effect, he only says that randomness cannot be a matter of pure Chance, but necessarily must be designed.

He didn't really go any farther with this, but to my perception his argument allows for the possibility of randomness, and hence Natural Selection, as the mechanism of change; but with this crucial difference: *randomness must have been designed,* he says.

If that's the meaning of Intelligent Design, I don't believe anything else is necessary to the theory. That says it all: it seems entirely comparable to my own statement that "God is in charge" of randomicity (though my statement is expressly theological, while Dembski's approach is mathematical and hence they are not subject to rational comparison). I'll have a little more to say about this in Chapter 9.

None of this is meant to imply Deism, the notion of a God Who is transcendent but not immanent, above Nature, not in it; Who created the universe but subsequently had nothing more to do with it, but simply allowed it to develop according to its own natural systems and laws. Yet, how could we have just now been talking about goal, objective, and purpose in Creation—as in gardening—after I went to so much trouble to dispute all that teleological hocus-pocus? Once more, a mystery! We cannot doubt that God had a purpose in Creation, as I had in spraying water on my garden. That is our faith, but you won't see it in science textbooks, because it's scientifically meaningless. As a result, the notion of Progress inherent in Nature is also meaningless: Progress must be toward something, must have a goal. As Christians we may believe in miracles, but if we do, we acknowledge thereby that in between miraculous events the world operates according to natural law. To that extent there is no disagreement between religion and science. Religion may continue to assert that an Immanent and Transcendent God is in charge of that natural law (and if it were not so He would not be able to suspend it for miraculous purposes) but I can't see why it should be up to religion to decide that natural law cannot be a function of randomicity, if so be that God has ordained that it is!

Playwright Tom Stoppard (quoted by George Will in *Newsweek*, 11/9/98) said, "The idea of God is slightly more plausible than the alternative proposition that, given enough time, some green slime could write Shakespeare's sonnets". If you insist upon competing alternatives, Stoppard is of course right.

But why must you? Suppose that is what God created green slime for! I say that God, Who may be presumed to know more about how such things work than I, could create and sustain a random universe, without making it non-random or anything at all other than what it is, and yet bring about His purposes; no less than I can achieve my gardening objectives with the use of random drops of water.

Speaking of mysteries and paradoxes of the faith, I wonder if it would be helpful to meditate upon the book of Job, a long and often tedious description of how Job and his friends wrestled with the question of how come God lets disastrous and ruinous experiences overtake people in this life. I think that Job believed as we do, that God is infinitely good, of boundless compassion, faithful in loving kindness and tender mercy. And he and we are asked to continue believing it in the face of fire and flood, hurricane and tornado, volcano and earthquake, war and famine, cancer and Lou Gehrig's disease, persecution and genocide, and even the Cross!

Jesus taught us that these things, like the sun and rain, fall on the good and the evil, the just and the unjust (Matt. 5: 45). This is the mystery that Job encountered and struggled with, and it is no less a paradox in our own day. The Lord finally answered Job without giving him an answer! In effect, He said, "I am God: who are you to rebuke and question Me? You don't even understand My creation—the world around you and how it works—do you think you ought to understand, or tell Me how I should do things?" Creationists and evolutionists alike, to all of whom the same questions apply, would do well to respond as Job did: "...what shall I answer Thee? I will lay my hand upon my mouth".

Keep in mind that Job's misfortunes must have appeared as entirely random events, even more so than the sunshine and rain. There were no epidemics of illness in the land, to which others were falling victim. There is no evidence of a dissolute lifestyle, the ill effects of which were finally catching up with him. Even were modern scientific investigations possible, the train of calamities that befell Job would defy explanation; his disease itself would likely be undiagnosable. All of it would appear entirely random, as it did also to Job and his wife and friends. He said to God, "...Is it good unto thee that thou shouldest despise the work of thine hands?... I am full of confusion..." (Job 10:3-15) So were Job's "comforters", who did their best to find reasons to explain away the randomness, but like Job, they also failed. Lev Grossman understood their dilemma; he said, "We need grand theories to make sense of grand events, or the world just seems too random". (quoted in TIME, 9/11/08).

No more than Job, can we ever be sure whether Satan is behind any of our own misfortunes. As frightening as it may be, it seems that randomness is often the only explanation within our power to make, for neither Job nor we can be satisfied with attempts to explain the world's calamities by our own or other people's sins (John 9:1-3). So here's my interpretation of what God might be saying to us of the third millennium A.D., adapting thereunto what He said to Job in about the first millennium B.C.:

The world does not revolve around you, that it should adapt itself to your needs and comforts. Neither were you placed in it for your own benefit, but solely by Me and for My reasons. The wealth, security and contentment that you have enjoyed were not of your own doing. They resulted from a random combination of good inheritance, propitious upbringing, fortuitous circumstances of weather and pasturage for your flocks (in Job's case; or of education and employment today). Nor were the disasters you complain of brought about either by your good or evil deeds. You control almost none of this; your faith in Me and your walk in My ways are the only things for which you are accountable.

You are a child of the universe. Just like it you are the product of a random combination of events: of genetic-social-physical-familial-economic-political and other forces. For this is what My whole Creation, as well as the dust of which you were formed, are like: a random combination of all the forces and materials that I brought together. Just as the mysterious, unknowable accidents of Nature brought you into being and determined your life and its good fortune as well as its near-destruction, so did comparable forces engender the creation of the universe and determine its operation and destiny. You are dust of the earth, made of and by the same materials and processes as the universe itself: you do not control these, nor can you escape them nor your religion prevent them!

Neither science nor faith has done more than scratch the surface of understanding. The evolutionist is not much less arrogant than the creationist when asserting his knowledge of The Truth. (He may be a *little* less so, because he acknowledges the possibility that new evidence could always appear and cause him to have to change his theories—or abandon them. But he doesn't really believe that will happen!)

"Wherefore I abhor myself in dust and ashes", concluded Job, and perhaps he set us a good example.

It may seem I've slanted my exposition of the book of Job in support of the argument for universal randomicity in Nature. Perhaps so. I happen to think it's relevant to Job's experience, and if it helps illuminate Scripture, it also illuminates our lives. God does not willfully cause suffering—yet He did not pass the buck to Satan. His response to Job's complaints was entirely based on Nature, as though Job "in sickness and in health" was a part of the world and should not expect to live or be treated as if it were not so. Arguably, the whole purpose of seeking Progress is to obviate or gain control over the randomicity inherent in Nature. When we fail at that we try, like Job's comforters, to explain away the randomness, and like them, we do it by invoking divine intervention. Their efforts illustrate the wisdom of Sir William Osler, who said, "The greater the ignorance, the greater the dogmatism". But God is telling us here that if we can't understand the world of which we are a part, neither do we understand Him, nor have knowledge of if and when He interposes Himself in Nature's processes. Christianity remains as much mystical as rational!

CHAPTER 8

COMMUNITY

...them that believed were of one heart and of one soul: nei-
ther said any of them that ought of the things which he possessed
was his own: but they had all things in common...Neither was
there any among them that lacked: for as many as were possess-
ors of lands or houses sold them, and brought the prices of the
things that were sold, and laid them down at the apostles' feet:
and distribution was made unto every man according as he had
need. (Acts 4:32-35)

Many Christians, who do not at all live in the manner these verses suggest, find them kind of an embarrassment. We have no real handy explanation for why we don't live that way. There's good reason to believe that such communal life persisted over some span of years, though we hear little else about it in the New Testament. It is referred to in the writings of Lucian *(ca* 125-192 A.D.) about the Christian community in Palestine (see Appendix to this chapter)—so it lasted at least 100 years.

The lifestyle here portrayed undoubtedly reflects some of the teachings of Jesus (e.g., Matt 5:42, 6:19, 25-34; 10:8-10, 19:21 -23; Luke 10:30-37, 11:5-10; etc.) and all such texts taken together have been quite an inspiration to people who would politicize the Gospel. I've mentioned G. B. Shaw's belief that pure Christianity is Communism; but a great many less radical, more or less socialistic views have arisen that equate governmental redistribution of wealth with the Kingdom of God. There's no doubt our materialistic orientation, as I tried to set forth in Chapter 6, helps account for the substitution of a political-economic welfare state for a spiritual Gospel. It follows, of course, that a market-oriented capitalistic system is considered pretty wicked from that point of view; if anything, it can be even more blatantly materialistic.

But things could be worse. It's probably better for the social-governmental system to be the enemy of the Gospel, than its imitator, or its sponsor, as in the case of the established churches of Europe or in the Roman Empire under Constantine. (I mean *spiritual* enemy, as when the government banishes religious indoctrination from the public schools; not flesh-and-blood persecutors.) The more effectively government provides for all needs of all citizens, offering cradle-to-grave security, the more it actually does, to the materialistic eye, resemble the Kingdom of God. It fulfills, or tries to, our Christian mandates to care for the poor, the sick, the imprisoned, the needy of multifarious description. There's nothing intrinsically wrong with that; if Christians won't do it, the government should. If we Christians no longer place our wealth "at the apostles' feet" for the benefit of those who lack, the government has power to take it away from us and fill in for our neglect of our duty. I thoroughly disapprove of all socialistic and government welfare schemes; yet in actual practice I have to support them and vote for their political advocates: they are the lesser evil, compared to our do-nothing toleration of poverty, hunger, sickness and all the other ills that Jesus told us we must care about.

For that matter, socialism is a pretty good solution to the material problems of society. My wife traveled in Scandinavia a few years ago. She reports a clean environment, contented populace, and apparent economic health in those countries.

Taxes run to about 60% of income or more. When she asked some people if that were not burdensome, they'd say, "Sure; but we don't mind, look at everything we get for it." And they do: jobs (or unemployment benefits), health care, education to any desired level, old age security—a nearly risk-free existence.

It is the Modernists' dream come true; yet it is not the Kingdom of God!—because it is entirely secular. The Church, and the role intended for it by its Founder, are elbowed aside, crowded out by the earthly kingdoms. Suppose a conscientious Christian in one of these countries took seriously his obligation to love his neighbor as himself, not as bleeding-heart sentimentality but as self-sacrificial performance of loving service. What would he do? Now, I didn't take the tour my wife did, and haven't studied the sociology of these countries, and in my ignorance of them I'm in no position to judge any of this; so I speak in generalities about socialism and welfare-statism as best I understand them. But I believe that what I say is not entirely inapplicable to the societies of Northern Europe, and is the reason I mostly oppose going down the same road in our own country.

So to get back to the question: I don't have any idea what my hypothetical believer would do to fulfill his commitment to Christ and his Kingdom! The whole array of human needs we are supposed to address—hunger, thirst, estrangement and nakedness (which in America I'd subsume as homelessness), illness and imprisonment (Matt 25:35-36) are already taken care of! By what loving works might his light be made to shine? Should he enter the church ministry? I'm all for that, but the truth is he'd be little more than a government bureaucrat!—for the government even purports to address the peoples' spiritual needs through its support of the churches. It is no surprise that in all these countries the church risks withering away. I mean, who needs it? Nothing else can more loudly and clearly demonstrate that the Church's mission of witness is twofold, spiritual and material; surely to convert people by persuading them of Christ's sonship, resurrection and lordship; but also to serve—to glorify God by compassionate good works. When this second task is neglected, or is taken over by the State, the first must seem irrelevant: and then the Church no longer appears to have any purpose. It becomes a social superfluity, and many rational people won't be bothered with it.

So much for Shaw and the Modernists and their socialized Kingdom of God. I heard these same arguments raised by Fundamentalist preachers long before the transformations in Northern Europe ever occurred and "welfare state" became a household word (so the above thoughts are not all original with me!), and history has borne out their objections. In the Middle Ages Islam nearly obliterated Christianity in the countries where it prevailed; and in our day a benevolent socialism threatens the same thing where it has taken hold.

But that isn't America's clear and present danger; I just wanted to be clear on what I am *not* advocating, even though I will be insisting that we do something about our social problems. In the preceding chapter we talked about the social-political perversion known as Social Darwinism, that followed Herbert Spencer's pseudoscientific attempt to apply the theory of Evolution to society. That perversion has taken hold in America: so deeply that much of our social-economic structure is derived from it; or to speak plainly, is built on a falsehood! I'm quite sure that Founding Fathers such as Jefferson and Hamilton, who were so bitterly antagonistic against each other over the kind of country we should be and the direction we should take, neither one could look at America today and say it's what they had in mind. As Shaw himself put it, "Would Washington or Franklin have lifted a finger in the cause of American independence if they had foreseen its reality?" (1903, *The Revolutionist's Handbook)* A predictably harsh judgment by the old communist and a strange one, given his devotion to the inevitability of Progress under impulsion by the Life Force!

It's not as though nobody else has thought about the problem. As I've indicated, socialist-minded critics, both secular and religious, have denounced our present system, citing its basis in self-seeking rather than generosity and fellow-feeling; and competitiveness rather than cooperation: elements for which their only counterpart offering is socialism and welfare-statism. But what about the Communitarian argument? It finds the Spencerian perversions troubling, but it does not propose radical government programs as the solution. I don't consider that the promotion of secular Communitarian principles is exactly the purpose of this chapter. Yet they are seen by many as a reasonable alternative to cut-throat social Darwinism, as well as to traditional Liberalism *(that* ought to arouse your interest!) In an Appendix to this chapter, I'll list some resources for your further education about it (there's much more: my computer search reported over 50,000 matches to "communitarian").

THE SOCIAL CONTRACT

...thou hast not lied unto men, but unto God (Acts 5:4)

Let's think about Ananias and Sapphira, the married couple who sold some property but withheld some of the proceeds for themselves, placing the rest with the Apostles in the common treasury. Following St. Peter's condemnation of this, they were struck dead (Acts 5:1-10). This text is frequently dusted off and preached on Stewardship Sunday, not only as an exhortation to give generously to the church, but also to be honest with yourself and God about how much you actually could afford to give; not to withhold, and then rationalize and make excuses: not to be dishonest. I won't dispute that exegesis of the Scripture, in deference to the multitudes and generations of preachers who have so used it. But I'm going to venture a different slant, which will not contradict the other, but look at a different aspect of it.

It was as if the couple had sold something for 10 bucks, then turned over 5 to St. Peter and the Apostles, telling them this was the actual sale price. In doing so, they clearly "lied unto men". But in what sense did they lie "unto God"?—had they held a preliminary word of prayer in which to advise God that 5 bucks was the full sale price? No; I suspect that what St. Peter called "lying to God" must have been a spiritual sin, not either a verbal, or a material crime like embezzling a little money, and I'd judge that this construction of what happened is mainly what enraged him. In fact he discounted the embezzlement itself, almost denying it: "...thou hast *not* lied unto men..."

A communal society like that described in the last verses of Acts 4 depends very much on the full cooperation of all its members, especially if it's fairly small and mostly poor (as I tend to suppose in the case of the primitive Church); but actually cooperation must be its basic premise regardless of other circumstances. As soon as it becomes permissible, or even possible, to cheat, withhold, break the rules, behave uncooperatively, the whole enterprise is put at risk. Human nature being what it is, other members of the community will be doing the same thing, later if not sooner, and the rules will no longer hold; distrust, jealousy and resentment run rampant; the social contract is terminated and the community itself is disrupted and likely ceases to exist. I think that is why the offense was so serious. At that stage of the

Church's history, it might not have survived a disruption of its basic contract. Ananias and Sapphira had committed themselves to that Church under the (understood, if unofficial) terms of that contract; and that commitment—to God, not man—was what became a lie when they violated it.

The Epistles of Paul are suggestive that similar problems were happening in some of the churches he'd founded. I think the reason they still persevered is the loving support and firm discipline provided them by St. Paul and his helpers (Titus, Barnabas, Timothy and the others). No such external guidance and support was available to the primitive Church in Jerusalem, and it might have died right there if the bad faith of some members had been permitted to go unchallenged.

It reminds me of a model of human behavior that social scientists talk about. It's called "the prisoners' dilemma", and here's how it works: suppose that two armed crooks are arrested on suspicion of a certain crime. They are isolated in separate cells. Each one is given the same instructions: "We know you are guilty; but we don't have proof, so we need your help. You face 20 years in prison. If you confess and turn State's evidence against the other guy, you go free—but he serves the time. If neither of you will confess, we'll still get you, because you'll serve a year for carrying a concealed weapon. If it happens that you both confess, you will still be granted leniency for helping us, and each will only serve 5 years."

What would you do? You no doubt want to act in your own self-interest, yet you need to consider what your partner might do. Maybe he will confess: then, if you stonewall, you'll serve 20 years!—or you could also confess, and then only have to do 5. But what if he remains silent?—then, if you confess, you go free! (whereas if you don't, you serve a year). It appears that no matter what your partner does, you are better off to confess! So what's the dilemma?

Here's the problem. Your partner is also thinking of his own self-interest and if he's as smart as you, he's thinking the same way. Go down that road, and you'll both rat on each other, and both have 5 years to sit and wonder if there's a better way.

Which there is! Perhaps words like "rat" may have clued you that I don't consider self-interest always to be the best approach. Let's assume further that these two guys are buddies; that they've been through a lot together, that they value their friendship and are accustomed to helping each other out on occasion. In short, they are a community, albeit a small one of only two members. That makes a difference, because what's most advantageous to the community is also what's best for its members. In this case, it means each serving a year—and then being still friends. Going free right away might be nice, but the partnership would be destroyed. One's freedom would be his wages for betraying the other.

This is what is known as the "cooperative solution" to the dilemma. The community's greatest good is achieved when neither betrays the other; when each accepts the smaller sacrifice for the greater good of the community.

That's why the story of Ananias and Sapphira is interesting to me. It anticipates the latest thinking of social science! That's why their monetary default is not, to me, the central concern in this story, but rather it's their spiritual lapse; the choice of self-interest over cooperation.

"Self-interest" is, of course, almost the name of our individualistic, "survival-of-the-fittest" American society. It isn't just in our financial institutions and business systems. Suppose there's a water shortage and people are asked to conserve. Cooperation would mean less lawn-watering, with all, or many yards turning a little brown. Any individual might reflect that if he cheated so as to rescue his own lawn, his extra water use would have a negligible effect upon the community-wide shortage, and nobody would be hurt. But if large numbers thought and behaved that way, their bad faith and self-interest would have a destructive effect on all. Any student knows that he can improve his own grades by cheating on a test, and yet not hurt anybody. But if almost everybody does it—engages in unfair competition— the grading curve is elevated and the advantage to any individual is lost, while the honest student stands to be hurt. Everybody knows that car-pooling on a large scale would greatly reduce air pollution in big cities. A strong public transportation system could do the same thing. So could bike-riding or walking. Speak for your own community, as to whether any of such cooperative practices for the sake of a common goal, are actually happening. These things depend upon consensus and consensual action. Community, in fact, depends, to a degree that we seldom think about, upon cooperation, upon shared sacrifice in a multitude of ways, upon all or most people doing their part: paying their share of taxes, supporting the schools, serving in the military, obeying the law, in general pulling their weight.

It's a paradox of our society that there is bitter competition in our systems of business, industry and politics: the leadership, so to speak, of people who on the contrary, are expected to be cooperative in most important respects. It's easy to see why we are not taught much about this. From earliest years our heroes and models are examples of competitive excellence. We are exhorted to emulate their fighting spirit all the while becoming good citizens; learning to be cooperative and sacrifice self-interest for the good of the community. It's not clear to me how this can be done! It's true that in athletics we're taught to value teamwork over grandstanding and this is actually a good example of the communitarian spirit; but I'm not sure how much the teamwork ethos carries over to other areas of life. In fact, I think we give pretty short shrift to any notions of self-sacrifice ("nice guys finish last") or of community concern, when we educate and train our new generations: as you'd expect, since we have little conception of or taste for such matters ourselves.

OWNERSHIP

As mentioned before, I did not make the Scandinavian tour with my wife. She tells me that in these countries, Denmark, to take one example, you seldom see trash littering the highways, parks or other outdoor areas, such as parking lots and playgrounds. In America we have individual "rights" such as to dispose of our hamburger wrappings and beer bottles in whatever manner we choose (regardless that in most places littering is against the law) and to avoid any personal inconvenience, such as lugging the stuff to a trash can. And yet we keep our front and back yards clean and free of litter!—because that is our own individual turf: the *pride of ownership.*

The Dane, I think, would consider the roadside—a part of his country—as his own turf and responsibility. I doubt that he'd believe it thoughtful or virtuous to seek a trash can, any more than you or I would as we put away our backyard barbecue refuse rather than throwing it on the lawn. I suspect that if you suggested he save himself the trouble and throw his trash on the roadside, he'd be quite puzzled, like, "Why would I do that? It wouldn't look nice." It's not that he values country more than self; I doubt that he sees any conflict of interest, or that he thinks of his own interest in the matter as being weightier or divergent from that of the community.

I'm not suggesting that Denmark is entirely a communitarian society. But I know that in spite of laws against littering, and our almost universal dislike or even disgust at our trashy surroundings, and our "adopt-a-highway" campaigns, and our use of prison work gangs to pick it up, the trash goes right on accumulating! In Denmark or here, the only way it can stop is if each citizen agrees to stop littering, and each to do his part in effecting proper disposal. It is his problem, not somebody else's, and if it's his problem then he owns it!—it can't be taken away or given away.

It is frequently said—and I may have said it myself before I knew any better—that "freedom" in America means you can "do anything you want". Whether it's to vote for my candidate or to throw my trash on the roadside or to open the school day with prayer (as long as it's to my God, not Mohammed's) or to have an abortion, nobody is allowed to tell me what to do. Communitarians can find themselves in conflict with the American Civil Liberties Union, which they consider to be often extremist in its promotion of various rights, without reckoning on the responsibility that any civil right imposes *upon others*. For example, from the '60's more or less to the present day we have heard arguments for such things as Welfare Rights, the Right to Health Care, Victims' Rights (in criminal cases), and the like. The social issues addressed by such "Rights" movements are real, but the language of Rights implies violation or discrimination, and thus is actually the language of victimology. It's not that the sick and the poor "...suffer/The slings and arrows of outrageous fortune/...The heartache and the thousand natural shocks/That flesh is heir to...", as Shakespeare would have it. Rather, they suffer because they are *victims* of somebody or something, and society owes them redress.

We are not here talking about those rights expressly provided for in the Constitution. Although these may sometimes require judicial interpretation, they are otherwise absolute and non-negotiable and in fact they mostly cost society very little. (My freedom of speech or religion takes nothing away from you.) Not so with the various Rights newly-minted by victimologists. Nobody has yet figured out a system for providing universal health care that we could actually afford; yet it's clear that the sick man's care would impose a burden on others. Welfare Rights: no different (my misfortunes are yours to pay for). The notion of Victims' Rights in criminal law has some appeal; arguably the criminal's constitutional rights—to a fair trial and all the rest—should be balanced by the right of the victim to be heard (and the term "victim" is more appropriate in these cases). The problem with that is that it's irrelevant: everybody already knows the victim has suffered, so it isn't necessary to make a scene in Court to dramatize the point. Besides, there's this notion that the law should be administered rationally, impartially and fairly, and made to serve its purpose in society, not to minister to the bruises or vengefulness of individuals. I mean, if testimony by the victims is to mean anything—to have an effect on sentencing, say, then the criminal's fate, and perhaps his entire life course thenceforth, might depend upon how convincingly pathetic or vengeful is the show that's produced by the hurt family; another criminal who by happenstance harmed a family less histrionically talented might get a lighter sentence. (Of course, if the law is to be administered on a rational basis—which is to say that emotional displays by victims or the defense are to be disregarded in favor of the facts of the case and the provisions of law—then the Victims' Rights argument has no meaning and the whole exercise is a waste of time.)

I certainly do not intend any of this to indicate any lack of sympathy for bereaved, hurt, or despoiled victims of crime—nor any lachrymose tenderness toward criminals, either. I just believe that in matters of Christian conduct, and of healthy, ethical living in general, we need to strive to be *Victors* over circumstance— "more than conquerors" (Rom. 8: 35-39). When we confirm our status as *victim,* when we concretize it to the extent of using it to determine the course of another man's life, we trap ourselves in that role. When our self-identity as *victim* is confirmed by assent of the court—in effect, having become a matter of law—how can we ever emerge from it and find either victory, in the Christian sense, or healing, in secular terms?

Once again, I do not mean to convey any lack of sympathy for those who in truth are victims of poverty, sickness, crime or other adverse circumstances not of their own doing. We wish, for society and for individuals, that such things not happen; but in so desiring we do not confer a *right* to be spared any unpleasantness. We only deny that "victimology" is the proper basis for a search for remedies. Here's why:

A major premise of Communitarians is that we need to redress the balance between rights and responsibilities in our social beliefs and policies. Indeed it may be their central doctrine. Rights and responsibilities are both valid concerns, but there's a difference between establishing those human rights needed to ensure a free society—which is what our Constitution does—and attempting to establish new rights intended to correct social ills. This latter approach, however widely approved and even adopted by a liberal society, is in fact not at all contemplated in the Constitution (and indeed, conservative Courts have a way of declaring them *unconstitutional* from time to time).

See, liberals would say the poor man has a problem, or the sick man, or the physically or mentally handicapped person; and they'd say these people have a Right to be spared such suffering, and their preferred means of accomplishing that is through laws and governmental programs, none of which might really alter the "victim" status of the sufferer, but only compensate him for it (which actually *rewards* him for it and fosters its perpetuation, as the behavioral psychologists would point out—cf Newcomb Simon quote, p. 117).

But suppose we transfer *ownership*. Suppose that, as an American, I considered our sickness and poverty as *my* problem. Suppose that, along with similarly responsible-minded members of my community or community group (perhaps my church congregation) we accepted ownership of the problem and responsibility for doing something about it. Sure, we have a "right" to ignore it, but Communitarians and, ideally, Christians want to redress the balance between rights and responsibilities. Now, you don't exercise that kind of responsibility by getting laws passed while the sick man worsens and dies, or the poor man starves or turns to crime. You *get him treatment,* or in the case of poverty, you find ways of getting him out of it. If I own the problem, as the Dane owns his highway roadside, then I can't pass the buck. It isn't his problem, or society's; it's mine, and I can choose to be irresponsible, or else to do something about it. Of course the problem may be too big for my own community group to handle. As I said before, until there is the will to fulfill our responsibilities in a Communitarian or other effective manner, government will have to do a lot of the job. Supporting this "interim" solution thus is also part of our responsibility. But it doesn't mean that I and my congregation can't get started. Taking just one case at a time, or taking any small first step, beats taking no steps at all.

"...the best way to help sustain a world in which people care for one another is to care for some." (Amitai Etzioni, 1993)

Ananias and Sapphira understood the little church's needs, and they gave to it—generously, I would suspect—but they never saw the need of the community as *their own* problem, or they could never have withheld from it. Conservatives are often thought of as "mean" because they oppose putting money into social programs, and I think that's more true than false. As Christians, haven't we generally dismissed a multitude of social ills as "not my problem", thus justifying ourselves in passing by on the other side of the road; unlike the Good Samaritan exemplified to us in Jesus' parable? Wasn't Jesus himself the "Good Samaritan" who made our problem his own and accepted both the responsibility for it and the consequences? Have you found any Scripture to show that we are not expected to "do likewise"? Read some of the Communitarian literature; sometimes you have to remind yourself that it's a secular movement, and not some kind of re-statement of Christian ethics.

Like Christianity itself, and like the battle against Materialism that we discussed in Chapter 6, a lot of it seems impossibly idealistic. There are two things to remember about this:

(1) Beware the near-universal tendency to say "don't want to" when "can't" is the real truth; and its corollary, to say "can't" when we really mean "don't want to". We find it more acceptable to say something's impossible, than to admit that we really don't want to be bothered, or to get involved, or to take the time and trouble, or to bear the cost. For people of good will and determination, far more things are possible than you might think at first, or might care to admit.

A historical preface to the second point I want to make: It is surely significant that the accounts of the young Church both in Acts and in the writings of Lucian refer to the church in Jerusalem or Palestine; i.e., to Jews. These people were Christian; but they were also mostly unreconstructed Jews, obeying the Law and bugging St. Paul's Gentile converts to do the same. It's a sure thing they were deeply immersed in the communal ethos of Judaism (see my discussion of this in Chapter 2, "I AND WE"). But the subjects of St. Paul's missionary ministry were Greeks culturally—individualistic to the core. We do not see in St. Paul's writings much reference to the communal nature of the church; I believe his own mentality was mostly Greek (hence his success with these people), having grown up himself in a Gentile city—just as American Jews think like Americans, not like Israelis. True, he used the body, of which we are all members, as a metaphor for the Church (in Romans 12, I Cor. 12, Eph. 4 and 5). But his Gospel was itself somewhat individualistic, stressing personal salvation by faith; and we may doubt that the Romans and Greeks he was writing to imbibed very deeply of the Hebrew tradition. Anyhow, regardless of anything in Scripture, history is unequivocal: in the dualism of individual *vs* community, Greek individualism has taken over our thinking and we, too, give little but lip-service to the Hebrew communal ideal of the Old Testament and the early Church.

(2) So, as to what's impossibly idealistic and what's not, remember that far more things can be accomplished by a community, a communal group, than by an individual. I know that in the course of this chapter some readers have started thinking, "How can I, a single, lone person; all by myself, take responsibility for, say, care of the sick? or the poor, or whatever else you may ask of me; or even of finding a simplified, non-materialistic lifestyle?" Answer: Maybe you can't, but *we* can!

In Mesa, Arizona, 2002, some high school girls, shopping for school wear, protested the excessively daring styles being offered in the stores. Note that they did not ask for "society" (the school board, the PTA, the State Department of Education) to pass a law or start some kind of program (e.g., a dress code); they *got together* and threatened to boycott the stores! In no time at all the stores began carrying a separate line of clothing selections for girls who wished to dress modestly. No teen-age girl could have achieved that, nor almost anyone else either. United, it was laughably easy. Together, they did not fear being different.

Indeed the Mormons, who include most of the girls I just mentioned (and where were the Christian girls, who abound in Arizona, but were not heard from?), have found a degree of balance between individual and community. They tend to be politically conservative (some would say "ultra") yet they have a welfare system of their own, and no Mormon goes very long in serious want. They can, it's true, get overbearing in positions of power (can't we all?) but in fact they do not depend much on political action. Their kids grow up with the understanding that alcohol, tobacco, drugs, teen sex and pornography are off-limits, so they are not much interested in legal curbs in these areas. They see to the education of their children, even to the college level (Brigham Young University). I think we could learn from them, including their requirement of full-time service to the church by all young members coming of age.

Perhaps we tend to identify communal groups with "cells", whether communist, terrorist, or other anti-social movements; but what of Christian cells in pagan societies; certainly like those of the early Church or like other Christian groups, often persecuted in their early history: Protestants, Puritans, Quakers, Huguenots. Of all these, only the Mormons, to my knowledge, have substantially retained their communal culture. I'm far from an expert on this, much less an insider, but I believe it could be called, to a degree anyhow, a *communitarian* culture. It seems to me these people consider themselves—not exactly persecuted any more but still as outsiders, self-consciously different, a slightly alien group within a larger society that bears them little sympathy and sometimes antagonism.

Hey!—didn't I just describe the Church (at least as it used to be)? I remember some of the Fundamentalist Gospel songs: "I'm just a poor wayfaring stranger", "I'm just a weary pilgrim, traveling through this world of sin", "I'm a pilgrim and I'm a stranger", "This world is not my home". It is easier to sing it than live it; but wouldn't we also regain a communal identity if we too had our own distinctive Christian culture, shorn of materialism; instead of being swallowed up in the secular culture around us, and barely distinguishable from it? The Fundamentalists are "sort of" trying to establish a Christian culture, and I applaud this; but its focus is all wrong. Its interest (like that of the larger society) is on political action, not personal and communal responsibility (and even where this interest does involve issues of social justice, it takes the form of seeking *governmental support* for "faith-based" programs). It is not much different from the liberals' focus on government as the solution; but it seeks *authority*, rather than government services. It takes no ownership of problems like abortion, drug abuse, or (in recent memory) alcohol. It only seeks ways to enforce governmental prohibitions against those who do have the problem. I won't be discussing narcotics policy; although the "War on Drugs" is understood by almost everybody to be a failure, I think the jury is still out, whether present prohibitions make any sense. Until we know what we're doing I think they should stay in place. But let's not imagine that either prohibitions and their associated enforcement measures, or prevention and treatment/rehabilitation programs are going to win that war. I know one thing: there's little or no such problem among Mormons.

Don't get me wrong. I don't claim that a Utah Mormon from West Bountiful is going to take "ownership" of the heroin addiction of a kid in the South Bronx. I say that there is in drug use a bit of behavior—a highly alluring one—which in his culture is not so much prohibited as unthinkable, and whose control by the government, or attempts thereat, are of little interest to him. It simply isn't their responsibility or their business, but his own and his community's.

MATERIALISM, AGAIN

What I'm saying about group consensus and consensual responsibility is abundantly applicable to any Christian testimony against materialism. I mentioned this in Chapter 6, and bewailed its absence from American life. I referred there to St. Paul's combat metaphors as models of the Christian struggle, and said that it's a useful way to remind us of the need to identify our enemies. It's useful in another way, too. A soldier in battle is not just responsible for the square foot or so of turf that he personally occupies. He's also responsible, most immediately, for his buddy and his squad. His company has most likely been assigned a specific objective, and he and the rest of his company are personally and jointly responsible to achieve it. If his company contributes to a successful divisional operation, and to a victory by his brigade and corps, he takes personal pride in having been a part of it (and personal humiliation in their defeat if it comes to that). He has, and knows he has, ownership of the problem and the outcome: he never imagines that it's somebody else's. In adversity he may gripe and make excuses, but a good soldier will never disclaim his responsibility to do his duty, nor doubt the commitment and willingness of his whole outfit to do the same.

In any war against Mammon—materialism—there may be little that can be done individually. Sometimes we hear of a family giving up the rat race and moving to the country to raise turnips and hand-wash diapers. I do admire and envy them, but nobody believes they'll make serious impact on American materialism as a cultural norm. In less spectacular ways, a person may streamline and simplify his life; but who will know? (though for our own spiritual well-being, I think we all should make the effort).

Let's admit that for any effective witness against Mammon, we need both a mass movement, like an army; and also squad, platoon and company-level skirmishers. Individual action alone won't do it. We need small cells drawn from local congregations, each with stated objectives, self-chosen or under plans from a higher command.

Let's admit that not only the individual but the small unit fighting alone would have a rough time of it. Contact—association or fellowship, regular and close and supportive—is necessary, or functionally there is no group, and practically there is no victory. Now I'm getting visionary!—but I wish Christians could accept the kind of war we're in, and make provision for fighting it effectively; not just spiritual provision, but literal. We should establish actual, literal communities, even with clustered housing!—giving communal supports both for living the simple life internally, and for ways of assuming ownership—responsibility— for human suffering both inside it and outside it. (But note the "neighborhoods" websites in the Appendix; housing is not the essence of community.)

Again, the military: soldiers, sailors, airmen and Marines gather together on bases and on ships. There they learn to support each other in their material tasks and their common morale, while learning the ways of coping with external forces identified for their purposes as "enemies". True, we have extensive Reserve and National Guard organizations. They contain loyal and capable servicemen; but they have no function unless called to duty for service or training. Then they have to emulate the Regular components; gather together to jointly perform the same duties; things they can't do alone, or in between periods of active duty. If we Christians are serious about our spiritual duties and the battles we face, do we not need a base in which to train and from which to operate?

My challenge in writing this chapter was not to find material for it, but to select the most pertinent out of quite extensive sources. I don't know whether I've succeeded. In this chapter, and this one only, I want to supply references; the subject is large enough, and important enough, and my capacity to set it forth limited enough, that I just want to facilitate the reader's continued exploration of it.

* * * * * *

APPENDIX TO CHAPTER 8

Lucian, a pagan writer, about 160 A.D. described the travels of Peregrine, a fictional wandering philosopher. Remembering that Lucian's genre was satire, this passage has nevertheless been described as an objective view of Christianity in his time.

Peregrinus Proteus

[Peregrine] "came across the priests and scribes of the Christians, in Palestine, and picked up their queer creed... the Christians, you know, worship a man to this day,—the distinguished personage who introduced their novel ideas, and was crucified on that account. [Peregrine befriends the Christians, and is later imprisoned.] The Christian communities put themselves to the expense of sending deputations [to prisoners] with offers of sympathy, assistance, and legal advice... they spare no trouble, no expense... You see, these misguided creatures start with the general conviction that they are immortal for all time, which explains the contempt of death and voluntary self-devotion which are so common among them; and then it was impressed on them by their original lawgiver that they are all brothers, from the moment that they are converted, and deny the gods of Greece, and worship the crucified sage, and live after his laws. All this they take quite on trust, with the result that they despise all worldly goods alike, regarding them merely as common property."

Lucian was just as unsparingly sarcastic about the Greek gods, and not surprisingly the "novel, queer, misguided" faith of the Christians easily lent itself to his acerbic pen. Yet the things he set forth as self-evidently absurd, are the things that we admire most in our forebears, and wish we could emulate.

Etzioni, Amitai, *Spirit of Community* (New York, 1993)
    General, broad coverage of the subject
Etzioni, Amitai, ed., *The Essential Communitarian Reader*
    (New York, 1998) In-depth discussions of selected topics
Frazer, E., *The Problem of Communitarian Politics: Unity and Conflict* (Oxford, Oxford University Press, 1999)

For a copy of "Communitarian Family Policy
   Statement": e-mail to: divinity.uchicago.edu/family/
   communitarianpolicy

On the Web:
www.city-journal.org/html/6_4_communitarian.html
   Communitarian Dreams…In short, it means coming
   clean about the real issues and recognizing that a serious
   Communitarian can no longer be a liberal.
info.bris.ac.uk/~plcdib/lect9.html
   Lecture 9. Communitarian Critics of Liberalism.
www.gwu.edu/~ccps/platformtext.html
   The Responsive Communitarian Platform
www.infed.org/biblio/communitarianism
   Communitarianism has become the focus of some debate
   and interest but what is it, and what implications does the
   Communitarian agenda have for education?
http://perc.ca/PEN/1998-ll/review
   Communitarian economics. An account of "Mondragon",
   a Spanish economic cooperative, and review of a
   book: Macleod, Greg, *From Mondragon to America:
   Experiments in Community Economic Development*
   (Octopus Books, 1997)

The Simple Life:
www.spiritualneighborhoods.org
   Reference to, and synopsis of, a book on development
   of structured cooperative neighborhoods; an apparently
   comprehensive treatment: Gabis, Alexander, *Managing
   the Spiritual Neighborhood* (Camp Springs, MD
   tinkerscreekpress@yahoo.com)

www.simpleliving.net

    The Simple Living Network

www.newdream.org

    Center for a New American Dream

www.pbs.org/kcts/affluenza

    ...the high social and environmental costs of overconsumption and materialism; helps to recognize and treat affluenza as well as educate the public.

http://southwestfacilitatorsnetwork.org/articles/
SFNApril2002W6.doc

    An extensive (4 pg.) review of a book: DuBois, Paul Martin, *The Quickening of America: Rebuilding Our Nation, Remaking Our Lives* (New York, 1995) Includes references to "intentional communities"—a good search keyword from which to turn up a lot more information; see also "voluntary simplicity" keyword

www.ic.org

    Information on ecovillages, cohousing, intentional communities, communes, student co-ops, urban housing cooperatives

www.meadowdance.org/basics

    The variety of Intentional Communities is nearly infinite: some are religious, some are not, politics run the gamut, they are large and small, rural and urban.

www.neighborhoods.org

    Neighborhoods are closely related to Intentional Communities and share in the experience of residential Intentional Communities.

CHAPTER 9

DARWINIAN EVOLUTION

These are the generations of the heavens and of the earth when they were created, in the day that the LORD God made the earth and the heavens, and every plant of the field before it was in the earth, and every herb of the field before it grew...And the LORD God formed man of the dust of the ground...and out of the ground the LORD God formed every beast of the field, and every fowl of the air. (Genesis 2:4-5, 7, 19)

I quote the second account of the Creation from the book of Genesis, because the first (in Genesis 1) is pretty well known, and I wanted you to note the differences between them.

These differences are self-evident and I probably need not dwell on them. This one relates a different sequence of events, and does not specify a six-day process, as does the first account in Chapter 1. It actually seems to suggest a single episode, or at least a single day.

For our purposes, we need only note that disagreements about how the earth, or universe, was created, go back a long way, to the actual writing of Genesis!—though God's hand is consistently affirmed, and that much we must accept unequivocally.

It seems to me we need nothing more than these passages to tell us that the Bible does not contain a scientific account of either cosmology, paleontology or biology! But I'm obviously wrong about that, because some people who know the Bible well persist in thinking that it does.

It does appear that if we accept the Bible as the infallible guide to faith and practice, though not to science, we haven't given up anything of spiritual importance. Nobody argues much any more about whether the sun revolves around the earth. We know it doesn't, though Scripture clearly says it does (Joshua 10:12-14), and this became Galileo's problem in 1610 when he said it does not, and the church stood by Scripture and maintained that it does. Here's what I think we might learn from that story:

The language of this Scripture is specific, concrete and unambiguous: "And the sun stood still, and the moon stayed... so the sun stood still in the midst of heaven, and hasted not to go down about a whole day". But God's intervention was not limited to lengthening the day: "...the LORD cast down great stones from heaven upon them...and they died...more with hailstones than... with the sword" (vs. 11). Combat in those days was "with the sword", that is, hand-to-hand with sword, spear or bow. There was no long-range artillery! Now, hailstones don't fall selectively upon Amorites or anybody else; they fall at random distribution (remember that discussion from Chapter 7?) When armies were locked in hand-to-hand combat, a mighty hailstorm would be an "equal opportunity" killer—it could not favor one side over the other. The story is not credible meteorologically. And the sun does not revolve around the earth like the moon; maybe we could believe the moon "stayed", but not the sun, which doesn't revolve in the first place. It doesn't make astronomical sense; and the author was not divinely inspired to tell the true facts about what happened on that day!

But: *it doesn't matter,* and is not worth arguing over! It is a historical fact that Israel occupied the land now known as Palestine, and it is an archeological fact that other civilizations preceded them there. Inescapably we have to assume that Israel conquered the land from its earlier inhabitants, just as the Bible says, and that they settled there, and made it their own homeland. We cannot doubt that God wanted it that way and, which is about the same thing, that He caused it to happen. Once more, the choice of methods, the actual way in which He brought about His ends, can only be His own decision. Indeed, if the Amorites were as numerous and powerful as the Bible suggests, we might even believe that their defeat by Joshua was miraculous! Surely we can believe that is so, without subscribing to details which if not viewed with the eye of faith, are simply ridiculous. The little boy said that faith means "believing what ain't so." Well, I'll be the first to assert, after Jesus, that we are required to have faith; but also to assure you that if it ain't so, you don't have to believe it!

As I said, the language used in describing these events is clear and explicit: "...the *sun stood still...*" There are plenty of people, specifically Bible-believing Christians, who have tried to interpret and explain the Creation stories in Genesis; to reconcile the account of a one-day or six-day Creation with the scientifically established age of the earth prior to the appearance of mankind, measured in billions of years. The language of these Creation accounts is a little less concrete and explicit than that in the book of Joshua. I think you have to bend it pretty hard in order to interpret it out of its apparent meaning—to reconcile it with the scientific account of the same events, though many Christians try. In the case of Joshua, there is no room for interpretation; we must flatly dismiss the literal meaning, if we are to make use of the common sense God gave us. Then why can't we do the same with the Genesis accounts, written in language so much less clear and compelling that Christian apologists, without at all surrendering their orthodoxy, see the possibility of reading into them meanings that are tantamount to dismissal?

WHAT ALL THE FUSS IS ABOUT

In Chapter 7 I referred to the random nature of the structure and function of all components of the universe. That view is not necessary to either religion or science, but it seems to me the only way to remove from Nature any supernatural—soul-like or godlike intrinsic life-force or other teleological element, which I believe both religion and science should disallow. That includes overt supernaturalism, such as Special Creation. When Christians say God is "in Nature", we do not mean that He is the hidden driver of evolution!—it is essentially a devotional expression: true, but not translatable (as far as I know) into the terms of science. I know that the concept of randomicity is a sticking point for many Christians, even as it apparently was for Einstein. After all, it is not a thing, like water, that God could manipulate and turn into wine; nor a force, like gravity, that He could reverse to make the axe-head float. It is a non-thing, a nothing, the absence of both form and function; you can't *do* something to it, because "it" doesn't exist. We have difficulty thinking that God is in charge of it. And yet John Milton, a devout Puritan Christian, in his epic poem, "Paradise Lost", referred several times to "Chaos and Old Night". The terms are drawn from Greek mythology. He speaks of "the reign of Chaos and Old Night... Spirits of the nethermost Abyss...ancestors of Nature". You don't have to believe in Zeus and Apollo to give the Greeks credit for being pretty smart. They said that Chaos not only preceded Nature, but that it is what Nature is made of! (i.e., the "ancestor" of Nature). As far as I know, they had no theory about how all this came about, for they knew of no God Who had arranged it that way. But to me, it's good to think that Stephen Jay Gould had a precedent, even a Christian precedent, for invoking randomicity in natural science.

Anyhow, I won't be discussing Creationism (the 1-day or 6-day model) or Special Creation (successive acts of divine creation throughout geological time, whenever new kinds of creatures did appear, as revealed by the fossil record; ones which are seemingly unexplainable by any theory of natural origins). That doesn't mean I accept everything evolutionists say. In the religious area, I can accept mystery. Both Scripture and experience convince me that our faith is not all rational but also mystical, full of paradox and the unexplainable. But in everyday life as in scientific considerations, I don't have to accept anything I can't understand or whose ostensible explanations don't make sense. In Chapter 2 I listed a few scientific dualisms, or paradoxes, which in fact I do accept; not because I fully understand them, but because both aspects of the dualism make sense (even though irreconcilable with each other) and because both aspects of a phenomenon are necessary. (You can prove that light is radiated in wave form, and alternatively that it is emitted in energy particles. Since you cannot logically discard either finding, it follows that both are necessary components of our understanding of light, energy, and electromagnetics.) But as we'll see, there are some things about evolutionary theory that seem just too incredible.

So, to begin at the beginning, modern cosmology sets the age of the universe at around 10 to 15 billion years. There have been a number of theories about its beginning. The most widely-accepted idea now is called the "Big Bang", a facetious term suggesting a massive explosion. Briefly and over-simplified, all the matter and energy of the universe—billions of billions of galaxies, each with millions or billions of stars (all of which taken together add up to about 10% of the total matter of the universe; the other 90%, "dark matter", is known mathematically to exist, but nobody can see it or knows what it is); all of this, I say, is thought to have been compressed into a single point, infinitesimally small but of near-infinite density, mass, and energy. This primal entity contained too much energy and matter to persist; it exploded—the "Big Bang"—and flung out into space all the countless electrons and other subatomic particles of which our universe has come to be composed. There are still competing theories about how the formation of stars and galaxies took place. As any explosion flings light and matter far and wide, so the early components of the cosmos were scattered in all directions by the force of the Big Bang. With nothing to stop them, they continue on their way: the so-called expanding universe; though now it's said that this does not explain the rapidity of expansion, but that it is abetted by "dark force"—unknown except that *something* seems to add to the centrifugal momentum.

Primordial clouds of matter and gas, the particles of which were subjected to mutual gravitational attraction to one another, gradually consolidated into swirling aggregations of discrete clusters, or what we call *galaxies,* so that each of these contains millions or billions of stars.

A star is a superheated mass primarily of hydrogen, which emits energy (heat and light) not at all by burning, as in the fireplace, but by nuclear fusion, as in the H-bomb. It generates enough power to cause its own fusion process to continue, which then creates more power, which causes further fusion, which..., in what we call a continuous chain reaction. Judging by the size of our local star—the sun—it will continue its chain reaction for several billion more years before running out of its hydrogen fuel. In the case of at least a few stars, clouds of surrounding gas and dust became consolidated and formed planets. Like the sun itself, these began their history as flaming balls of energy. Being tiny compared to the parent star, they cooled more rapidly, and in most cases became solid objects, like Earth or Mars, with or without a surrounding atmosphere.

When the earth cooled sufficiently, probably around half way through its 41/2 or 5 billion-year history, life began. Nobody knows how; Creationists may claim to know, but they don't. They only know Who created it, but not how; in this as in so many other matters He has His own ways "past finding out" (Job 9:10, Rom. 11:33). Life did begin, and something about it, like the chain reaction that fuels the sun, fostered its own self-perpetuation. It is thought to have started as an undifferentiated mix of chemicals and water, or "soup" that, like the stars and planets gravitating into solid bodies out of primeval cloud, began to differentiate into discrete lumps of matter, and eventually became organisms—plant and animal cells.

We don't really know a thing about these early stages of life. There's no possibility of any fossil record of them, and all is speculative. It doesn't matter whether we find this hypothesized sequence of events credible or not; "we" can't disprove it any more than "they" can prove it. But at the organism, or cellular stage, we're on more solid ground. The existence of such one-celled plants and animals is known, because the world swarms with them, even today as bacteria and protozoa, and there are even reports of their fossilized remains having been found in rocks dating back millions of years in age.

We have observed in our own lifetimes that these creatures *evolve*. We keep devising ways to kill them with chemicals called antibiotics. First there was sulfanilamide, to kill the streptococcus and the staphylococcus. Then the pneumococcus, the gonococcus, and the syphilis spirochete were found to be done in by penicillin; and at last even tuberculosis succumbed to isoniazid-rifampin treatment. I need not emphasize that this is not a complete list: bacterial meningitis, leprosy, and even a few virus-caused diseases, among countless others, can be treated with medications.

Nor is this a complete listing of the drugs we use, because here's what happened: Like humans, no two germs—even of the same species—are exactly alike. Out of, say, a thousand patients with pneumonia, and out of a thousand million pneumococcus organisms infesting the lungs of each patient, maybe one such germ will survive the penicillin bath that has wiped out all the others. Out of a thousand such individual survivors, perhaps one will be coughed up out of the recovered patient's lung, and transmitted to another person. Out of a thousand such persons perhaps one will be in a relatively debilitated state, with a depressed immune system and an enhanced susceptibility to infection. Consequent upon such an utterly random series of events, this person develops pneumonia, which is to say, a descendant of the original "survivor" organism lodges in his lung and is not immediately destroyed by his body's natural defenses; and it reproduces by dividing into two copies of itself. Each one of them bears the parent cell's genes that conferred ability to survive in the presence of penicillin. Each daughter cell does the same, and before long the person is severely ill with pneumonia. He will of course be treated with the standard remedy, penicillin, in expectation that within hours the fever will go down, pain be relieved, breathing restored to normal, and in a few days the patient would be well.

The trouble is, it doesn't happen! This particular strain of bacteria was *penicillin-resistant,* and so was the disease it produced. The long and the short of it is that the germ has *evolved,* through survival of a new type that is fitted to live in a different environment—one drenched with penicillin.

Dozens of new antibacterial drugs have been produced, a constant supply of new ones being needed to kill germs that have developed resistance to the old ones. It is the best-known example, in Herbert Spencer's not-quite-accurate term, of "survival of the fittest". (The fact is, we are in the early stage of *running out* of antibiotics that work, because the organisms we treat with them are developing resistance faster than we can produce new drugs; but that's another story.) Each new incident of reproduction, whether of streptococcus or horse or hamster or human, displays a greater or lesser degree of *variance;* in a word, no two organisms are alike. There can be major variations—known as *mutants*—such as colored mice producing albino offspring; but most are minor and have little effect on the appearance or survivability of the progeny. But even minor changes can sometimes confer survival value, and these often apply when severe environmental change is taking place.

For example, body tissue normally is a suitable habitat, or environment, for disease organisms. When that environment is flooded with a toxic substance (meaning penicillin) they cannot survive. Except for the very rare mutation, a bacterial progeny of such different metabolism that it can live in the new environment, the race of organisms could not continue. And in fact, so assiduous are we with our treatments that the original strain of, say, tuberculosis bacilli, is becoming to all intents and purposes extinct in some parts of the world, leaving an entirely new race of resistant organisms.

Here's another real-life example of how evolution works; hypothetical but a probable approximation of reality. Wild oxen are widely distributed, from tropical Asia (water buffalo) to temperate North America (bison) to the high near-Arctic plains of nothern Asia and Tibet (yak), as well as the zebu and aurochs (now extinct, but the supposed parent of all Western cattle - as is the zebu of the Indian Brahma breed). They are closely related; all can be and have been domesticated. Like the bison and domestic cattle (Beefalo), all are likely cross-fertile with each other. The tropical water buffalo is short-haired. The bison is shaggy, and in winter especially, it grows a coat of long hair which mats against moisture and cold. The yak is a hairy caricature of the winter bison, and it survives sub-Arctic temperatures and weather. Though these are sufficiently distinct to qualify as separate species, it is almost a no-brainer to assume that they descended from some kind of primordial wild ox, whose progeny got themselves separated geographically, and in the exigencies of their respective climatic conditions—tropical, temperate and Arctic— were able to develop adaptive features which would enable them to survive such conditions and reproduce, thereby transmitting these adaptive features to their offspring. That being so, who can doubt that the best-adapted would be the ones to produce the next generation? So we end up with three species that differ from each other, in hair length more than anything else; for no better reason than that as the climate cooled, long hair became more adaptive than short. Either northward migration or the onset of an "Ice Age" could account for the new environment that required new adaptations; but the fact of variation between individuals and between generations, and the differential survivability of the best-adapted variations, is almost self-evident.

This process was called "natural selection" by Darwin, and it is the fundamental process of Darwinian evolution.

THE THEORY OF EVOLUTION

The theory of evolution derives originally from Charles Darwin's book, *The Origin of Species* (1859) and, to the best of my knowledge, little or none of it has ever been disproved. It includes—as does my own discussion of it—mankind's own descent from pre-human, or so-called "lower animal" ancestors. I've read that Darwin was a faithful Christian throughout, though clearly aware that he was creating problems for some believers. I've also read that he utterly lost any religious faith—talked out of it by his own theories. I don't know; but I know that some evolutionists remain Christian and some do not. And I'm sure of this: that Christians have done as much or more than evolutionists to create conflict between science and religion, ever since the case of the church *vs* Galileo in 1610, right up to the present time.

I use the traditional term "theory of evolution" even though some scientists claim that it's now established fact, or natural law, and no longer a mere theory. I don't know about that; I believe that something at least a little bit like evolution has to be the truth of the matter, but my mind is so full of uncertainties about so many details, that I consider many important aspects of it to be still theoretical. I'll devote a little attention to these later on.

No responsible evolutionist claims to know how life began, much less whether it began as an act of God or of a natural process. Whatever it is and however it got here, *Life* is the subject matter of biology, which starts out with it already in existence. Darwin's approach to it began with observations about domestic animals—the well-known fact that animal breeders constantly encounter variations in their stock, and that only by careful selective breeding can they maintain or improve the characteristics of any particular variety. Conversely, by breeding selectively for off-breed characteristics—a different color, say—a whole new variety can be developed.

On his Pacific voyage of exploration to the Galapagos Islands Darwin made many related observations; for example, of finches of a type known from their mainland counterparts but different in some ways—and even different from the finches found on different islands in the same chain. He thought that many of these examples of variation were substantial enough to qualify as separate species of finch. It reminded him of the domestic development of, for example, dozens of varieties of pigeons—highly developed from a common ancestor by selective breeding. It occurred to him that some primordial finch whose descendants found themselves in separate and isolated geographic locations could in time have given rise to the different types that were now observable. The basis for it was the aforementioned fact, well-known to farmers and stockmen, that every member of each generation varies, in greater or smaller degree, from each other and from their parents. The only thing that determines the characteristics of future generations is *selection*. The breeder selects for the characteristics he desires, whether milk production or meaty conformation, in the case of cattle. In Nature, with no human hand intervening, who or what does the selecting?

Darwin had been impressed by the writing of British clergyman and economist Thomas Malthus. His writings were of a predicted crisis in human affairs, when a rapidly increasing population's requirements for food will exceed the earth's capacity to produce it, and he saw the necessity for the poor, the sick and handicapped, as well as the victims of war, plague and natural disaster, for all such to succumb in the competition for nurturance. Darwin reasoned that the same principle will apply in Nature: no ecosystem can accommodate unlimited population growth of any species. He conceived of a "struggle for survival", a competition for limited food and other resources among the members of an excess population. Thinking about what might determine which members survived, he hit upon the concept of "natural selection": the process by which Nature herself chooses individuals for survival and, of course, for reproduction. Just as a stockman chooses individuals to breed (and butchers the rest) because of having characteristics that he wants to transmit to the offspring, so Nature provides for intergenerational transmission of characteristics favorable to survival, by allowing individuals that lack them to succumb.

We don't really know how great a leap it was for Darwin to move from this simple—actually self-evident in retrospect—concept to the idea that all life, in all its forms, has likewise developed and altered due to the cumulative effects, over long eons of time, of successive variations between parent and child generations. It is not true, as sometimes supposed, that the competition is necessarily violent. We may conceive of the "survival of the fittest", to use Spencer's term, as being functions of size, strength, speed and the like, of length of claw and strength of jaw. But intelligence, improvements in vision, in mothering and nurturing, in food-gathering methods; development of new instincts and self-protective devices, all may also contribute to meeting the goal of all life: reproductive success. (Survival itself is not the "name of the game"; it's no benefit to a species unless genes for the traits that enable survival are transmitted.)

Maybe this is a good place to clarify a statement made in Chapter 7. Talking about God's creations, we said that they are perfect and not capable of improvement. That is, of course, a thoroughly Creationist viewpoint. The evolutionist would deny it, and say instead that all species are "in process"; they are here and now subject to Natural Selection; to continuing change and development. If you believe in Progress, as also discussed in that chapter, you could then assert that the species is indeed being improved. Without making such value judgments, the evolutionists would simply say that "perfect" is a subjective and inappropriate term for the process of change in directions that we may or may not approve of! Though I don't agree with Creationism, I'll stand by the illustration I gave in that discussion. Whatever else it might be, evolution is exceedingly slow. It's a sure thing that rabbits, and Man for that matter, have not evolved significantly during human history, and there's nothing wrong with the idea of a perfect rabbit: a common-sense notion, and for any practical purpose, a true one.

I see some problems with the idea of natural selection. (I have neither the qualifications nor any interest in a comprehensive and educated refutation of Darwinism. I do believe we're all entitled to think for ourselves, as opposed to adopting a blind, dogmatic oppositionalism, and I wanted to share some of the things I think about.) For example: a fly is currently buzzing around me. Its body is built for flight: not only in the possession of wings, but in the lightness of its structure, and the incredibly specialized nature of the muscles that operate its wings; all of these features being necessary for flight, but valueless for any other purpose.

How in the world could some terrestrial animal have learned to fly? Can anyone claim to understand by what process some tiny primeval slug developed a set of muscles which are totally useless except for flight, by which to propel a set of primordial structures which were not wings, but only that out of which wings might some day evolve? Exactly what kind of survival benefit could have been conferred, by which the said animal proved to be superior for survival and reproduction than his fellows who were not so endowed? It is simply not conceivable what small evolutionary developmental steps could have brought about these structural changes; and even more mysterious to me, how could terrestrial patterns of *behavior* have evolved into flight patterns of behavior?

Similar, more scholarly arguments have been advanced by Lehigh University's Michael J. Behe *(Darwin's Black Box)* from the standpoint of physiology rather than physical structure. He points out, for example, that the clotting of blood is not just a single event but a complex series of chemical steps which follow successively, like a row of falling dominoes in which each one sets the next in motion. It's self-evident that all the steps have to be working, or the process couldn't succeed, nor operate to ensure survival of its possessor. How can step-by-step development account for a process in which every component has to be in place at once? and for many similarly complex life functions that have to be complete from the onset?

Somewhat similar arguments are elaborated at book length in *Darwin on Trial* (Intervarsity Press) by P.E. Johnson. The book is well-named: the author, though obviously a student of natural history in general and the theory of evolution in particular, is actually a lawyer. His book, in essence, consists of a series of arguments about the seeming inability of gradual changes to account for fundamental differences; he succeeds well in establishing (in my mind, at least) "reasonable doubt" about natural selection. Ever the lawyer, he rests his case at that point and he'd clearly have won it in a courtroom. There, you don't have to prove your client's innocence. You only have to establish reasonable doubt of his guilt. The jury need not determine who is the real culprit, but only that there is some doubt whether he is actually the accused. Johnson doesn't give us any clue about the real process by which life develops. In his foreword he explicitly rejects "creationism", defined as a literal six-day creation *ex nihilo* in 4004 B.C. (Ussher chronology). He leaves plenty of hints that he suspects something like *special creation* to have occurred whenever a new and really major departure took place; for example, when water-dwelling creatures, adapted to their habitat by such equipment as fins and gills, began to walk the land and breathe the air. Any conceivable series of small mutational modifications, each conducive to survival by improving the creature's adaptation to his watery environment, would enhance the odds of his reproductive success and therefore his progeny's comparably advantageous position in the struggle for survival—*in water*, rather than leading in the direction of possible future minor changes, the cumulative effects of which would include, among other things, legs and lungs. The fact of adaptive selection—almost self-evident—nearly or entirely contradicts the notion that variation might eventuate in structures and functions not at all adaptive to a creature's contemporary environment, but to a future different and hostile one. Johnson (apparently) and others postulate divine intervention at such major departures in the course of natural history, this being the only conceivable explanation of such seeming impossibilities. In a word, they invoke the miraculous—not only in the affairs of men, but of worms, bugs and lizards. I find this both scientifically and theologically offensive. But in so doing, Johnson and his sympathizers appear to me no more irrational than the evolutionists themselves. Here's why:

The truth is that *nobody* has a clue about the origin of such major departures.

Darwin's book, *The Origin of Species* is also well-named; and its arguments are to me persuasive. They are hardly any less so as re-interpreted by Steve Jones, in his book, *Darwin's Ghost* (New York, 1999). The author fancies himself Darwin's ghostwriter, and he essentially re-writes The Origin of Species, using the same chapter headings and subdivisions, but substituting his own language, that is, the language of modern genetic science. It's not that he despises Darwin's lack of scientific support for what is, after all, an almost entirely intellectual *tour de force,* one not based on the science of biology but only on descriptive natural history. To the contrary, Jones is the profoundest admirer of Darwin's perceptive genius, his ability to formulate without or nearly without the benefit of scientific data, that system which now constitutes the foundation of biological science and which only now is getting the support of hard scientific data such as that derived from the study of genetics.

But both Jones and Darwin are talking about the "origin of *species*". Not only are different species of animals (within a given genus or family) so closely related that they can sometimes interbreed and produce fertile hybrid offspring; but there are actually examples where two species are well-defined in their respective primary range, but in the geographic area between such separate ranges there appear all the "minor intermediate variations" that are postulated to have appeared during the differentiation of the two contemporary separate species through their evolutionary development.

The suggestion that such creatures descend from a common ancestor is, as I said, a no-brainer, even though it took a brain of genius caliber to make it originally. But try to find an explanation for what I referred to above as the "major departures"—i.e., for differences occurring above the species level. Creation-minded apologists invoke miracles. Biologists invoke Evolution! Now, you can't explain a phenomenon by the phenomenon itself. Not logically, at least; you can say rain is caused by wet weather, but you haven't answered any questions. It's no better at all to assert that the major departures in natural history were brought about by Evolution! Read a book or article, or watch a TV documentary in which the marvels or peculiarities of a plant or animal are portrayed. The author or narrator cavalierly states that Evolution accounts for them.

What Darwin said about the origin of Species, and what I suspect may be true, simply doesn't translate to the origin of the biological Genus, Family, Order, Class, Phylum or Kingdom—the larger and more differentiated groupings under which life forms are classified.

I want to talk about just a couple more examples of this, though there are hundreds and multiples of hundreds. Consider the hummingbird. This creature approaches a flower and hovers over it, motionless except for the beating of its wings 25 or more times a second. There it inserts its long, tubular bill and sucks out nectar from the base. Now, there are at least three conditions necessary to enable such behavior:

There must be the peculiar *flight* machinery and pattern, nearly unknown elsewhere in the animal world, unless in insects. There must be a highly specialized system of digestion and *metabolism,* to enable the birds to live on a diet of nectar and, it is thought, the occasional miniscule bug that is picked up in the feeding process. And third, there must be the unique *instinct* that drives the whole complex of behavior. All these features are inherited—carried in the genes, which are subject to variation and mutation. But imagine an ancestor of the hummingbird which did not possess these structural, functional and behavioral features; and then try to imagine what small incremental variations could have led to what we have today. How could an instinct to feed on nectar develop in a bird that had not the metabolic capacity to digest and utilize it, nor the necessary bill type and the ability to hover, so as to extract nectar in the first place? And how could the requisite bill and wings develop in a bird that had no instinctive proclivity to use them for their extraordinarily specialized function, and that made its living from some other food supply than flowers? How could the physiologic ability to digest and metabolize nectar develop in a bird that lacked the equipment or impulse to obtain it? It boggles the mind.

In some South Pacific islands there dwell several varieties of birds called "megapodes". Unlike most other birds, these creatures do not brood their eggs by way of hatching out their young. Instead, they bury them in a mound of rotting leaves and grass, the heat of which is sufficient to reach about 100 degrees, the temperature required for chicks to develop in the shell. Indeed, it is more than sufficient: the birds are obliged to give constant attention to the pile, scratching away superficial layers of material so it can cool, if it should get too hot, and then burying them deeper when necessary to conserve or increase the heat needed to incubate them. I don't think I have to explain what's mysterious about this bizarre system of hatching eggs. How did these birds develop the instinctive behaviors involved? How do they know the correct temperature, and how do they determine the temperature of a clutch of eggs buried out of reach, and how do they know the method of maintaining proper temperature?

Such questions motivated me to buy Steve Jones' book, *Darwin's Ghost*, for I'd read that it was strong on evolution of instincts. It is; but most of his discussion of it is about the honeybee. (I can't really be satisfied with his answers to these kinds of questions about bees but at least he tries.) In the same chapter he mentions the megapodes. His explanation: there is fossil evidence that some dinosaurs incubated eggs the same way. Now, that is what I would call a non-answer! Let's assume, along with most evolutionists, that birds descended from dinosaurs. Let's assume that the original birds were like megapodes; or at least resembled them in their reproductive behavior, inherited from their ancestors, as Jones suggests. Let's assume that the more common bird behaviors—nest-building and brooding—are relatively recent, having developed by evolutionary small steps from the primordial megapodal method (and for now, let's not take time to ask how *that* happened). The questions have not been answered at all, but merely moved back to a prehistoric point of origin. If we can't comprehend the behavior of contemporary birds, we're no better able to account for that of dinosaurs! (I believe the American alligator uses a similar, if somewhat simpler system of hatching eggs. I don't know where they learned it, either!)

With his use of genetic science, Jones gives a much clearer and more satisfying account of animal descent. Given the existence of, say, hummingbirds of the biological family Trochilidae, it is readily imaginable how different varieties developed over time, due to geographic isolation, environmental changes, variation in the kinds of flowers available, sexual selection, etc. But Trochilidae are utterly different from all other birds, in at least the three characteristics that I described, and no author or other expert has persuaded me that he understands how such characteristics could have arisen.

Though I accept Jones' assurance that genetic science can be helpful in understanding biological relationships, and hence the descent and change through time of the world's organisms; I know that some of its findings have been exploited and sensationalized. Especially in the relationship of man to the higher ape families (gorillas, chimpanzees, orangutans) we frequently hear that these animals have (as variously stated) 90 or 95 or 99 per cent of genes that are the same as humans'. I guess the point of this is to try and establish how similar we are to them.

Well, in the first place, no matter what scientists say, we are no more like them than anybody can tell at a glance, unless he's blind. No laboratory finding can disabuse us of the common-sense differences that we can readily observe. I don't know a lot about this, but in a general way I'll try to clarify. Genes are chemicals in the chromosomes that carry, in a marvelous sort of code, all the specifications for creation of an individual offspring. Genes, essentially, are locations on a string-like protein molecule called deoxyribonucleic acid, for most purposes mercifully referred to as DNA. Most mammals have rather similar numbers of genes and comparable DNA content. Despite these likenesses, there are differences in organization and sequence of genes within the DNA molecule, and these affect what is transmitted to the offspring. So the raw count of "shared" genes between species is actually not very informative.

Nevertheless, it is obvious that humans are more like, say, gorillas, than like armadillos or zebras. Yet even such different creatures as mice can have as much as 70% correspondence with humans in gene structure. In other words, truly immense diversity is accomplished with a relatively small proportion of the total gene endowment. From that perspective, it doesn't seem quite so amazing if two species that actually do bear some resemblance have an even greater percentage of gene correspondence; there's lots of room in that one or two percent variation for huge differences. The popularized and sensationalized statements about this are never made with any explanation of that perspective.

Like Darwin, Jones, Johnson, Behe or anybody else that I know of, I have no idea, either, how the major departures in life's developmental process could have occurred. I just know that they did. It is an easily observable scientific fact—and in science you don't make allowance for mystery or miracle!

WHAT ARE THE CHOICES?

Suppose you try and pretend for just a moment that the theory of evolution were entirely true. Forget all the problems and misgivings and whys and wherefores. Imagine it is true, and you have to make the most of it! Now, assuming, as you should, that this does not mean there is no God, just how do you think Genesis should have accounted for Creation? You'd want it to be divinely-inspired truth, but it couldn't use the present language because (so you keep telling us) you think that rules out evolution. So should it start by describing the Big Bang?—and indicate that somewhat later (perhaps something like this) God sent a lightning bolt to strike a puddle of amino acid soup—maybe having first explained where *that* came from—such as to reconfigure and combine its elements into a strand of DNA?—and then to state in greater or lesser detail how this eventually led to the evolution of mankind?

With all my admitted lack of comprehension of details, you may think I'm gullible, and maybe I am, but I have to believe that something at least a little bit like evolution has to be the truth of what occurred. *Life is there;* the forms we see were not created *de novo* in six days; the fossil record is also there, and in the supposed 4000 years since the Flood, it is not possible for bones, shells and plant material to have been turned to stone (fossilized). Life as we know it *did have to develop* somehow. And even knowing that much, I could not rewrite Genesis to make it conform. Everything I could make it gain in scientific accuracy according to the latest theories, would be at the cost of its inspirational and devotional value; and isn't that what it's for? I think I want to leave it alone, and assume that it does not rule out Evolution or any other rational theory of origins.

Christians are mistaken to agitate for Creationism to be taught in the schools, the way the church held out for Joshua's Long Day against Galileo. And I think that if by some miracle Christians unanimously decided this very day to quit fighting evolution—with or without having changed their minds in the matter itself—neither the faith nor the nation would be the least bit endangered.

The newspaper recently quoted a public school teacher. She does not dogmatically teach evolution, but finds ways to permit her students to specify their own ideas of where life and the world come from. I have no doubt that in the process she manages to teach at least the outlines of evolutionary theory, but what strikes her the most is this: the children have no difficulty distinguishing what is science and what is religion!

One was quoted as saying, "I have two ideas. One is that God made everything. The other is that we evolved after the Earth was created by the 'Big Bang'". (He might be willing to approve of my ideas about mystery, dualism and paradox!) So if your own kids are at least as bright, they will not be fooled by the pretensions of Creationists at being scientific; nor those of evolutionists that their beliefs refute the Bible!

The same newspaper issue carried two "comment" articles, one by a creationist local school board member, and one by a local college professor of biology. I am not nearly as much appalled by the *beliefs* of creationists as by their almost unbelievable twists of logic. Though there have been somewhat scholarly attempts to formulate a positive theory of life based on Genesis, for the most part Creationism is entirely negative. It is devoted to shooting holes in evolutionary theory, which is easy to do, as shown by my own examples—and I can think of countless more of them—but a proclamation of what could *not* have happened is not a scientific theory. It is a proclamation only of ignorance—mine as well as theirs—about *how* it might have happened.

But the thing is, these people claim that their views constitute valid *science* which should be taught in the schools (regardless that its foundation is the Bible); but that evolution is a *religion* (and thus should *not* be taught) because of its foundation upon a thesis or faith that "random change produces complexity". They've even dug up supporting court decisions; but I don't base either religious or scientific beliefs on the opinion of lawyers!

Once again, it all depends upon one's understanding of the Bible. Another newspaper article quoted a minister who said that Creationism is not just a theory, but an essential ingredient of his faith. He said, "The only way to believe in the Creationist account is to believe in the authenticity of the Bible. In my mind, it's either all right or all wrong...if we don't believe, can we believe Jesus Christ is who he said he was? If that's questionable, then is there no eternity? It goes on and on. The same is true of Genesis".

He's right: you can't believe in Creationism unless you believe in what he inappropriately called the "authenticity" of the Bible. He referred, of course, to the literal verbal inspiration and infallibility of the entire text of the Bible. If I accept the Bible as the only infallible guide to faith and practice, it seems to me I must have granted its "authenticity" even if I can't accept it as an infallible guide to biology and cosmology.

What we have here is the "slippery slope" argument used habitually to support rigidly dogmatic positions against any encroachment of flexibility. A nun was instructing her class of girls in reasons why they should not chew gum: "Any girl who would chew gum will probably go on to smoke cigarettes; and any girl who would smoke will probably start drinking. I hope I don't have to tell you what a girl who drinks might do!" Don't let the camel's nose under the tent. Don't give an inch, or they'll take a mile. If a girl chews gum she is boarding the slippery slope and is bound to end up in a brothel. It is reminiscent of a number of actions by the American Civil Liberties Union, for example by challenging Christmas displays on public property: every slightest shadow cast by religion upon the public sets off the alarm bells. If we tolerate this, what's next?—presumably an established church, mandated by Federal law. The National Rifle Association is just like it, even opposing a ban on plastic handguns (which have no conceivable use but to smuggle onto aircraft), lest it lead to prohibition of all firearms. Don't flirt with the slippery slope!—so if you don't believe Joshua made the sun stand still, or that the universe was created in six days about 6000 years ago, then you're going to end up denying Jesus Christ and losing your salvation.

It isn't so, and I'm Exhibit A to demonstrate that.

SO HERE'S HOW IT IS

To be fair, I have to admit that scientists have proposed answers to many of these puzzles. To be unfair, I'm not going to discuss them (except Steve Jones' explanation of the megapodes' curious reproductive habits, as I mentioned above) even though if I offered persuasive, plausible arguments it might help someone to accept evolution. But I won't, because (1) I couldn't do a good job of it, having so many questions myself, (2) I'm not interested in trying to get you to change any of your beliefs, (3) the explanations themselves (at least the ones I've seen such as Jones') are not that persuasive, (4) this chapter is too long already, and I've got to end it before you lose interest (if it's not already too late) and (5) if you want a really decent discussion of all this, enter the keyword "darwin" in your computer's search engine.

But I have to refer you at least briefly to the ideas of Kenneth J. Hsu. I'm pretty sure he is the scientist cited by Johnson in his book who said, "In China we can criticize Darwin, but not the government. In America, you can criticize the government, *but not Darwin!*" And that's what he did, by flatly denying the doctrine of natural selection, which, as we've seen, was Darwin's foundation postulate. Hsu turned Spencer's philosophy around: not that our cut-throat social and economic system stems from Darwin's "survival of the fittest" notions, but that Darwin himself invented the doctrine out of his own submersion in class distinctions (according to which, his own privileged social status meant that he had received from his ancestors a superiority over the lower classes); as well as his need to place mankind at the pinnacle of all life; to show that man's grandiose station in nature is due to his being the best and fittest of organisms.

It is widely accepted now that the dinosaurs abruptly became extinct at the end of the Cretaceous geologic period, some 65 million years ago, as a result of the collision with Earth of a monstrous meteor, of asteroidal proportions. The following cataclysm of fire, smoke and dust would have been like—but much more severe than—the "volcanic winter" of scientists, or "nuclear winter", that they call for as the consequence of nuclear war, and it would have been fatal to most of the land-based animal life of the period.

Hsu concludes two major lessons from this (and extensive other studies): that drastic environmental change after great cataclysms is the primary cause of mass extinctions, rather than competition for food by better-equipped organisms; and that development of new species takes place very rapidly (i.e. not by a prolonged process of gradual small changes) in a planet depleted of life, with virtually all of its land mass available for migration and settlement—but presenting a whole new set of environmental circumstances consequent to such mass extinctions, evidence for which he claims to have found at multiple periods of Earth's history. Such natural selection as may occur, he says, serves to *stabilize* the organism's adaptive structures and habits, not to change them into precursors of some new organ that might some day be useful in some new environment. In a discussion of all this in *The Great Dying* (New York, 1986) he describes the blind loyalty (which he compares to Christian fundamentalist dogmatism) of biologists to their Darwinian belief.

Well, he would be of no help to six-day Creationists. But for others who wish to challenge Darwin, he may have contributed some food for thought. He hasn't answered any of the kind of questions I raised on pages 175-181; but I'm pleased that he concludes his book with a Bible verse that he thinks reflects on the idea of natural selection and survival of the fittest, Ecclesiastes 9:11, "...the race is not to the swift, nor the battle to the strong..."

Of course, there has developed more recently the theory of Intelligent Design (herein ID). I don't really know much about it, but it has always seemed to me to be another version of P. E. Johnson's (apparent) belief in divine intervention at any point of major—and otherwise seemingly unexplainable—changes such as from respiration in water to air-breathing, or from oviparous to viviparous, or as in some of the examples discussed earlier. But as mentioned in Chapter 7, William Dembski's mathematical investigation of randomness—from which he concluded that it has to have been designed—is of much interest. ID of randomness itself appears to me a solid answer to the anti-Darwinian denials that random changes can generate complexity: not if this is what randomicity was designed for! I see a basis here for reconciliation between science and religion (which we should be striving for, if both are true). If an Intelligent Designer (which I assume we're free to call God) is behind randomicity—or is *in charge of it,* to use my own language from Chapter 7, then the claim that randomness cannot generate complexity simply has no meaning or value. Just as evolutionists need not admit that God created the world, though a Christian evolutionist believes He did; so an evolutionist need not believe in ID, even though the Christian who accepts the random origin of life and the universe is nevertheless confident of God's hand in it all—because He started it, in His design of randomness.

Which is not to say that any of this should be taught in the schools, nor touted as an alternative to Darwinism. If randomness were "designed" in such a way as to accommodate biological changes that we don't otherwise know how to explain, then so be it. But:

(1) promulgating ID in biology class is making a metaphysical statement. No student in college biology class, and few in high school, would be so naive as to hear of "intelligent" design without also understanding that an Intelligence is being posited to account for it. To claim, as its proponents do, that ID is not theology because God is not formally referenced, is to assert a distinction without a difference. You could talk about miracles or eternal life without mentioning God and likewise claim that it isn't theology; but if you believed that, you'd be deceiving only yourself.

(2) If ID is not distinct from theology, it is also not any kind of alternative or refutation of Darwinism. ID requires

nothing more than designed randomness; for if its proponents are honest, they must admit that merely this would be compatible either with Darwinian natural selection, or with cataclysmic change as suggested by Hsu. (The latter has proposed a flat-out contradiction to Darwin; but a non-theological one, which may be why the religionists haven't picked up on it.)

Back in my own Fundamentalist days, whenever a discussion of evolution came up, I'd say that I certainly didn't believe in it, but on scientific grounds, not on account of anything in the Bible. Because of my interest in birds, and with some knowledge of egg-laying (oviparous) reproductive systems, I had long since decided it was impossible for oviparous species (the primitive, probably reptilian, ancestors of mammals) to evolve by small steps of gradual change into viviparous creatures (that gave birth to living young). I haven't moved very far from that position. I think now that something—not necessarily classical Darwinian evolution but maybe something a little bit like it, or something more like Hsu's cataclysmic extinction scenario, has to be the truth of the matter. I don't know what the "something" might be, and I don't believe that evolutionists know either. I know that evolution is going to be taught in the schools, and in absence of any other reasonable basis for the sciences of geology and biology, I accept that this is how it must be.

If you want your children to be well-educated, particularly in the sciences, and most especially if they are to become professionals in a field of biology or geology or medicine, you had better not interfere with their learning all they can about evolution! You can help them to study it as a theory rather than a settled law of nature. You can help them to be skeptical of its claims (which is not the same as negative and oppositional). But don't require them to believe the world was created in six days!

You can also help them to a balanced view of Scripture, that will allow them to cherish it for its spiritual content, and laugh off the silly criticisms of smart-aleck cynics who reject the whole Bible because its ancient authors had never studied Biology 101. And you can encourage them to hold fast the faith, even while having to hear the militant unbelief (as they may) of some of their teachers.

To be a well-educated person, you have to know the theory of evolution and the science of genetics, at least in broad outline. You must realize that the mechanisms of heredity ensure both the continuity of species and the variability of individuals. You also have to concede the evidence of life's development through millions of years, from some original chemical organization that came into existence and had within its own structure the capacity to replicate itself, all the way through ages in which plant and animal lines originated and differentiated and became in succession the worms, mollusks, amphibians and mammals; or the bacteria, mosses, ferns, and flowers and trees, of contemporary Nature.

But also: in order to be a rational, open-minded person, you have to admit the uncertainty—or even contradictory dualism—in our understanding of how all these developments occurred. Evolution can explain some part of it, and I think Christians ought to admit that, but other parts it cannot. It is, and is not, an answer to the mysteries of life.

It occurs to me that religionists and evolutionists see themselves in much the same way. Both conceive themselves (with at least a grain of truth, in either case) as under attack; their fundamental, basic beliefs under challenge by the other side. And they both react with exaggerated defensiveness. Religionists denounce evolutionary teaching, though they haven't a shred of an alternative scientific biological theory. Evolutionists react with condemnation of religion, or with outright attempts to disprove it.

Between the two, I think the evolutionists have more reason to feel defensive. They don't try to shut down churches, but militant Creationists use political maneuvering to get their teachings prohibited from the schools' curricula. Wouldn't it be great if Christians could offer armistice and peace: graciously accept teaching of evolution in the schools, and *along with that* foster in their youth that open-mindedness which is the essence of the scientific approach (and helpful also in Bible study!) both as to the merits and the gaps in the Darwinian understanding of life. Maybe evolutionists, no longer under attack, could be less defensive and dogmatic themselves. Maybe they could more candidly admit the deficiencies in their theories (and only by recognizing these can they ever study them in search of answers). Maybe they could come to see the divinity in Nature and its origin. Maybe some might be converted!

But more to the point of this discussion (though not more importantly, in the greater scheme of things) our youth would not be forced to choose between loyalty to their parents and church—to "believe what ain't so", as against the dictates of their schooling and of their own rationality.

CHAPTER 10

OUT OF THE CLOSET

At the beginning of Chapter 1, I introduced myself as one with a "conservative" outlook on life and public affairs. But reviewing the issues I'm discussing here, and the positions I'm taking on each, I am wondering if I'm not only kidding myself, but trying to pull a "bait-and-switch" on readers who actually are conservative and who may feel misled as they read on and find out what I'm really saying.

In other words, am I a closet Liberal who, like members of other despised minorities, tries to hide it and resorts to deception to get himself accepted? Once again, this book is not about me—but I have to think about my credibility among the Christians who I hope may be among my readers.

It's hard to conceive of any kind of compromise or middle ground in most of these issues—Creation vs. evolution, or abortion vs. no-abortion, or between straight and gay; and so with a lot of the things we tend to quarrel over. I don't have any answer to that. For a number of these questions, I have to conclude that "both are true", as you've undoubtedly noticed. That is not just a dodge, an escape from clear thinking. I believe profoundly in the broken state of the world, a state that we've seen (Chap 2) results in many irreconcilable opposites and that lends a dualistic cast to creation. Most especially does it refer to mankind; the noble and glorious crown of creation—the children of God—and also the fallen, contemptible, misbegotten vassals of Satan.

> *Oh man! Thou feeble tenant of an hour,*
> *Debased by slavery, or corrupt by power,*
> *Who knows thee well must quit thee with disgust,*
> *Degraded mass of animated dust.*
> *(Lord Byron)*

"Both are true" of every human being, and of most human affairs, in which we do well if we can discern the lesser evil.

So I do not find fault with any tendencies in myself or others that run toward the "liberal" side of things; but here's why I still consider myself "conservative" in spite of all:

During my formative years from age 11, I grew up on a game preserve and pheasant farm. I loved the work, and indeed it constituted my career plan through high school and part of my college years. In connection with it, I pretty much lived and breathed *conservation*, though back then I understood the term to refer to the development and preservation of game habitat. As far back as the fifties I'd become a member of the National Wildlife Federation, the only conservation organization I was then aware of. As ecology and environment became public concerns as well as household words, I fell very naturally into the ranks of the concerned.

Here's my point: as I began to develop political consciousness beyond the "hiss Roosevelt" level of sophistication, I was pleased to find that as a Republican I was also a "conservative"—because I thought that was identified with my major interest, conservation. As a country boy I held typically libertarian views as to individual rights, and was happy again to recognize that Abraham Lincoln and the Republicans were the party of freedom (you already figured—right?—that I grew up in the North!)

194

I was both pleased and complacent with all this until one day—I was already in college by then—I was told by an up-in-years farm hand I knew that Roosevelt "cares about the little man"! That's what he told me, and I respected him, and I've never forgotten it. It was nearly twenty years more before I ever actually voted Democratic, and longer than that before I ever figured out the contradictory ideas I had developed back on the farm.

How could it have ever happened that the Democrats became the champions of individual (civil) rights and environmental protection?—and how did these and other issues ever get tagged as "liberal" when my whole "conservative" indentity had developed out of them?

And there's this: circumstances, which otherwise need not interest us here, had made it seem important to me to be not just a country boy, but a *poor boy*. It wasn't quite true, even though back then in Depression years, just about everybody was more or less poor. All the more reason I wanted to identify myself as poor like the other kids; calling one of us "rich" would have been as opprobrious as calling him "yellow" or "sissy". This is why I was shaken to hear that Roosevelt and the Democrats cared about the "little man"—that is, about people like me, as I saw it—and thus to surmise that the Republicans did not.

I have mentioned how it was that when I got into serious Bible study under my guru, Helen, I would sometimes turn up various kinds of textual difficulties in Scripture. But until my "moment of truth", if it was that, upon confronting Elisha and the bears, I managed not to let it concern me. Actually I think it is pretty common to use *denial* in coping with troublesome questions. We not only refuse to face them, but deny our own refusal; i.e. we don't even admit there's a problem. This must also have been my defense against any contradictions in political matters. I favored, and voted for when old enough, Republican candidates until 1960, and even then I switched because of my personal disfavor toward Richard Nixon, and not because of any change of philosophies or political outlook. Never, to my present recollection, did I give any further thought to whether my candidate cared about the "little man" (still my psychological self-image, even though having become a successful physician).

I won't repeat any more of the story from Chapter 1 about how my denials came unglued. But I do want to insert one follow-up note. I discussed there my problems with "witnessing", namely, that I couldn't do it, at least not in the manner to which I'd been instructed. For quite some years I lived with persistent, unmitigated frustration, and more than a slight sense of guilt. Eventually I gave it all up: I'd stop trying to do what I can't or be what I'm not, and go on to work with what talents I do have; though always feeling a sense of defeat in the matter, nor ever escaping the sense that I'm a second-class citizen of the Kingdom.

But here's what happened a few years ago, in a church that, during my Fundamentalist years, I'd have dismissed sight unseen as liberal, Modernist, and maybe heretical. I heard a sermon titled "Evangelism Styles Unpacked". It described six styles of witnessing, each based on Biblical examples. The Confrontational style of St. Peter (Acts 2:14) was a "frontal assault" that requires confidence and courage. The pastor observed that "some people" are able to use it!—such as, I guess, my mentor, Helen—but not me! The Intellectual style is based on St. Paul's work in the Athenian agora (Acts 17). The Testimonial style, exemplified by the blind man who received his sight (John 9) simply involves bearing witness to the works of God one has actually experienced, whether of healing or other extraordinary blessings. The Interpersonal style was used by Matthew (Luke 5:27-29) who threw a party for his publican friends so they could meet Jesus. Multiple and deep interpersonal relationships are used to bring friends to Christ. The Invitational style is shown by the woman at the well (John 4) and is available to those who are more comfortable inviting people to come and hear others teach or tell about Jesus. The Serving style is exemplified by Dorcas (Acts 9:36,39), who may or may not have spoken much verbal testimony, but whose endless acts of kindness and service to others pointed them to Christ. If that's Modernism, we should see a lot more of it!

I wish one of the three Baptist ministers at my old church had told me these things. How different my life might have been! Perhaps they didn't understand it either, I don't know. Anyhow, I wanted to bring some closure to that part of my story.

As time went on, though no longer a "little man", I still felt that somebody should care about them. I also read a little history. I realize now that the unknown backwoodsman, Abraham Lincoln, was cultivated and promoted by wealthy railroad and manufacturing interests whose concern was not at all about slavery, but only to keep the South rural and poor and dependent on them. (For me, it's easy to see why Southern states wanted to rebel against a government that seemed intent on taking away their livelihood—their dependence on slave labor being only one aspect of it. That their perceptions were correct is shown by the history of "Reconstruction" under the Republicans after Lincoln's death.) After a 140-year span, it appears the GOP has not changed its spots. So where does a person go, be he ever so conservative, if he does care about the "little man"?

George W. Bush, a philosophical and intellectual pantywaist, also had to be engineered into the presidency by powerful business, oil, and other would-be puppeteers. Whatever eminence may be accorded to him by history, it will stem from his happening to be there when America was attacked. No less so Abraham Lincoln; but I do believe Lincoln was his own man, and never served as the catspaw of his promoters. As to Bush on the same question, he appears to be firmly in their pocket.

In fairness to my readers and myself, I consulted sources to try and find the proper label for myself. A recent op-ed item in the newspaper quoted the late John F. Kennedy: "...liberalism is not so much a party creed or a set of fixed platform promises as it is an attitude of mind and heart, a faith in man's ability through the experiences of his reason and judgment to increase for himself and his fellow men the amount of justice and freedom and brotherhood which all human life deserves."

A beautiful sentiment, and a wildly irrational one. Nobody ever got elected, or won a political argument, because of the attitude of his mind and heart. In fact, you never can know another's mind and heart except by his actions. Nobody anywhere on the political spectrum would deny the goal of increased "justice and freedom". Yet one may pursue it by means of social programs to help the "little man" while another would try to benefit business and industry, with the idea that greater prosperity will benefit all.

In another column, the Boston Globe's Jeff Jacoby said that he was inspired by William F. Buckley's National Review, which held forth the "...importance of individual freedom, the dangers of a too-powerful government, the blessings of a free market, the imperative of fighting Communism, the indispensability of faith..." Neither vague and fuzzy, nor at all unreasonable. And an appeal to "faith", as I understand it, is something higher and more reliable than man's "reason and judgment", as Kennedy would have it.

My favorite Conservative of all, New York Times' columnist David Brooks, wrote this not long ago, concerning the purpose of conservatism: "...positively using government to give people the tools to run their own lives." Hardly a comprehensive definition, but as far as it goes, it's one with which I have no problem whatsoever.

So I turned to the dictionary and the encyclopedia. Combining and summarizing a great many words, I find this:

Liberalism is a political philosophy based on belief in progress and the essential goodness of man. It stresses individual autonomy, liberty, freedom, and equality of opportunity. Though standing for individual freedom from restraint, it accepts state interference in the economy to foster free competition and a self-regulating market. It is concerned with political liberties and civil rights.

Conservatism is a disposition to conserve what is established; a social/political philosophy based on traditional values, stressing social stability and continuity of established social institutions. It rejects sudden radical change, while maintaining the idea of progress by gradual development (I found nothing very direct or clear about limited government, fiscal restraint and balanced budgets; nor conservatism's historic and current affinity for the interests of big business and the rich. Only implied is its consistent indifference to problems of the "little man").

I also encountered this: *Religious Liberalism* is a movement in modern Protestantism emphasizing intellectual liberty and the spiritual and ethical content of Christianity. Inferring what is not said, but is consistent with my own observations, *Religious Conservatism* must therefore emphasize intellectual conformity and the legalistic content of Christianity. If that's so, 'nuff said: I'm a religious liberal!

I don't know. As to civil rights, equality, autonomy, I guess I stand with the liberals, though I don't yet understand how these conservative values got transferred out of the Party of Lincoln. I want individual "freedom from restraint", and of course that implies what today is considered a "liberal" view on things like homosexuality and abortion. But I have a severely limited faith in the essential goodness of man and the idea of Progress (see Chapter 7). As to state interference in the economy, I am profoundly skeptical. It seems to me both heavy-handed and inefficient, but it is certainly the lesser evil compared to the almost *laissez-faire* preference of today's conservatives. It's an issue that we'd now refer to as "government regulation", and there's no doubt who stands for more and who wants less of it. Solely because it may be the lesser evil, I guess this issue leaves me grudgingly and un-optimistically liberal.

All that is almost entirely based on mental operations, an intellectual or rational (to me) set of opinions. In my "mind and heart", I'm still a country boy. I love my life and don't want big government interfering with it. I love my country the way it is, and worry that it may be changing. I love classical and folk music and I detest rock 'n roll. I love Renaissance art and comparable representational modern works such as those by Andrew Wyeth. I can tolerate Monet, and enjoy Dali, De Grazia and a few others, but beyond these, almost anything modern leaves me unmoved, if not contemptuous. I love Tennyson, Wordsworth, Shakespeare, Longfellow, Poe, and even some modern poets, to the extent they emulate the classic style: Rudyard Kipling, Robert Frost, Robert Service and Stephen Vincent Benet. Most other modern poetry is utterly incomprehensible to me. I loved "Shane", "Around the World in 80 Days", and "Casablanca"; Sid Caesar and Elaine May, Charlie Chaplin, Abbott and Costello. I can't abide

Madonna, Sly Stallone, John Travolta, or any modern "action" movie. I'm appalled at the morbid fascination with sex and violence in entertainment.

I am impressed, and frightened, by the concern with "traditional matters" in the 1946 abridgement of Arnold Toynbee's *A Study of History:*

"In a famous passage Polybius" (Greek historian, 206-128 B.C.) "lays his finger on the practice of restricting the size of families, by abortion or infanticide, as the principal cause of the social and political downfall of Greece in his day...We shall pass...to the artistic techniques of architecture and sculpture and painting and calligraphy and literature ...[and ask] why our own traditional manners of music and dancing and painting and sculpture are being abandoned by a large section of our rising generation" (written before the advent of Rock-'n-Roll).

"...is the explanation a loss of artistic technique? Have we forgotten the rules of rhythm and counterpoint and perspective and proportion which were discovered by the Italian and other creative minorities... in our history? Obviously we have not. The prevailing tendency to abandon our artistic traditions is not the result of technical incompetence; it is the deliberate abandonment of a style which is losing its appeal to a rising generation because this generation is ceasing to cultivate its aesthetic sensibilities on the traditional Western lines. We have willfully cast out of our souls the great masters who have been the familiar spirits of our forefathers; and, while we have been wrapped in self-complacent admiration of the vacuum we have created, a Tropical African spirit in music and dancing and statuary has made an unholy alliance with a pseudo-Byzantine spirit in painting and bas-relief, and has entered in to dwell in a house which it found swept and garnished. The decline is not technical in origin but spiritual. In repudiating our own Western tradition of art and thereby reducing our faculties to a state of inanition and sterility in which they seize upon the exotic and primitive art of Dahomey and Benin as though this were manna in the wilderness, we are confessing before all men that we have forfeited our spiritual birthright. Our abandonment of our traditional artistic technique is manifestly the consequence of some kind of spiritual breakdown in our Western civilization..."

He was discussing reasons for the breakdown and disintegration of civilizations. He did not lay it all at the feet of artistic taste; this was one of several related and parallel tendencies that have worked on the world's civilizations (since the Greeks and before that) to bring about their decline and fall. It is given that none thought at the time these trends were taking place, that they were signs of decay. As in our own day, the people probably thought they were making Progress! I think warnings like these ought to be heeded.

When I was a kid we played marbles and jacks; we spun tops and roller-skated in the streets; we played tag, hide-'n-go-seek, buckity-buck and relievo, sand-lot baseball and football. Now it's action toys, video games and other amusements both solitary and sedentary. I do not believe that any of these trends represent advances at all. As George Bernard Shaw might have said, they are not progressive, they are only modern!

I don't believe in any "progress" at all, that's going to make things any better. Improvement would come if we could do away with modern fads in education, modern economic trends like globalization and the modern business and industrial mania to consolidate, to squeeze out the mom-and-pop grocery, the corner drug store, the "5 and 10", the neighborhood family doctor, the family farm, the small business, and all the wonderful features of both community and economy, that traditionally made our country a great place to live. They're gone; and a great part of the blame has to rest with so-called "conservative" policies that were actually radical, serving not social stability, but the very changes—massive, abrupt, and fundamental—that I just described.

Don't misunderstand me. What you just read was only cheap nostalgia. I know that the old schools were segregated by both race and socio-economic status, that neighborhood drug and grocery stores probably could not offer today's variety of products, that the family doctor often could not match the quality of care offered by today's multi-specialty clinics, that the "5 and 10" flourished in a day when hardly anybody could afford to buy almost anything costing more than a dime: those were not the "good old days". I only mean to emphasize the contradictions between a philosophy of stability and traditional values, and the practice of radical change under today's conservative leadership.

So I guess calling myself "conservative" in Chapter 1 was putting my heart over my head. It's true emotionally, yet I feel betrayed by today's conservatives. I began this in 1996, and at the end of Chapter 1 I was trying to find reasons to vote for Bob Dole instead of Bill Clinton. I could not, and actually I think the Clinton administration was pretty successful even if the man himself is scum. I never liked or trusted Al Gore, and I'm sure I'd have happily voted for John McCain. In spite of his immense attractiveness to the vast middle-of-the-road electorate of both parties, and hence his almost certain clean victory, he fell victim to the primary campaign of George W. Bush, so massively financed by the same patrons who had rescued him from bankruptcy, made him wealthy, and propelled him to the Texas governorship. McCain's crucial defeat, of course, came at the hands of South Carolina's Christian fundamentalists, who valued Bush's "born again" profession over the quality of his human and political make-up; and whose tactics involved a massive whispering campaign falsely alleging McCain's having fathered a Black Child. (In spite of all that, Bush almost certainly lost the general election—though that is not known for sure and never will be.)

I know a lady who said that even if she didn't know anything else about Bush, she'd have voted for him "because he's a Christian". As I confessed, speaking of Jimmy Carter, I am somewhat susceptible to that kind of thinking, though I don't approve of it, and it was far from my only reason for favoring Carter. After all, it is the easiest thing in the world for an utterly corrupt or totally incompetent politician to garner Fundamentalist votes by the simple expedient of coming out against abortion, evolution and homosexuality. I have no doubt that some office-holders have done just that, and it's a shame that some people give these charlatans their vote for no better reason.

Anyway, Carter was a lifelong believer, whose simple faith was well-integrated with his personality and career. He lacked the zealotry of the recent convert. I truly believe that he considered his faith to be the source of personal assurance and the ground of ethical conduct, but seldom if ever a clear directive governing political, administrative and policy decisions. I wish I could think that about Bush.

I'm sure of one thing. If there were a Communitarian Party I'd be a member. Read some of the references I provided in Chapter 8. Communitarian philosophy rejects typical liberal programs of welfare-statism, primarily because it transfers to government the virtues and responsibilities that should belong to the community. It rejects a number of the ACLU positions, because these are advanced as a matter of individual civil "rights", with no regard given to individual and community *responsibilities.*

They define "community" as any grouping of people in recognizable and supportive relationship to one another. The most fundamental community is the family; that is the first object of concern, and the ideal family is the basis, or at least the model, for larger groupings. The movement's major emphasis is not political but moral. (Too bad that can't be said about the Evangelicals!)

The Green Party is of interest. They certainly stress cleaning up politics—countering or abolishing the influence of big money—a keen interest also of Amitai Ezioni, the pre-eminent Communitarian spokesman. And of course the Greens are thoroughgoing environmentalists and I like that. Their vision strikes me as nearly Communitarian, but their programmatic proposals suggest an emphasis on *rights* (health care e.g.) and dependence on government.

As to the Republicans, the "little man" is still not even on their radar, and I care about that. Furthermore, though the "war on terrorism" is a dreadful necessity, they additionally took us into war against Iraq, which I opposed from the start. I never believed that we knew what we were doing, and I was right. And also, it is an unprovoked, pre-emptive war that is based on two fallacious ethical assumptions:

–that the ends justify the means; and

– that might makes right.

No action so based can be called moral.

The expression "axis of evil" was coined by David Frum, Bush's speechwriter, but he has made it his own, and used it enough to stir counter-reactions. North Korea and Iran, the other "evil" designees, prudently perceived a threat to themselves, as well as to Iraq, and reacted with hell-bent development of nuclear weapons. Anyhow, "evil" is a moral term, not political, and is perhaps most often understood as theological. So the whole Muslim world saw in the phrase a declaration of religious war against Islam; and what could have been a political conflict—however ill-advised—was converted in many Muslim eyes to a holy war in which all of worldwide Islam is obligated to join. It's hard to imagine any words more thoughtless, irresponsible, and costly in lives and treasure in all the annals of foreign relations.

But that's not all. The Project for the New American Century, a Washington "think tank", has been advocating "regime change" in Iraq, as well as establishment of a strong U.S. military presence there, since 1998 (and frankly advocating war *at that time* to congressional leaders). Its membership includes top leadership figures in the neoconservative movement, many of them having also become involved in management and policy matters in the Bush White House and Pentagon. Their aim is global military and economic hegemony by America; in a word, a new Nazism. One such neocon leader, William Kristol, editor of the *Weekly Standard,* in October, 2001 published (and maybe wrote) "Once we have deposed Saddam, we can impose an American-led international regency in Baghdad..." And of course we know from the Downing Street memo that the decision for war had been made well before any ostensible justifications for it had been factually established or adopted. Events so far suggest that this Administration is hewing to the PNAC line.

THE BIBLE

I also have to come clean about my use of Scripture. It's clear that I utilize Bible texts to create or support various positions, and these are often dependent upon a wholly literal meaning of the text. Nobody could do this without subscribing to the *authority* of Scripture, which in many readers' minds must translate to mean the literal, infallible, verbal divine inspiration thereof.

But not in mine. I make no apology for my use of Scripture. It isn't a gimmick to try and cultivate acceptance by Fundamentalists. I believe I've been open about some passages that I consider doubtful—regarding St. Paul's ideas about women and sex, about Joshua's Long Day, about a cranky Elisha and his ferocious bears, and about the 6-day Creation.

When I was younger and a Fundamentalist myself, we used to proclaim that the Bible IS the Word of God, in opposition to Modernists who confessed only that the Bible CONTAINS the Word of God, thus leaving themselves free to discard whatever portions of it they didn't like; and these might include anything from various historical and scientific matters, to theological ones such as the divinity of Christ. If *they* didn't believe it, then it couldn't be the Word of God!

I hope I've stopped short of that level of arrogance. I think we must consult Scripture in seeking out the Holy Spirit's guidance; and when He uses it to speak to us, it is by definition the Word of God. (But so may be a sermon, a hymn, a poem, a sunset or a meadowlark, the birth of a child or the death of a loved one. He can speak in many voices; yet the Bible remains pre-eminent, because it is not just the Word, but *words* that are mostly specific and unambiguous, unlike our emotional responses to the beauties or tragedies of life.)

Still, maybe it's kind of a stretch, trying to sort out one's political philosophy from the teachings of the Bible. There's too much opportunity to find support for one's preconceived notions. The farther we get from questions of faith and ethical practice, the more hazardous the territory. Younger readers especially, may not remember when older women—and some not-so-old—wore their long hair twisted and coiled into a knot or bun, which they pinned to the top of their heads: the "top-knot". There was a preacher who thought this arrangement unseemly, and he determined to oppose it. Strapped for Biblical support for his position, he finally found a phrase in Matthew 24:17 around which to build his sermon: "top not come down".

I'm probably as guilty as anyone, of wanting to find Scriptural proof-texts to support positions or beliefs that I actually hold because of personal inclination or even prejudice. All the more reason why I *do not* write on these subjects to convert others to my way of thinking.

I write them to show you that beyond prejudice, there really are such proofs—legitimate and rational Scriptural reasons to take these positions. You are welcome to find your own proof-texts to support the opposite sides. Neither of us is going to prove the other wrong, and that's OK—for once again, I am not trying to prove you wrong. As I've argued before, life—and especially the Christian life—is filled with mystery and contradiction, and more often than not there is truth on both sides: "both are true", as I've said so often.

I would like you to admit, not that you are wrong on this or that issue, for you may be right in your own way, and your proof-texts as good as mine; but maybe you can admit that I may be right also, my proof-texts appropriate and my exegesis of them reasonable. I would like you to abandon your negativity on public/spiritual issues about which there can be no agreement between the sides, nor any clear and final victory for either side, nor any foreseeable benefit to the nation or advancement of the cause of Christ, even if you could win.

The question of abortion, especially, is likely to be answered emotionally, not rationally or Scripturally. The same for evolution and homosexuality, though less starkly so, since they are at least discussed in the Bible (abortion is not). It's hard to have an open mind concerning things about which we feel so strongly. But you're in good company: think how it must have been in Apostolic times for Jewish Christians to be told that they could, despite scripture, eat pork and not circumcise their sons! Read Acts 15 about the mighty conflict that developed out of this, which nearly split the Church. And consider the endless sabotage these same Christians committed against the ministry of St. Paul. In view of his furious reaction to them (see Gal. 1:8,9) it's hard for us to remember they were actually Christians! But by the Holy Spirit the Church has come to the more permissive (or liberal) view.

So here's my approach to Scripture: I lack significant knowledge of the Higher Criticism of the Bible, as well as commitment to any theory of cover-to-cover verbal inspiration, so I have simply tried to treat its passages with respect. I assume that it means what it says, so I've followed some rather elementary rules of interpretation:

First, as I said in Chapter 1, I accept the Bible as the one infallible rule of faith and practice, and by "faith" I mean historic Christian belief as set forth in the Nicene and Apostle's Creeds. However, in matters of both faith and practice, Scripture still requires interpretation; so secondly, a Biblical statement has to be understood *in context:* of the immediate passage or argument of which it is a part; of the author's known views or purposes, as set forth in the rest of his writings; of the overall message or world-view of the Old or New Testament, and when applicable, the known facts of history or science. And finally, I look at any Biblical passage for what is said there by or about Jesus Christ. (Thus, his attitudes about women and sex trump St. Paul's; though I don't think anything else he taught does so.)

I've mentioned Joshua, Creation, Elisha and St. Paul so often, and again just above, that some will think I've pounced on them like a chicken on a June bug, clucking and waving them at you so insistently as to seem that I want to disprove Scripture by pointing at them. The opposite is true. I cite them to make specific points, and do not generalize from them. I use them repeatedly without making recourse to other examples simply because I don't know of many other passages that are importantly problematic. To me, the near-total lack of such textual problems speaks to the reliability and authenticity of the rest of it. As to all the other nit-picking questions and issues that get raised, I like to remember the comment by historian Hugh Trevor-Roper, when Adolph Hitler's bodyguard and his chauffeur were found to have given discrepant testimony about the burning of Hitler's and Eva Braun's bodies: "The truth of the incident *is attested by the rational discrepancy of the evidence*" (emphasis mine). I guess he means that a too-perfect congruence between different accounts suggests collaboration, and a suspicion that the evidence was "cooked"; minor discrepancies suggest genuineness of the event itself. (The same principle ought to be applied to various other New Testament incidents, the Scriptural accounts of which reveal slight variations; differing reports of the Resurrection offer a good case in point.)

I have already cited St. Paul's own disclaimer of divine inspiration of some of his views (see p. 63). I've also suggested how the stories of Joshua's Long Day, and of Elisha's bears, though not historically accurate (in my belief) can yet be the Word of God when He uses them to speak to us (p. 16, 236). The same for the Creation accounts (p. 182, and Chap. 3 generally).

But the question remains: how can the Bible be the Word of God if it contains even a few unacceptable portions? Here's how I think of it:

The expression "Word of God" essentially means God's *revelation* of Himself. The Word of God is not a book but a Person: "In the beginning was the Word, and the Word was with God, and the Word was God...the Word was made flesh and dwelt among us, and we beheld his glory, full of grace and truth" (John 1:1-14). "...his name is called, The Word of God" (Rev. 19:13). For people who want to know what God is like, the answer is simple: He is like Jesus Christ: "who is the image of the invisible God" (Col. 1:15), and "...Christ, who is the image of God" (II Cor. 1:15). To see God's revelation of Himself, we look at Jesus Christ: "he that hath seen me hath seen the Father" (John 14:9). I don't mind referring to the Bible as the Word of God, and I often do so, but it is not divine like the true Word. It is unquestionably part of God's revelation, but that revelation was only completed in Christ. We may revere the Bible, but we do not accord it attributes of divinity, as we do Christ himself. We do not ascribe to it perfection, infallibility or omniscience, because these characteristics belong only to God and we flirt with idolatry when we find them anywhere else.

I know some of the arguments that are used in rebuttal of such views as mine, and I know some of the counter-arguments to support them; but I spare you, and myself, for the reason that I'm only trying to explain myself, not to persuade you. I am a Christian and I accept the Bible, and I use it freely to help me understand the faith and practice that should guide my walk. I also use it to try the things that others want me to think and believe, or to say and do. You should do the same, and I know perfectly well that you can find as many, and as good, proof-texts for your beliefs as I can find for mine. We are all members of one Body, and we are not commanded to agree—only to love one another.

WHERE WE'RE COMING FROM
AND WHERE WE'RE GOING

I hope that in the above discussion I've indicated where I'm coming from, as regards the set of beliefs from which I've derived my positions on some of the issues of the day. Let me also try to be honest about what I think it means for you.

Years ago, the *Readers Digest* printed an account of a meeting of a so-called Anti-Vivisectionist society. To these people, all animal experimentation was considered vivisection. At this meeting, a representative of a medical school spoke, and he used the occasion to describe what was actually done with white rats, guinea pigs and other laboratory animals, how they were obtained and cared for, and especially, what benefits all this was providing for people, particularly children. He concluded his presentation with a question to the audience, "Do you want to save the children or the rats?" With one voice they screamed back, "SAVE THE RATS!!"

To some readers, this may not be self-evidently the wrong answer; but most of us value children over rats, and regardless of our solicitude for animals, we think that using them in humanely-conducted experiments is a lesser evil than to allow preventable suffering by our children. That is, we think that the humane impulse, noble as it may be, should be kept in perspective, and not be allowed to become the single and sole determinant of every position or decision, the answer to every question; to be what we now call a "litmus test", the result of which tells all we need to know about any issue. Here's an example:

Following the 9/11 attacks on America, the Rev. Jerry Falwell is said to have opined that they represented God's judgment on us for homosexuality, abortion, etc. (though I believe he later recanted). Is it at all ironic that these are bugaboos equally or more so, to Muslims? And is it strange to find Christian NGO's (non-governmental organizations) teaming up with the 53-nation Organization of Islamic Conferences in U.N. debate? The fear was that a humanitarian measure to fight AIDS might offer protection to homosexuals; or that a women's health care initiative might be tolerant of abortion.

See, we get so fixated on things like these, and so obsessed with our driven battles against assumed evils, that we lose sight of all else—just as we base our voting patterns on them and not on the character of the candidate or to whom he may be indebted. In my Fundamentalist days, much was made of our principled objections to the National Council of Churches of Christ in America and the World Council of Churches of Jesus Christ, of which, obviously, our own churches never became members. Our Scriptural basis for this was II Cor. 6: 14-17: "Be ye not unequally yoked together with unbelievers...what part hath he that believeth with an infidel?...come out from among them, and be ye separate..." The point being that we considered the "mainline", non-Fundamentalist denominations to be modernist or even pagan – "infidel"—and not worthy of our fellowship. I don't know how it is today; perhaps little changed, but how far have we come when the "infidels" alluded to in St. Paul's advice to the Corinthians, might include other Christians, but not Muslims!—with whom it seems we may become "yoked together" if they happen to agree with us on the "social issues".

And today's Fundamentalists do have just such "litmus" tests, and they use them consistently. A recent TV interviewee was reminded of policies of the Bush administration that actually took money out of the pockets of middle-class people like him and used it to favor big business and the rich. He said he realized a vote for Bush was a vote against his own interests, but because of the "social issues", Bush would get his vote. We do get obsessed with things like homosexuality and abortion, to the exclusion of matters more crucial to the nation, to ourselves, and even to the faith.

Practically nobody is exempt from one fact: we have problems with that which is new, unfamiliar, perhaps contradictory to our settled beliefs. By "problems", I include a thoughtless, ill-considered, over-enthusiastic and probably emotional rush to acceptance (such as seen in people like Huxley and Spencer in Darwin's day, as mentioned in Chapter 7); or conversely, and I suppose more commonly, a likewise thoughtless, "knee-jerk" oppositionalism.

But again, I want to emphasize to Christians of all varieties of religious confession, that I am not interested in persuading anybody (or creating opposition either) to the positions I represent, on subjects like Evolution, Abortion, Homosexuality, or any other of the purported "enemies" that I am trying to de-fang. (If you do find that any of these positions are of interest to you, I urge you not to consider them on the basis of anything I might say, but in light of your own study of Scripture.) Meanwhile, here's what I *am* interested in:

In the public life of the United States there is a fine line that has to be drawn both in official policy and in the mind and conscience of every believer, and that is the line somewhat carelessly referred to as "separation of church and state". It would be inappropriate, or "is" inappropriate in the case of some issues, for a church or organized religious coalition to take political action in support of a particular issue or candidate or platform or party. There is potential political muscle in such groups, and it cannot fail to be a temptation on their part to use their power, and on the politicians' part, to solicit its use. But there are three things wrong with doing so:

1. Our Lord Jesus Christ was God incarnate, "...the Word was made flesh...and we beheld his glory,... full of grace and truth." (John 1:14) We should not presume to enlist him, or flatter ourselves that we can use his glory, in pursuit of worldly political goals, no matter how righteous or justified they may be. Furthermore, he is infinitely attractive because of his person—full of grace—and because of his message—full of truth. In his name we can attract people, but we should be attracting them to him alone. It's a "bait-and-switch" scam to invite people to come to Christ, then tell them they have to support our political agenda to be "real" Christians.

2. Christ called us to give service, not to exercise power. Christians of today sometimes think their organizations should mobilize voter power to fight for this or that side of a public cause, be it taxes, welfare, or abortion. We ought to keep in mind that Jesus repudiated the use of power by his followers: "My kingdom is not of this world: if my kingdom were of this world, then would my servants fight" (John 18:36). You'll never convince me that this means only physical power and military fighting, rather than political power, because I don't think it does. When we fight for our causes, we are not fighting for his kingdom, but our own, nor are we giving service in so doing. All of that is OK to do—only not in his name!—because he forbade it!

3. There is serious, grave danger that a religious group may even be fighting *against* the Kingdom of God. To mince no more words, let me go ahead and name the Christian Coalition; though the shoe may fit others, it is the most prominent and the most blatantly political. Just how Christian is it?—that is, how well does it represent Christ and the Gospel? Here are some of the

things it has accomplished (remember that we are judged by our fruits, not our good intentions):

    – It has given popular expression to, and degraded, the term "born again", which is now often not recognized as a spiritual condition or experience. It may refer to any simple change of mind; or to a category of believer (popularly, an unsavory category) in the same sense as Protestant or Evangelical; that is, almost devoid of defining content. It has even found its way into popular music. One song says, approximately, "in your arms I'm born again", and John Denver sang that upon encountering the Rocky Mountains he was born again. Maybe he was—I'm not the judge—but how many seekers after new life and regeneration will come to Christ for it after being assured by a beloved troubadour that it means coming to Colorado?—or even, that it means finding love and sex? I think this perversion could have been avoided. Though I don't use the term much myself, I treasure it too much to want to see it cheapened.

    – It has created both fear and repulsion among many liberal elements of our society, some of them unquestionably Christian, but many others being people we most fervently ought to "covet for Christ", but who instead have been driven off, perhaps forever, by extremism, irrationality, and unapologetic power manipulations.

    – It has succeeded in identifying the Gospel with right-wing politics. The problem is not just that this alienates liberals, as noted above, but that it could lead almost anybody to think that opposition to personal freedoms is what the Gospel is all about (and to decide they aren't interested); when in fact they may not have heard the Gospel at all, and now have found incentive never to hear it.

    All of which is not to deny that there are worse organizations than the Christian Coalition, and my purpose is not to trash it or bash it. Especially, I don't want this book to be perceived as some kind of a liberal political tract, or worse, one that would use religious jargon to justify and promote what some will consider irreligion and its left-wing causes. It is, after all, the activist Evangelicals themselves who have succeeded in identifying their personal moral beliefs as political issues. I do not do so. Though there are legal-political implications to some of these questions, my purpose is actually to *remove* personal moral issues from the political scene. So I wanted to clarify my intentions here, before going on to the subject of Abortion. It may be the hardest for some people to deal with, though I think the Scriptural basis for what I say about it is as strong as for any of the other subjects I discuss.

CHAPTER 11

ABORTION

If men strive, and hurt a woman with child, so that her fruit depart from her, and yet no mischief follow: he shall be surely punished, according as the woman's husband will lay upon him, and he shall pay as the judges determine. (Exodus 21:22)

In case of doubt about the above passage, *mischief* means injury or damage (Heb. *ason*, mischief, injury), and *strive* means struggle (Webster) or fight, engage in strife. I said in the last chapter that abortion is not discussed in the Bible. I think that's true, though it is mentioned in this one verse. If *mischief* ensues, as discussed in subsequent verses, there can be serious consequences which are imposed according to the severity of injury to the woman. But without any such damage done, the miscarriage itself is penalized with fines, about like any property damage (and not like a *murder,* which fundamentalists seem to think is the essence of induced abortion.)

Mosaic law is pretty specific as to the details of everyday life, as well as of more major and less common matters. If you make a loan to somebody, you mustn't take his millstone as security; if you lend anything to a man, you mustn't go to his house to retrieve it, but wait for him to return it; if you use an ox to tread out grain for winnowing, you mustn't muzzle his mouth

(Deut. 24, 25). There are many regulations dealing with sexual and reproductive matters, including homosexuality (see Chapter 5) and bestiality. It is just hard to believe that abortion would never be mentioned, if it were indeed a matter of serious concern to Moses—or to God, if we believe He inspired these laws.

Only after the introduction of Christianity was any real effort made to suppress abortion, first in canon law and later in civil law. Opposition to it was based on the sanctity of human life. (This and other references to the history of abortion law are mostly based on a great discussion of the subject in *The Sanctity of Life and the Criminal* Law, by Glanville Williams [New York, Alfred A. Knopf], 1957). In ancient times, human life was thought to begin 40 days after conception, following the speculations of Plato; or at quickening, according to the formulations of St. Thomas Aquinas. Only since 1803 has life been legally defined as beginning at conception. At any rate, it is clear that disapproval of abortion is intrinsically theological in origin. No purely legal theory can support it.

Nevertheless, let's get this straight, above and before all else: *abortion is wrong,* categorically and absolutely; no ifs, ands or buts, no whys and wherefores, or moreovers and howevers, and no exceptions.

The silliest argument I've ever heard is whether "life begins at conception". The father's sperm and the mother's ovum are necessarily alive. When they fuse to form the fertilized egg, or zygote, the life of a new individual begins. If it were not alive (as can happen) it would simply be expelled with the menses. Otherwise it is fully alive, and it is not a goldfish, goat or gorilla, but a human life, a human being. It is always wrong to destroy life, though for food and other purposes it can be necessary. It is the gravest of wrongs to destroy human life, though even this may also rarely be necessary. When there is maternal eclampsia prior to the stage of fetal survivability, or when the pregnancy is extra-uterine—abdominal or tubal—both mother and fetus will die unless the pregnancy is terminated, thereby allowing one of them (the mother) to live—clearly a lesser evil, yet an evil regardless of that.

I hope this point is clear. Actually, I doubt if anybody, however strongly pro-choice their convictions, really thinks abortion is virtuous. That includes me, and the problem is that the question of good and evil is irrelevant. Some people want to outlaw abortion, for no reason I've understood, other than they think it's evil. But evil, as grounds for prohibitory law, is mostly irrelevant, and is becoming entirely so with time and the evolution of legal philosophy. The reason is that law is becoming more secular. It used to be thoroughly intermingled with theology, and we had criminal statutes against Protestantism in some countries and Catholicism in others; against Judaism and witchcraft, against working on the Sabbath (erroneously identified as Sunday), against adultery and fornication; and alcohol, on the theory that it leads to all the evils attendant upon drunkenness. Our First Amendment prohibits theologically-based law.

Hear that great Republican, Abraham Lincoln, on the subject of prohibitory laws: "A prohibition strikes a blow at the very principles upon which our government was founded... Prohibition goes beyond the bounds of reason in that it attempts to control a man's appetite by legislation, and makes a crime out of things that are not crimes."

I am not a legal philosopher, but I believe that from a layman's standpoint we establish laws for two reasons: to secure liberties and to maintain public order.

Thus, at the most basic level, we prohibit government from taking away the lives, safety and property of citizens; and then we likewise prohibit individuals from doing it. So things like murder, theft, rape and arson are outlawed, not because they are evil but because you can't tolerate things like that in an ordered society. Conversely, things that we can tolerate are not to be taken away by the government: they are what we call liberties. It's true that liberties may collide: my freedom to go where I want to doesn't mean I can trespass on your property without permission; so we may enact laws to limit freedoms—again, in the interest of public order—but only when my freedom may impair your rights. Otherwise, I may claim what Justice Brandeis pronounced as the "right to be let alone".

I have the conscientious right to define good and evil in my own way. Some people believe it wrong to serve in the military, and the government defers to them, allowing for conscientious objector status, regardless that most of us think it wrong for them to avoid service. The fact is that good and evil are religious concerns, and are none of the government's business, and my or your belief that something is wrong is simply no ground for outlawing it.

A timely example of this appeared in today's paper, just as I was preparing to print this chapter. A new abortion controversy has cropped up, and a County Board of Supervisors member held forth his opinion on it. "It's a fundamental right, the right to life. That's just a very core belief of mine. To me, that's just something that's not negotiable", quoth he. I happen to have some strong beliefs of my own. I believe that personal opinions—one person's "core beliefs" (even if shared by others)—are not a basis for public law. I believe that bigots should not be eligible for public office. Fortunately for the Republic, my beliefs will never become law. Nor should his!

PERSONHOOD

And the LORD God formed man of the dust of the ground, and breathed into his nostrils the breath of life; and man became a living soul. (Genesis 2:7)

In Chapter 3 I discussed the fallacy of *anthropomorphism*—of ascribing to non-human creatures the characteristics or rights of people. I submit to you that the human embryo or fetus, though human, is not a person. Legally, our 14th Amendment is what tells us who a citizen is, and in that context, "citizen" means someone who has constitutional rights; and as far as I can see, the term "citizen" is co-extensive with "person": "All persons born or naturalized in the United States ...are citizens thereof". Note that to be a citizen you have to be born, and the so-called "right to life"—an expression taken from the Declaration of Independence—extends to "all men". In context, and as elaborated by subsequent law, this means all *citizens*, including women—but not the unborn, because the 14th Amendment excludes them. The argument that prohibition of abortion can only be established by a constitutional amendment is correct, and without it, the Supreme Court in *Roe v Wade* was thus justified in striking down such prohibitory laws.

It happens that the Scriptural concept of personhood is similar. Notice in the above quotation from Genesis that the physical human form is not a "living soul" until it receives the "breath of life".

And think about Ezekiel's vision of a valley full of dry bones. In the vision, the bones came together and were furnished with sinews, flesh and skin. So Ezekiel prophesied as God commanded: "Come from the four winds, O breath, and breathe upon these slain, that they may live...and the breath came into them, and they lived" (Ezek. 37: 1-10). Here's the thing you have to understand: throughout this passage, the Hebrew term translated into the English words "wind", "breath", and "spirit" (as in verse 14) is the same word: *ruach*. In the Genesis verse above, the word for "breath" is *neshamah,* and this also means "spirit", and is so translated in Job 26:4 and Prov. 20:27.

The same is true in Greek, in which *pneuma* means both "wind" and "spirit", as in John 3:5-8; or "ghost", as in Matt. 27:50. It also refers to "breath", as in the cognate words *empneo* and *ekpneo,* to expire or breathe out (see Luke 23:46 and Acts 9:1).

Latin usage is the same. *Spiritus* means "spirit", "breath", "vapor". Its derivatives in English, besides "spirit", include "expire" (to exhale [breath], or to die—to give up the ghost, to stop breathing); and "inspire" (to inhale; or to move or influence by the Divine Spirit, or in other ways). "Spirit" itself means not only the incorporeal essence of a person or some other invisible entity, but also the distillate ("vapor") of wine or fermented grain mash.

I'm told that in Japanese and some African languages the same applies, namely the identity of breath and spirit. In most modern languages this identity has been lost to us, and we can only imagine the quarrels that might have arisen among Bible translators of words like *ruach, neshamah,* and *pneuma,* to assign the appropriate meaning in English, as in Luke 23:46, where Jesus "gave up the ghost" (King James), or else he "breathed his last" (New International Version). I think the former is better suited to the context, but it is not a more accurate translation.

Now, here's the point: persons are spiritual beings, and any creature without the spirit—flamingo, fox or fetus—is not a person. As we see in Genesis, a human form without *neshamah* is not a "living soul", and as Ezekiel saw, without *ruach* there is no Israelite. And as with Jesus, when somebody expires there are not two different events taking place—giving up the ghost and ceasing to breathe—but one thing only: *ekpneo,* the exit of breath and spirit, *pneuma;* a single entity, regardless that the English language has no comparable word to express their common identity. After it happens, the body is still there, but as with Ezeklel's bones, there is no person.

And inside the womb there is similarly no person, and for the same reason. That which departs at the last breath is not different from that which enters at the first.

WORDS, WORDS

I know how hard it is in Latian verse
To tell the dark discoveries of the Greeks
Chiefly because our pauper-speech must find
Strange terms to fit the strangeness of the thing.

(Titus Lucretius Carus, 1st Century, B.C.)

I'm sure that most people will find difficulty with the concept of identity of spirit with breath or wind. I do myself, so my ability to explain it to you is pretty limited. To start with the bottom line, it's in the Bible!—and as with other mysteries of the faith, what I may be unable to explain, I still have to accept.

Consider John 3:8, "The wind bloweth where it listeth, and thou hearest the sound thereof, but canst not tell whence it cometh, and whither it goeth: so is every one that is born of the Spirit." I am not sure exactly what this means, but it does underscore the Hebrew/Greek association between wind and spirit; because *pneuma* is here the word used for both "wind" and "Spirit". Compare John 6:18, "And the sea arose by reason of a great wind that blew". In this case, the word for "wind" is *anemos*, by far the most common Greek word translated "wind" (and used in English for anemone, the windflower, and anemometer, an instrument to measure wind velocity. It was passed into Latin as *anima*, which also means both breath and soul). The words variably translated "Holy Ghost" or "Holy Spirit", *hagion pneuma*, are found in very many locations. It seems to me that the word implies a relatively gentle blowing, perhaps more comparable to English "breeze". *Anemos*, though, always refers to winds at least strong enough to propel a ship, and more often to a strong wind or tempest. I don't know whether that helps.

I am not able to think like an ancient Greek or Jew, who had at least some concept of what we call "spirit", and who named that entity the way we see it today in Scripture, *ruach*, or New Testament *pneuma*, "breath", and "wind". They apparently saw no contradiction or conflict of meaning in such a usage; perhaps as in our own terms "wind" and "breath", which can be used interchangeably for some (not all) purposes. In our minds, it may be too much of a stretch to apply the same principle to "breath" and "spirit". We cannot clearly understand how (1) our spirit, the numinous and immortal essence of our being, can be also (2) the air that our lungs exchange countless times every day. Maybe they are not, in any concrete, non-mystical sense (especially if we consider that "spirit" itself is not a concrete but a mystical entity, almost necessitating that its identity with breath be understood as a mystic concept); but given the Biblical testimony, it seems to me the burden of proof is upon those who claim that the fetus, untouched by breath—*ruach*—can yet be a person, a spiritual being: one possessed of *ruach* (the spirit).

There are ways in which English usage reflects all this. In medicine, *pneuma* means "lung"; pneumonia and pneumonitis are diseases of the lung, and pneumothorax means air in the thorax, or lung cavity. In mechanics, *pneumatic* means air-filled or air-driven, as a pneumatic tire or pneumatic drill. And in theology, *pneumatology* means the study of spirits, or the doctrine of the Holy Spirit. So we do recognize the Greek usages. But these are English words only by courtesy; they are more like anglicized Greek, for we have our own words for air, wind, breath and spirit. There can also be this objection to my linguistic analysis: that the Greeks had their own quarrels and theories about the beginning of life, or *animation*, without—as far as I can tell—making any reference to *pneuma*. Prior to animation, the fetus was regarded as a part of the body, or *viscera*, of the mother. Only the Stoics put the time of animation at the first breath following delivery. Other estimates dated it at anywhere from 30 to 90 days after conception. But it seems that what was supposedly infused into the embryo or fetus at animation was *zoe* (life) or *psyche* (soul); not *pneuma*, about which Greek mythology and literature have little to say. Virgil's *Aeneid* speaks at length about disembodied spirits encountered by Aeneas in his visit to Hades; but Virgil was a first-century Roman, and he wrote in Latin. I don't know with what choice of terms he referred to these ghosts; the complaint of Titus Lucretius Carus, mentioned at the beginning of this section, may well have applied in Virgil's case also! I have to judge that in Greek culture (and language) there was little pre-Christian concept of Spirit as the essence of humanity. But not so in Hebrew culture and language, as shown in the creation and "dry-bones" passages cited above; and it is that Hebrew concept expressed in Greek language, rather than the pagan Greek philosophy, that we find in the New Testament use of *pneuma*.

226

To anthropomorphize the fetus is a great fallacy—to ascribe to it the characteristics of personhood such as civil rights. It should not be Christians who discount or deny the significance of the human spirit; who assert that because a (fetal) body exists there is a complete person, and therefore one capable of sin and salvation, and susceptible to murder. Please review the discussion (pp. 44-47) of what a human being—a *person*—really is: a *spirit*, not just animated meat. A body, living or dead, fetal or adult, by itself is not a person. So we ought to be guided by the Biblical principle of identity between breath and spirit; and consequently the attainment of fully human status—personhood—with the first breath, at birth.

Our common sense (when we care to use it) also confirms that this is so. We do not consider a fetus as a person. We don't count it in the census, or pay it welfare benefits, nor enter it in the church membership, or put its name on the Sunday School roll. We couldn't, because it doesn't yet have a name, and that's because we don't know whether it's going to be a boy or girl. And we use an expression like "going to be" *because it isn't yet!* If the mother miscarries, we don't hold a funeral, and the couple do not thenceforth call themselves "parents" or ever say "We had a child" (unless there were living children). When we dream of Heaven, we do not envision hordes—millions and millions—of aborted embryos and fetuses surrounding the throne of God; or is that because St. Fulgentius was right (p. 109)? There is practically no usage of language or custom that indicates a belief in fetal personhood.

Not only that, but the "product of conception" may not be a "person" by anybody's definition. It can be a tumor of placental tissue that forms a cluster of grape-like structures called *hydatidiform mole*, a benign growth; or a malignant one, a *choreocarcinoma,* which is rapidly fatal to the mother if not treated (i.e. *killed).* Though the life of these anomalies began at conception, their removal is medically necessary; they are not "persons" and destruction of non-persons is not murder.

There are other possibilities. The fetus may have *acardia,* a missing heart, or *paracephalus,* having only the stub of a head and defective trunk or limbs, or *anencephalus*—no head at all, or *pseudoencephalus*—a head with the brain cavity filled with a vascular (blood vessel) tumor. There can be identical twins, of which only one develops to term, while the other becomes a *teratoma,* consisting of only a rudimentary head or other body parts attached to or enclosed within the body of its sibling. In effect, a kind of tumor that may require surgical removal from its viable twin. Though all these are products of conception and fully alive (however, *acardia* and some others cannot survive birth), there is simply no sense to an undiscriminating designation of personhood to them from the moment of conception, nor any reasonable way of distinguishing, among the wide variety of possible abnormalities—from harelip to *anencephalus,* which ones should or should not deserve civil rights protection.

There is nothing that can already be what it is yet becoming, and the fact is that no fetus and no thing can be a person, in the absence of *ruach,* the breath and spirit of life.

PRACTICALITIES

Look: *everybody* opposes abortion in principle. *Nobody* thinks it a good thing. No doubt it is more abhorrent to some than to others, but that is not what makes the difference in political attitudes. That difference is between those who think their personal disapproval of it should be translated into law, binding upon all others; and those who think that a woman may decide for herself what, in her own individual case with guidance from her conscience and her doctor, may be the greater or lesser evil. And I assure you that carrying an unwanted pregnancy to term and delivery can be an evil. Seldom an unmixed one, of course—but who other than the affected woman can weigh these things? There must be a multitude of illustrative circumstances, but take one example: suppose a woman realizes that she carries the genes of some dreadful hereditary disease, maybe Huntington's chorea, that she does not want transmitted to another generation. Birth control can fail; and when that happens, what should she do? She must answer that question, not I. All I can do is try to assure that she actually does have a choice—the freedom to work out her own answer in one way or the other.

In terms of the previously suggested purpose of law, to maintain public order, it seems that prohibiting abortion in a case like this would have a negative public impact. It would almost assure the development, around mid-life of the as-yet unborn, of hideous suffering and handicap, as well as huge private and, almost certainly, public expenditures for the care of the afflicted, whose death will not be swift and merciful, but long drawn-out and agonizing. And before the victim's mid-life, there would likely have been the production of yet another generation of sufferers to follow. Conversely, to tolerate abortion is to create no conceivable impairment of public life and order. No person is harmed by the procedure, including the fetus, which is not yet a person. The regrets, depression, self-hate and guilt sometimes encountered later by the woman are not unexpected; she did a grave wrong, as I freely admit, but she harmed nobody else, she made her own decision (and could have made an even worse one, if on balance the abortion were indeed a lesser evil than the alternative), and just like the rest of us—at least those of us duly conscious of our own iniquities—she will have to seek forgiveness and peace the best way she can. Unless she comes to me personally with her troubles, it's none of my business—and it is none of yours! Two things to remember about this: (Psalm 51:17) "...a broken and a contrite heart..." is necessary to forgiveness; and, (Matt. 21:31) "...the publicans and the harlots go into the kingdom of God before" the hypocrites who condemn them. Have a little compassion (Matt. 6:15) "...if ye forgive not (others) their trespasses, neither will your Father forgive" yours.

Speaking of dreadful diseases, it seems the question of stem-cell research has become entangled with the abortion issue. Perhaps I've said enough already to indicate that I see no sense in valuing an embryo consisting only of a few cells, to the point that it must be frozen and preserved alive forever—or else consigned to the dumpster!—rather than to be made available for research into curative uses of it.

When abortion was legalized following the *Roe v Wade* decision, it appears there was a gradual annual increase in the number of abortions performed. (This cannot be known for sure, because there can be no accurate count of illegal acts, such as the number of pre-1973 abortions). What is known is that there were millions of abortions annually, both before and after 1973. The major change was that the procedure came to be performed in hospitals and special clinics, by skilled operators under sanitary conditions. Septic abortion, hysterectomy to control hemorrhage, inflammatory sterility, and other deplorable complications, so common before, became nearly unknown. Again, outlawing abortion worked *against* public order, and it would do so again if prohibition were restored. (There is evidence, going back thousands of years, of women obtaining abortions. They've always done it, and it's a certainty they always will, *regardless of risk or law.*)

There are instances of pro-life and pro-choice women who, however much they disagree politically, do agree that they want to do something about abortion. They get together to provide interventions—perhaps to emulate the Salvation Army and offer counseling, and shelter if needed, to pregnant women, as well as adoption service when desired. Any program to encourage healthy adolescence shorn of morbid preoccupation with sex, is likely to help. Sex education is probably good to offer, but it contains a trap. When we teach home economics or driver's ed, it's clear that we expect students to use their skills, in driving or cooking. In sex ed, we must somehow contrive to give useful information along with the stipulation that we *don't* want it used!—that is, until fully mature and/or married. This is certainly one among several places where *values education* ought to be part of the curriculum.

From a political standpoint I believe that—as is usually the case—some compromising is necessary. Many pro-choice people believe the right to abortion on demand is absolute for all women. They tend to see various related legislative proposals as attempts to weaken that right, infringe on its universality, and to take a step toward abolishing it entirely. But in public life, very few absolutisms can be justified.

I've heard the example given, of a (hypothetical) girl of 15, in her first trimester of pregnancy: should she have an inalienable right to the services of an abortion clinic without parental knowledge of it?—or, which is a different question, without parental consent?

See, children in our society do not have all the rights of free adult citizens. They often attempt to act like adults, say, by drinking or sleeping with boys, but when they do, they still remain children, and do not acquire adult rights just by trying to preempt them. We most always object to attempts at establishing a "nanny state" in which multiple laws are passed to protect us from ourselves; but when we do object, we're talking *as* adults *about* adults. But we do protect children; nobody wants to repeal anti-child labor laws, or compulsory school attendance, or controls over child pornography, drinking, or statutory rape. Appropriate controls over abortion of minors (but not prohibition thereof) are necessary, and we risk becoming extremists ourselves if we can't accept even such reasonable limitations.

(I do think that some such restrictions may be advisable, but I do not necessarily endorse any specific measure, including that one suggested in the above paragraphs. I've heard it claimed that this limitation might have adverse effects on the girls concerned, and I don't know the sociology of it enough to be able to say. Yet I maintain that "pro-choice" advocates should keep open minds about the various restrictions that get considered.)

THE DOWNSIDE

I said that abortion is wrong, for the reason, above all else, that it destroys life. Arguing, in spite of that, for its acceptance, opens the door to even greater problems. The more that destruction of life becomes commonplace, the more it is accepted and tolerated. That is, to a greater or lesser extent we become insensitive. We become less and less tender toward life and more open to its brutalization and destruction. That way lies infanticide, euthanasia and eugenics.

Actually, I can see room for discussion of these subjects and of the possibility that a rational case could be made for them (though I certainly couldn't make one myself at present). What worries me is that we could drift into them, not for rational reasons but because a progressively insensitive public doesn't care about life any more. Though I've disparaged the "slippery slope" argument (Chap. 7) because it's so easily invoked in desperation to refute scary ideas; yet it can be a reality. The wide gate and broad path always leads downhill.

We see it already: a professor of bioethics at Princeton, Peter Singer, argues for performing infanticide, in cases of severe deformity or handicap, e.g. His argument is not very far from my own: that the infant is "not yet a person". I don't know what grounds he has for asserting this, but I'm pretty sure they aren't Biblical!—because Biblically, a completed person comes into existence when an infant acquires *pneuma,* which in English is both breath and spirit.

So again, we must find ways of cultivating Reverence for Life, as Albert Schweitzer expressed it, and combating abortion and all else in our culture that cheapens life rather than furthering its preservation. I do not believe that outlawing abortion would contribute to establishment of a more humane society. I can see that tolerance could accomplish the opposite, if we let it, and I believe we should not tolerate evil, but combat it; only with better weapons than futile legalistic prohibitions.

It's a sure thing that when liberties are abused, they stand to be lost. It seems to me that conservatives should rejoice at the challenge of combating a social evil in the voluntary way, without reliance on governmental Big Brotherish punitive meddling and intrusion into private life and affairs. But then I've admitted not understanding today's conservatives.

Anyway, if you care about children, including the unborn, here's what you do. You find ways to:

 –combat alcohol and drug abuse
 –combat AIDS and VD

–combat domestic violence

–combat divorce, infidelity, desertion, child abuse and neglect

–eliminate teenage pregnancy

–support public and private child care and health care

–support environmental conservation and minimize environmental pollution.

And also, if you care about what our self-righteous leaders are beginning to talk about as a "culture of life", you:

–do something about childhood and general starvation

–do something about global epidemics

–do something about war.

And if you care about your country, you abjure greed and materialism, and work against their becoming cultural norms; and you divert your energy into these and other constructive efforts, and away from your self-serving pursuit of power and your faux-moral political crusades!

If all this sounds *liberal*, get out your Bible and show me just what's wrong with it.

A contemporary footnote to this chapter:

In January, 2006 a world-wide Islamic uproar ensued upon the publication, in a Danish newspaper, of a dozen representations of Mohammed, some purported likenesses, others in cartoonish caricature. It is, of course, forbidden to Muslims to make any representation of the Prophet—much more, to poke fun at him. Protesting Islamists clearly believe that Danes—and Americans, and Christians, and Jews, and Buddhists, and Kenyans, and Bolivians, and Australians, and Russians, and everybody else in the world, must live under the same prohibitions as their own. I suspect that most pro-life Americans would regard such a restraint of freedom unacceptable; if they themselves are not interested in cartooning Mohammed, they still would understand why someone else ought to be free to do so: "...if you disapprove of something, then don't do it!—but don't try to impose your beliefs upon others!"

I support that sentiment entirely! –whether relating to cartoons or abortion.

CHAPTER 12

BEARS

...As Elisha was going up by the way, there came forth little children out of the city, and mocked him and said unto him, Go up, thou bald head, go up, thou bald head. And he turned back and cursed them in the name of the Lord. And there came forth two she-bears out of the wood, and tare forty and two children of them. (II Kings 2:23-24)

Isn't this a strange text? For a long time I didn't know it was there. It sure doesn't get taught to little children in Sunday School!

I mentioned it once to a minister, and he wasn't aware of it either, though I know he had read it, as he had the whole Bible. I think we tend to apply selective inattention to some texts, because if we really perceived what we were reading and thought about it, as we're doing with this one, it could create problems: what does it mean, and how can it relate to other Scripture, in which we are taught that Christ loved little children and said we must become like them? (Matt. 18: 1-6)

My own first reaction to this passage was simply to disbelieve and reject it (Chapter 1). I still don't believe it is literally and historically true, but I consider it the Word of God nevertheless, because I believe God has spoken to me by it. Maybe He can to others as well, if we may look somewhat more humbly at the text, and see what we can learn from it. Let's start with Elisha, the character himself. In three ways, he is to be seen as a type of Christ.

He is, of course, the servant of God, the prophet of holy truth. He is the proclaimer of that redemption which follows repentance and obedience; the messenger possessed of miracle-working power who, though fully heir to the infirmity and mortality of the flesh, never used his powers in his own behalf: not to restore a decent head of hair, and not to descend from the cross .

Secondly, Elisha is harassed; if not quite persecuted, he was at least mocked. Though this point won't bear much stretching, still the image of the Suffering Servant, so pervasive in Old Testament Scripture, is expressly Christ-prophetic.

That being so, we must interpret very carefully the third aspect of Elisha's typology: that Elisha *cursed* those who mocked him, and therefore presents the question whether Christ, as so typified, may do the same. Let's look at the record.

One morning, hungry for breakfast, Jesus and the disciples approached a fig tree, hoping for a bite to eat. Finding none, Jesus said, "No man eat fruit of thee hereafter forever." Next morning, coming the same way, they found that the tree had withered away. St. Peter referred to Jesus' action as his "curse" pronounced upon the tree, significantly, *for its failure to bear fruit* (Mark 11:12-14, 20-21).

"Bearing fruit" is a well-known New Testament metaphor, referring to what today we would call *behavior,* for there can be evil fruit as well as good fruit. "Ye shall know them by their fruits"; read Matthew 7:16-23, in which, again, a tree is to be destroyed if it "bringeth not forth good fruit". In case of any doubt as to its meaning, Jesus' metaphor is followed by his explanatory warning—*and his curse*—not for a failure to confess

Jesus as Lord, but *for failure to do the works he commanded:* "I never knew you: depart from me".

And here is what is meant by "good fruit": read John 15:1-12. In summary, "Love one another", which means doing the works that show love; i.e. Christ's commandments (v. 10). Once again, the vine that bears no fruit is "withered", cast away and burned (v. 6).

Or try this: In Matthew 25:41 Jesus says, "Depart from me, *ye cursed"*, in his final judgment of the sheep and the goats upon his throne of glory (Matt. 25: 31-46). Notice three things about this passage: (1) Although in this account the "sheep" address him as Lord, they are not "blessed of my Father" because of having accepted Christ as their own personal Savior; they are blessed because they gave sustenance to the hungry and thirsty, shelter to the stranger, clothing to the needy, care for the sick and support to the prisoner. (2) Notice again Christ's curse *even though the "goats" also confess him as Lord;* and we are inevitably reminded of the previously-cited warning, "Not every one that saith unto me Lord, Lord, shall enter into the kingdom of heaven, but he that doeth the will of my Father which is in heaven." (Matt. 7:21) (3) Many people read this passage (as I think we should) as a warning to the individual: that an empty faith, not bearing *fruits* of faith, deserves, and may receive, Christ's curse. But the literal Biblical language does not refer to individuals. It says that this is Christ's judgment upon the *nations,* (v 32). Though we believe (taken in the entire context of Scripture) that it is the individual who may or may not be saved and enter Heaven; yet we can hardly doubt, upon reading this text, that nations also can be blessed or *cursed!* I take this to mean that not only individuals but also *nations must face judgement, and according to the same standarts!* Check Matthew 21:43, "The kingdom of God shall be taken from you, and given to a nation bringing forth the fruits thereof". Sounds like a curse to me!—or at least an awfully dire warning. And again, what's wanted is *fruits;* perhaps I have set forth already in sufficient detail what "fruits" are expected of a nation that seeks God's blessing and fears His curse.

But wait a minute. Let's think about this verse some more, in the light of history. Jesus is saying the Kingdom of God shall be taken away from "you", and the context seems to require that he means the nation of Judea. Now, that nation ceased to exist some forty years later, so whatever else you think this passage means, it is at least in that sense prophetic.

But to what "nation" was God's kingdom then given—one that brings forth the fruits thereof? None that I know of, whether ancient or modern.

We saw in the passage previously discussed, concerning the Judgment of the glory throne, that the scriptural word "nation" can and probably should be seen in two different ways: to refer either to literal nations or to individuals. Perhaps in this latter verse (21:43) Jesus again gives the word two possible meanings: either individuals or whole countries. We've noted before what amounts to an ambiguity to our modern American way of thinking: the Scriptural lack of precision as between the individual and the nation. But since we do make such a clear-cut distinction, I think we must be obliged to apply Scripture to both meanings. As we discussed in Chapter 2, the ancient Jews may have been less cognizant of the distinction between the two concepts than we are, deriving personal identity less from personhood than from national citizenship. Anyhow, I think that Jesus here refers to "you" as the People of God, who happen to have been at that time coextensive with a political entity, the nation of Judea. Thus, he says, the Kingdom of God will be taken away from a nation (though not from the people of God, as we can see now), and be given to a People of God who are not politically a nation, but are spiritually defined: that is, the Church (I Peter 2:9-10,"... ye are a... holy nation...the people of God..."). Yet I suggest we take the dual meaning of "nation" seriously, even if it stems more from a Greek and English mentality than Hebrew. Thus the old "nation", meaning both the spiritual People of God and the political entity known as Judea, should be seen as having a successor—as Christ warned that it would—both spiritually in the Church, and politically in any nation that pretends to "successor" status for itself. But from all we have seen, it is quite clear that any such nation that refuses or ceases to bear fruit, risks Christ's curse! (as does the Church itself: Rev. 2,3).

Let's examine one more passage that may help our understanding. In a dreadful indictment against the scribes and Pharisees (Matt.23:13-36) Jesus pronounces eight curses ("woes") upon them. In each, these people are called "hypocrites" and brief or more lengthy citations are given, which taken together and summarized, simply say that their affectations of religious piety were unsupported by their deeds. Devoted to understanding the commandments in meticulous detail, they overlooked the *meaning* of the law, and God's intent that it be used for the betterment, not the oppression, of His people. So much is this so, that they will not receive His call to repentance, and moreover persecute those who deliver the call.

All this we know, and however much we may dislike the notion of Christ as one who may pronounce curses, it's set forth here in inescapable clarity. And here's a sobering thought: though the parallelism is imperfect, in approximate terms the Pharisees were the *conservatives*—indeed the "fundamentalists" of their day. They revered and believed the Scriptures and, at least by their own lights, were faithful to them. Apparently they tried with some diligence to make converts (v.15). But their besetting sin was hypocrisy (Luke 12:1), and this is not something that disappeared with Pharisaism or the destruction of Jerusalem. For us in the population at large and in the "liberal" churches, our besetting sin is lukewarmness, apathy, doubt, faithlessness, skepticism; in a word, *unbelief*. For Fundamentalists, it is hypocrisy, and in Scripture these two are equally condemned. But hypocrisy may be more dangerous to the soul, for it comes disguised: it wears the mask of faith and piety, so that however conspicuous it may be to the onlooker, it can go entirely unrecognized by the hypocrite himself.

Look again at verse 15. Scribes and Pharisees (and contemporary Fundamentalists) "compass sea and land" to make converts. Though this was spoken with disapproval, it was apparently less than two weeks before the risen Christ was commanding exactly this of his disciples (Matt. 25:19-20). (Here again the word "nation" is used, even though "nations" don't get baptized. It does seem to me that we, who make rigid distinctions between the individual and the group or nation must remember that people who did not do so were the authors of Scripture; and so try to read what they were saying, not what we think, and allow, whenever possible, that both are intended.) Notice that Christ's command was twofold: to "baptize" (make converts), and to teach his commandments, presumably in hope of obtaining compliance with them!

Now, I am entirely happy at the revival of Christianity in our country, even though led by Fundamentalists. But why hasn't this spiritual growth been accompanied by concomitant decreases in poverty, crime and imprisonment, homelessness and ill-health? Aren't these the things we're to be held accountable for at the Great Judgment? A huge proportion of the Bush electorate is

Christian, and rightly or wrongly they consider him in their debt. What payoff are they asking for? According to Time magazine (Feb. 7, 2005) they want a constitutional amendment banning gay marriage, more restrictions on abortion, and above all, non-"activist" Federal Court appointees who are not "threatening to religious liberty and to the institution of the family".

Where are the requests for succor to the sick, the poor, the homeless, to abused children and women, to the forgotten inmates of our ever-expanding prisons? Is such succor only desired by Jesus and the so-called "liberals"? And what's this about "activist" judges? For the most part, the judicial decisions Fundamentalists hate are those *enhancing* liberty: freedom from racial segregation, from discriminatory sexual and reproductive prohibitions, from prisoner abuse by law enforcement agencies and personnel. As for religious liberty, they certainly have not displayed the (apparently) desired prejudice toward Christianity, but have instead consistently ruled in favor of the minority religions or unbelievers. The "threat to religious liberty" consists in our no longer being able to impose our God, our beliefs and our Scriptures upon innocent school children and other people of different belief or no belief.

A current shibboleth is that judges must not "legislate from the bench" but only interpret the Constitution. Maybe they got into "legislating" a little, when they decreed inter-district busing of schoolchildren, but that seems to me a fairly rare example. The way I look at it, the Constitution "ain't broke"; it is the Fundamentalist Christians who want to "fix" it, with amendments to prohibit flag-burning, certain marriages, abortions, and other unpopular freedoms. These freedoms, or rights, were not invented by activist judges. Have you ever read the 9th Amendment to the Constitution?—"The enumeration of the Constitution, of certain rights, shall not be construed to deny or disparage others retained by the people". Ideally, this means our rights or liberties include everything not specifically prohibited by law (when such laws are constitutional). It is not liberals or liberal judges who are trying to infringe these liberties, but conservative Christians—whose true mandate is not to control other people's behavior, but to relieve their suffering.

(I know I've stated my objection to religious politicking [p.214-216], and I'm not now necessarily advocating that we should be leaning on the President for greater social welfare expenditures, or the like. But if we're going to twist arms, at least it should be on behalf of others—the needy—and not merely to advance our own partisan interests.)

As I mentioned in Chapter 1, when I was a Baptist, there existed almost a denial of our responsibility in social areas. "Do-gooder" churches and "uplift" programs were pretty much scorned: what good is it to give people food and clothing if they're unsaved? Spiritual needs have priority; get them converted, save their souls, was the only duty of the Christian that I was ever taught. Jesus said to teach the nations *all* things whatsoever I have commanded"— not just one thing. To whatever extent I became a "child of hell" like any Pharisee, I'd like to blame the Baptists for it, but I don't think the Judge wants to hear alibis and finger-pointing and blaming others, for he did indeed send me in abundance the Bible verses, hymns, prayers, and if not sermons, at least books, enough to have let me correct my errors of pride and denial. But there it is: if we have not taught our converts the necessity of giving individual and corporate service through love, we make them, in Jesus' words, a "child of hell" *like ourselves,* for we invite upon ourselves the curse of which these passages warn us (Matt. 23:15).

We are told that Elisha was "mocked" by the little children, and hence his curse upon them.

I tell you that we mock the Savior when in his name we give honor to the rich, and use our political influence to help in taking from the poor to further enrich them; when in the name of Christian morality we seek opportunities to gain power rather than provide service; when we advise people that God hates them because of their sexual orientation; when we scorn the hungry, the poor, the homeless, the sick and the prisoner, forgetting that when we do so we scorn Christ himself.

You do not, of course, expect or want the votes of these people in your political schemes (though I imagine such could be obtained, if you showed yourself caring about their troubles). So it's important to you that their numbers (and hence their adverse votes) be kept down. So you must be hoping that existing programs will have a modicum of success, lest their numbers increase. Speaking of the various social programs that in principle you disapprove of and would rather abolish! Is it wrong for me to talk about mocking and hypocrisy?

If we as Christians do not intend to feed the hungry ourselves, we have no moral right to oppose food stamps and school lunch programs. We mock Christ when we oppose governmental proposals to care for the sick, yet allow a quarter of the nation to go uninsured and pretty much uncared for. We mock him when we self-righteously point the finger at criminals and gangs, and brutalize them with ever more harshly punitive measures, by way of denying our own responsibility for social evil—after he told us that in visiting the prisoner we visit him. We mock him when we name as enemies those Christians or others who are unable to believe that the world was created in six days in 4004 B.C., but ignore "weightier matters of the law, judgment, mercy, and faith" (Matt. 23:23). We mock Christ, born an Asiatic Jew, when we discriminate against modern Jews, and Asiatics, and others;

and when we acquiesce to our own historic genocide of Native Americans, and when we live comfortably with the consequences of our enslavement of Africans. We mock him when we piously demand prayer in the schools for *our* children, but fail to provide safe schools and decent education for "theirs". We mock him when we hypocritically wring our hands over "secular humanism", a near-Christian ethic, because of its invasion of our education and other public arenas; even when we know our Constitution requires that public policy be kept secular.

All of us, as a nation, do these things, not just the Religious Right, and so we as a nation invite Christ's curse (N.B. not because of abortion, homosexuality or teaching evolution; the Judge on his throne mentioned none of these). But even in our own nation, Christians stand in particular peril. Whatever we may say, the truth is we believe in "cheap grace". We have his commandments but ignore them; we know of his curse upon what we do, but are indifferent at best and more often in denial, and self-righteously and proudly, in the very name of our Lord, advocate and perform those things which mock his life and word.

And speaking of "activist" judges, where are they when we need them?—to protect us from that exemplary Christian, John Ashcroft, who reportedly had himself *anointed with oil* (Mazola) upon learning that he was to be Attorney General. Our nation, under him, and of course under his boss, the president, now engages in arbitrary and indefinite imprisonment, "rendition" (a euphemism for *kidnapping)* for transport to foreign jails and torture centers, all on mere suspicion, while promoting piecemeal but steady shredding of domestic civil liberties.

When I was a school-kid, we were thrilled and inspired by the words of Patrick Henry: "Is life so dear and peace so sweet, as to be purchased at the price of chains and slavery? Forbid it,

Almighty God! I know not what course others may take, but as for me, give me liberty or give me death!" The answer to his question today apparently is, "Hell, yes!" We will pay any price for "Homeland Security"; including our liberties and our national dignity, if only somebody will protect our cowardly existences. And we thought stories about selling our souls to the devil were all ancient mythology!

We have the potential to change what is wrong through service, but we rather perpetuate it in our quest for political power. Here's another curse: "That servant, which knew his Lord's will, and prepared not himself, neither did according to his will, shall be beaten with many stripes...For unto whomsoever much is given, of him shall much be required." (Luke 12:47-48).

At this exact place in my writing I happened to see Ralph Reed, then Executive Director of the Christian Coalition, on "Meet the Press", broadcast in the middle of the December, 1995 budget standoff. Reed is not, to me, an inspirational speaker; all the more remarkable the impact of his quiet, sincere earnestness as even in brief responses he is able to portray a vision of a simpler, non-bureaucratic method of providing for human need, within a morally positive structure under "voluntary" group efforts.

"Almost thou persuadest me", Ralph. But then I began thinking—it's all talk:—the hungry are *not* being fed, the homeless sheltered, or the lives of criminals redeemed; and in the same broadcast indeed, Reed's primary point was made, if I understand him, that we have to cut back—spend less—cut off "benefits" to these very people and the programs intended to help them. We are not doing the things our Lord commanded, and we oppose efforts by others to do so!—and how will we answer him in that day? "We wanted to help, but the stingy, compassionless

Republicans wouldn't let us?"—I might choose that, but I can already hear, "Depart from me" before I get half the words out.

Or maybe, "we had hoped to, but there were no funds for it, after the Democrats wasted all our resources on foolish Great Society gimmicks." Can you really believe that will fly? We may find He cares neither about alibis nor partisan politics.

Ralph Reed and others think that voluntary charities will suffice to change the system and provide what those in need require. Reality check: *they aren't doing it*—hardly even a small portion of what needs to be done; it's only talk and fantasy. It's only an excuse to try and justify lower taxes: discontinue these Federal programs, you say, and leave the money with us who earned it, and we will care for those in need through our voluntary ("faith-based") services.

Believe that, and you are in great danger—not only of Christ's curse, but of somebody peddling you gold bricks, swampland in Florida or the Brooklyn Bridge in exchange for your life savings!—for you must be gullible indeed.

You know *exactly* why you want your taxes cut. You were born and raised, most of you, in my own materialist, individualistic world whose highest values are commercialism, entertainment and consumerism; and none of this would have to be written if the vast majority of Christians were not equally as conformed to that world as all the rest of society. You want lower taxes *not in the least* so that you can give more money to charity, but to have more for yourselves. You want more and better consumer goods, not more food for the hungry; a bigger house in a nicer neighborhood, not shelter for the homeless; ability to pay for private schooling for your children, not quality education and a safe school environment for all; better and more comprehensive health benefits for your family, not healing and health care for the poor; safe streets in your own neighborhood, not prison reform or prisoner rehabilitation. Ever since the late 60's governmental support and tax funding for social, health and correctional programs (other than mere expansion of the prison system) has in fact been low-priority and sometimes cut back or abolished (perhaps deservedly so, in some cases); but there has *never been any serious* recoup of lost programs, services and funding by any effort, charitable or governmental.

For a moment, let's just pretend. Let's say Congress in one blow abolished Welfare and all its Federally-funded relatives and descendants, call it Workfare or food stamps or Medicaid or Medicare or Job Corps or school lunch and all the rest, on the theory that private charity could now take care of human need and the needy. Let's pretend that the entire cost of the abolished programs would be applied to a tax reduction and returned to the taxpayers. And let's imagine that every taxpayer family tithed, so that a tenth part of the tax savings or refund went to Christian or other charities for the poor. And of course we'll assume that these private charities would to no extent at all divert their funds to unnecessary administrative, bureaucratic or wasteful purposes.

Do you seriously want to say (a) that everybody, Christian and other, is going to tithe, and that if they did, the poor could be adequately provided for at a tenth of the present cost? or maybe (b) that everybody (including the rich, who do pay a great proportion of all income taxes) will return the entirety of their tax savings to programs for the poor?—and that this amount will now be sufficient to provide for them, when it never before has come even close? Why in the world are people asking for a tax cut, if that's what they're going to do with it?

Nobody believes that. I certainly wasn't hinting at it in Chapter 8 (cf. "Ownership", p. 157 ff.) The Communitarian vision is not at all like what I'm talking about here. It isn't about money, but about *responsibility:* "A communitarian perspective recognizes that communities...have obligations ... the duty to be responsive to their members...(it) does not dictate particular policies; rather it mandates attention to...the social side of human nature; the responsibilities that must be borne by citizens, individually and collectively..." It maintains no objection to public programs; but "The government should step in only to the extent that other social subsystems fail, rather than seek to replace them." (Quotes from "The Responsive Communitarian Platform", ref. p. 170). Here are some examples of how Fundamentalists have the Communitarian (not to say "Christian") approach all backwards:

Around each Christmas season, and occasionally throughout the year, we are treated to media accounts of the unselfish, the heroic, the caring and generous, the bearers of love and the "points of light" which do abound in this society. Has it ever occurred to you of the Religious Right that people really love this stuff?—that they admire, and long to see, generous and genuine "no hidden agenda" acts of compassion?—that if you were interested in service more than in talk and power-grabbing—in displaying the humility and servitude that Jesus commanded and exemplified—you would be less feared and your mission more trusted?—that even those liberals who love to trumpet their "compassion" might "see your good works and glorify your Father which is in Heaven"? (Matt. 5:16), and maybe even seek to support you and join your efforts? (not to say, seek to acquire and emulate your faith). Who ever feared and resented Mother Teresa or the Salvation Army?—or begrudged their support?—because everybody knows their mission is service.

I never heard of any anti-abortion activism by the Salvation Army. Yet they have of a certainty prevented more abortions than all the howling, vicious mobs that picket women's clinics and harass and intimidate their clients. All they do is provide a chain of Florence Crittenden Homes in which unwed mothers may complete their terms and deliver and arrange adoption if desired, in privacy and dignity. Much more could be said, but for now and in the present, the truth is that you are not interested in service. You are interested in power. You want to control the Republican Party, and through them the American government. You want to control what goes on in our schools and in our bedrooms. You want to censor our books, classrooms, films and broadcasts. "Ye know that ...princes... exercise dominion, and the great exercise authority...*But it shall not be so among* you...whosoever will be great...let him be (a) servant" (Matt. 20:25-28). And what if you profess to serve but do not? Like the son who said, "I go sir" and went not (Matt. 21:28-31): even publicans and prostitutes enter the Kingdom of God before you. You are like the man bidden to discipleship who answered, "Lord, suffer me first to go and bury my father" (Luke 9:59). A laudable sentiment, and not contrary to a life of faith; but *"first"*? And will you plead at the Throne, "First we had to try and get control of Congress and the White House and get our taxes cut"?—and do you think it will sell?

Look: Jesus and his disciples were hungry one Sabbath and having no food of their own, they began to pick a few heads of wheat, to eat the grains (Matt. 12:1-8). The Pharisees who criticized them for doing labor (i.e. reaping grain) on the Sabbath, did have at least a technical excuse for their meanness: the law of Moses forbade such work. But ought they not to have spared the necessity of either labor or criticism, by giving food themselves to the hungry? "Depart from me, *ye cursed*...for I was an hungered, and ye gave me no meat". And are you so different from the Pharisees?—are you not equally condemning of, say, food stamps—and public welfare generally—not despite but specifically *because* they provide "handouts" to what you call "Welfare Cadillac Queens"?

Can you still say, "If we had been in the days of (the Pharisees) we would not have been partakers with them"? (Matt. 23:30). *Au contraire:* there are now today, here in America, the homeless, the hungry, the mentally and physically ill, the prisoners, the deprived and needy in a thousand ways, that you are not ministering to, that you have no plans or intent to provide for beyond some vague notion that *some day* "private charity" will take care of them, at no cost to yourselves—but not until you and your "compassionate conservative" colleagues can collaborate in the destruction of what little is now being done by the government; while you devote yourselves instead to the very opposite of "compassionate" objectives: to legalistic and persecutory battles against abortion, homosexuality, evolution, and such efforts that never filled a hungry mouth or sheltered or healed or visited a needy person—and all in the Name of Christ! "Wherefore be ye witnesses unto yourselves, that ye are the children of them which killed the prophets. Fill ye up then the measure of your fathers... *How can ye escape the damnation of hell?*" (Matt. 23:32-33)

So is the One we worship "gentle Jesus, meek and mild" who loved little children and succored the widowed and the handicapped, the sick and the wayward?—or is He the mighty Judge, the Alpha and Omega, the Christ Who cleansed the temple in anger and pronounced curses on those persons and nations who mock Him?

Both Are True!

We certainly ought to pray to our loving Savior for personal and national healing. Maybe we also should ask of the righteous Judge that we be cursed with nothing more fearsome than rampaging bears.

APPENDIX

Not long ago I saw a television segment on some aspect or other of homosexuality. It was pointed out that in the Netherlands there seemed to be no big problem over homosexual marriage, and a Dutchman being interviewed for the show was asked, How come?

He said, "In Netherlands we have *separation of church and state*".

Huh?

That shibboleth is so often used here in reference to ourselves, by me among others, that it clearly must have a different meaning over there. The man went on to explain himself. He said that in his country the government does not "marry" people; only the church may do that. And, apparently, they marry whom they please, regardless of sexual orientation.

In a Theodore Robinson painting done in France of a wedding procession, the bride and groom, followed by all the wedding party, are on their way from the town hall, where they had undergone a civil registration, to the church where they were to be married. As you'd expect in a largely Roman Catholic country where marriage is a sacrament of the church, it can't be performed by justices of the peace or other government agents!—at least not during the Third Republic, and perhaps still so now.

As a loyal fan of William Shakespeare, I've long observed that the numerous marriages portrayed in his plays *(As You Like It, Romeo and Juliet,* etc.) were always performed by priests directly upon request—no civil license apparently even having been heard of in his day.

How and when did it become the case that American clergy have "the power vested in me" *by the state* to pronounce marriage, which historically (and properly) has always been a religious, not governmental institution? And to compound matters, a government agent, such as a justice of the peace, has the same power to pronounce marriage, while a clergyman may not marry a couple without their first having obtained a license from the state.

This is not "separation" but *commingling* of church and state!

It seems to me that, as in the Netherlands, our problems with homosexual marriage could be solved by such a separation. As I mentioned in Chapter 10 we may be encountering some confusion about proper church-state boundaries; so even solving the problem as to this one issue would still leave us with a need for more clarifications. But maybe it's a place to start. I'm not a lawyer and can't seriously propose "model legislation", but I've had enough dealings with Federal and several states' laws that I may venture to string together the kinds of provisions that might stimulate preparation of a competent state legislative proposal. When writing Chapter 5 I worried that we may not have time to debate the issue of homosexual marriage: and now developments in California, Massachusetts and the White House have made my fears a reality. Impetuous development of legislation, which I may seem to be proposing, is not the best kind of response to complex questions such as this; but maybe it is at least no worse than impetuous constitutional amendments that write in stone government control of the religious institution of marriage. So hoping it's not too late, here's my suggestion:

ARTICLE I.   A BILL,

Providing for establishment of civil union status of couples in this state; amending (Sec. _____, Art. _____, Chap. _____, [name] state statutes); establishing a clear line of separation between government and religion; prohibiting discrimination as to the rights, privileges and obligations of couples united in civil union and of those united in marriage; authorizing state recognition of civil union between couples of the same sex; reserving to religious authorities the power to recognize a civil union as marriage or to withhold such recognition; and providing for equivalence of marriage and civil union in all legal matters.

ARTICLE II.   SHORT TITLE

This bill may be known as "the marriage and civil union act of 20 _____".

ARTICLE III.   PREAMBLE

The legislature of the state of _____ finds:

1.   THAT marriage has historically been considered a divinely-ordained institution and one governed by the laws and traditions of religious groups;

2.   THAT action is therefore appropriate, to clarify and strengthen the role of religion in such governance, and to limit any needless state intrusion into it;

3. THAT demographic, economic and public health interests require the state to recognize, and record the establishment of, unions between couples;

4. THAT such recognition by the state does not constitute marriage, which is not a secular but a religious institution;

5. THAT the requirement of equality before the law necessitates that the state make available to all couples the rights, protections and obligations of legally-recognized unions, irrespective of religious construction of the union or lack thereof, or the identity or difference of sex between the members of such couples;

THEREFORE,

ARTICLE IV   BE IT ENACTED by the legislature of the state of _____:

ARTICLE I.   CIVIL UNION

Section 1. There is established in this state a legal relationship between any two persons qualified therefor, to be known as "civil union".

Section 2. All couples married before the effective date of this Act, in any state or country, shall in this state be deemed to be living in the status of civil union; notwithstanding that they may also be in the status of marriage, under the laws of such state or country.

Section 3. Marriage shall for all purposes be recognized and acknowledged by the state as a religious institution, not to be authorized, performed, established or pronounced by any person acting as state agent or other secular authority. But marriage itself shall not be demeaned, nor its relevance diminished, by any provision of law; and to this end, marriage retains its legal status regardless that it may only be ordained and established by religious authority. Notwithstanding, legal marriage shall not be established under any religious auspices for a couple not possessing a certificate of civil union, as provided herein.

Section 4. Throughout all the laws of this state, any reference to marriage or marital status, (but not to divorce or marital dissolution) shall be deemed to include equally the status of civil union, and the provisions of such laws shall be construed to apply to civil unions and to members of such unions. For all purposes a member of a civil union may represent himself or herself as "married" without violating any public law, even if such representation constitutes violation of a religious law or tradition in cases where no religious recognition of the union has occurred; provided that whenever relevant to a court proceeding, disclosure of a person's technical marital status may be required by a judge, and solely in such cases may the statutes governing perjury be applied.

ARTICLE II   ADMINISTRATION

Section 1. The state shall impose no requirement of licensure upon any couple desiring legal recognition of their civil union or their intended civil union. The state and all political subdivisions thereof which have formerly issued marriage licenses shall, on the effective date of this Act, discontinue doing so and shall instead offer civil union certification, and the offices maintained by such political entities, heretofore known as the "marriage license" office or its equivalent, shall be re-designated the "civil union certificate office" or a comparable term. The certificate's form and content, and the charge for obtaining such, shall be prescribed by the state department of health.

Section 2. Section _____, Article _____, Chapter _____, (state statutes) is (are) amended, to read:

(here the writers of legislative proposals would have to substitute, in place of rules and procedures for obtaining a "marriage license", procedures and qualificatory requirements, which actually could be similar or identical, for obtaining "civil union" status; and such status would thereby be established in finality, without, in the state's option, necessarily requiring any further ceremony.)

Section 3. Qualification for civil union shall be open to all couples regardless of race, citizenship, sexual makeup of the couple, or political or religious affiliation, without discrimination except for age, polygamy and kinship limitations as provided by law.

Section 4. When an agent of the civil union certificate office is satisfied that all requirements have been met for establishing the civil union of a couple, a certificate of civil union between the two parties named on such certificate shall be provided forthwith for signature by parties of their current full names, even if one of them uses or intends to change his or her surname following establishment of their union. Any member or members of the issuing agency may be designated by the head of such agency to sign in witness upon the certificate, and the signature of the agency's head shall likewise be inscribed on the certificate, either by hand or in printed facsimile. The state may require signature(s) of up to two additional witnesses to be provided by the couple. The certification of civil union shall thenceforth be on public record, and additional information about the couple as required by the state bureau of vital statistics, shall also be recorded. Any such additional information beyond names shall be confidential, shielded from public disclosure.

Section 5. Upon issuance of a certificate under the provisions of this Article, a civil union between the two parties is established; as is the legitimacy of any offspring born to or adopted by the parties at any time. The issuing agency shall honor any request by the couple for additional ceremony, the contents and format for which may be furnished by the couple, or a standard brief ceremony may be offered by the agency. The scheduling of any ceremony shall be at the agency's convenience. It is not permitted in any civil ceremony to state or imply that a marriage is being ordained thereby; provided, that the ceremony should include vows by both parties of permanence and faithfulness.

Section 6. Following issuance of a certificate of civil union, any couple desiring marriage may apply therefor to any religious group or authority. The power of such group or authority to conclude and pronounce marriage is not vested by the state but by applicable rules, laws, customs or traditions held by the religious group.

ARTICLE III.   SEPARATION OF RELIGION AND GOVERNMENT

Section 1. No provision of law shall impair the liberty of religious groups or their members, or the religious authorities thereof, to offer or to refuse marriage to any civil union-certified couple for any reason, including but not limited to reasons of religious law, and no grounds for suit may eventuate from such an offer or refusal. Religious law or religious authority may determine what persons shall be empowered to ordain marriage, without supervision or interference by the state.

Section 2. Divorce or dissolution of a civil union is a state function, as had been its original establishment. It shall be governed by the same or amended laws now applicable to divorce. Following completion of the procedures, neither party to the former union shall be eligible for the title "married".

Section 3. No provision of law shall be construed for any purpose as establishing an authority over or any overlap between governmental and religious jurisdictions, as to religious matters, including but not limited to marriage.

ARTICLE IV   EFFECTIVE DATE

This Act shall become effective on _____(date)

Comments:

ARTICLE in italics indicates subdivisions of the proposed legislative bill; ARTICLE in Romans is a subdivision of the actual law when enacted—the statute as it would actually appear in the law books. Items in parentheses are either optional or they require information to be supplied, that I don't have.

As also stated in Chapter 5, I still assert that it is unwise, unnecessary and probably unacceptable for any government entity (court or legislature) to define a homosexual relationship as "marriage". Whether it's wise for a church or the couple themselves to do so, is not a matter for government to decide. I attempt here only to show a way for all persons to enjoy constitutional liberties, while making it at least legally possible for a traditional definition of marriage to be maintained.

I'm adding here a few explanations and clarifications, and if I have mangled the legal language, I hope that these may undo the damage.

ARTICLE 1. Section 1. The term "civil union" is awkward, and I'd welcome a creative alternative; the term is not necessary to the rest of the proposal.

Section 2. The term encompasses all couples in legal relationship, so it is necessary to "grandfather" existing marriages into it.

Section 3. As long as two types of relationship are being recognized, it is important to avoid any difference of legal weight to either of them.

Section 4. An alternative would be to go through the entire body of a state's laws and amend any references to marriage or divorce or homosexuality. I can't do this, even for my own state and hardly for 49 others, and I suspect it is unnecessary, given a blanket provision such as this.

Persons united in civil union should not have to choose between checking the "married" or "single" box on job applications, tax returns, or others of the multitudinous forms we have to complete at times. Nor should issuing agencies have to create new forms, when the technical distinction is rarely of material consequence (don't ask, don't tell). It is my view that authorizing homosexual couples to check the "married" box at the top of a medical history or other form does not constitute state establishment of homosexual marriage!

ARTICLE II. Section 1. Obtaining a marriage license today is tantamount to getting married, from the state's point of view, except for the politically trivial requirement that somebody, religious or secular, conduct a ceremony to make it so. Actually, I think ceremonies are important—that is, to me; but if they are not important to the concerned couple, it makes little sense to require it.

Section 2. Here again, the peculiar or unique provisions of any state's set of laws would have to be reviewed, to eliminate contradictions or to fill in gaps.

Section 4. Mostly a re-statement of Sec. 1 of this Article.

Section 5. Again, a gentle nudge toward a ceremonious entry upon union status.

Section 3, 6. OK?

ARTICLE III. Section 1. Under this proposal, religious groups are at liberty to conduct their own affairs regarding marriage; the sole limitation under state law being that prior civil union status be obtained. This is, or should be, no more burdensome to the couples or the churches, or constitute greater domination by the state, than is the current requirement of a marriage license prior to actual marriage. For some couples (those not wanting a religious ceremony) it would actually simplify matters.

Section 2. Civil union is a state-sponsored arrangement, and only the state can dissolve it.

Throughout, the assumption is that government rightly has no more business in the area of marriage than in baptism or Holy Communion. Its need for demographic, health, economic, educational and similar data can all be subsumed under a proper state function, that of enabling civil union status.